Instructors:
Your time is valuable.
We're here for you!

SAGE COURSEPACKS: OUR CONTENT TAILORED TO YOUR LMS

We make it easy to import our quality instructor and student content into *your* school's learning management system (LMS).

- **NO NEW SYSTEM** to learn

- **INTUITIVE AND SIMPLE** to use

- Allows you to **CUSTOMIZE COURSE CONTENT** to meet your students' needs

- A variety of high-quality assessment questions and multimedia **ASSIGNMENTS TO SELECT FROM**

- **NO REQUIRED ACCESS CODES**

CONTACT YOUR SAGE SALES REPRESENTATIVE TO LEARN MORE:
sagepub.com/findmyrep

SAGE coursepacks

For use in: Blackboard, Canvas, Brightspace by Desire2Learn (D2L), and Moo

D0219010

SAGE
Premium Video

BOOST COMPREHENSION. BOLSTER ANALYSIS.

- SAGE Premium Video **EXCLUSIVELY CURATED FOR THIS TEXT**
- **BRIDGES BOOK CONTENT** with application & critical thinking
- Includes short, auto-graded quizzes that **DIRECTLY FEED TO YOUR LMS GRADEBOOK**
- Premium content is **ADA COMPLIANT WITH TRANSCRIPTS**
- Comprehensive media guide to help you **QUICKLY SELECT MEANINGFUL VIDEO** tied to your course objectives

The
Hallmark Features

- **REVISED CHAPTER-OPENING LEARNING OUTCOMES** focus readers' attention on the themes of the chapter and act as a helpful roadmap.

- **INTERSTATE TEACHER ASSESSMENT AND SUPPORT CONSORTIUM (INTASC) STANDARDS** are now connected in every chapter.

- **EACH CHAPTER FEATURES STORIES FROM TEACHERS AND CLASSROOM OBSERVATIONS** that bring authenticity to the content.

- **END-OF-CHAPTER PEDAGOGY** supports student comprehension by summarizing learning outcomes, listing important key terms, providing journal prompts, and positioning succinct review questions that speak to the chapter's themes and content.

- **TIMELY TOPICS** including the STEM, STEAM, and Maker Movements, student diversity, school safety and gun violence, the enormous role that technology plays in teaching and learning, sexual orientation and gender identity, and more are explored.

- **SAGE COURSEPACKS** allows instructors to import high-quality content into their school's learning management system (LMS) with no access codes.

- **SAGE EDGE** provides students helpful tools, including eFlashcards, practice quizzes, a customizable action plan, and more, all in one easy-to-use online environment.

- **AN ALL-NEW END-OF-BOOK GLOSSARY** provides clear definitions for all of the key terms used in the text.

teach

Fourth Edition

teach
fourth edition

Sara Miller McCune founded SAGE Publishing in 1965 to support the dissemination of usable knowledge and educate a global community. SAGE publishes more than 1000 journals and over 800 new books each year, spanning a wide range of subject areas. Our growing selection of library products includes archives, data, case studies and video. SAGE remains majority owned by our founder and after her lifetime will become owned by a charitable trust that secures the company's continued independence.

Los Angeles | London | New Delhi | Singapore | Washington DC | Melbourne

teach
Introduction to Education
Fourth Edition

JANICE KOCH

Emerita, Hofstra University

SAGE

Los Angeles | London | New Delhi
Singapore | Washington DC | Melbourne

FOR INFORMATION:

SAGE Publications, Inc.
2455 Teller Road
Thousand Oaks, California 91320
E-mail: order@sagepub.com

SAGE Publications Ltd.
1 Oliver's Yard
55 City Road
London EC1Y 1SP
United Kingdom

SAGE Publications India Pvt. Ltd.
B 1/I 1 Mohan Cooperative Industrial Area
Mathura Road, New Delhi 110 044
India

SAGE Publications Asia-Pacific Pte. Ltd.
18 Cross Street #10-10/11/12
China Square Central
Singapore 048423

Senior Acquisitions Editor: Steve Scoble
Senior Content Development Editor: Jennifer Jovin
Associate Content Development Editor: Chelsea Neve
Content Development Editor: Kathryn Abbott
Editorial Assistant: Elizabeth You
Production Editor: Jane Martinez
Copy Editor: Diane Wainwright
Typesetter: Hurix Digital
Proofreader: Eleni-Maria Georgiou
Indexer: Joan Shapiro
Cover Designer: Gail Buschman
Marketing Manager: Jillian Ragusa

Copyright © 2020 by SAGE Publications, Inc.

All rights reserved. Except as permitted by U.S. copyright law, no part of this work may be reproduced or distributed in any form or by any means, or stored in a database or retrieval system, without permission in writing from the publisher.

All third party trademarks referenced or depicted herein are included solely for the purpose of illustration and are the property of their respective owners. Reference to these trademarks in no way indicates any relationship with, or endorsement by, the trademark owner.

Printed in the United States of America

Library of Congress Cataloging-in-Publication Data

Names: Koch, Janice- author.

Title: Teach : Introduction to education / Janice Koch, Hofstra University.

Description: Fourth Edition. | Thousand Oaks, California : SAGE, [2019] | Includes bibliographical references and index.

Identifiers: LCCN 2018041133 | ISBN 9781544342573 (Paperback : acid-free paper)

Subjects: LCSH: Teaching—Psychological aspects. | Multicultural education.

Classification: LCC LB1027 .K578 2019 | DDC 371.102—dc23 LC record available at https://lccn.loc.gov/2018041133

This book is printed on acid-free paper.

21 22 23 10 9 8 7 6 5 4 3

• Brief Contents •

• Detailed Contents •

• Preface •

For the college or graduate student, making the decision to become a teacher is often fraught with uncertainty, complexity, and confusion. What should I know? What courses do I take? How do I get certified? How can I be sure this career choice is right for me? Although some aspiring teachers approach this journey with more personal confidence than others, most find it challenging to make the transition from the college classroom to their own classrooms. *Teach* is designed to help them meet that challenge. I wrote this text in response to colleagues who felt I could speak to future teachers plainly and clearly.

The most important task of this text is to invite readers to look inside themselves to their own dispositions for teaching and to look outside of themselves to the demands of an ever-changing culture filled to the brim with iPhones, iPads, tablets, laptops, and endless text messages. Choosing to become a teacher requires that one analyzes his or her own personal strengths and weaknesses to ask if this profession is a "good fit" between one's personal and cognitive attributes and the demands of the teaching profession. This is not a simple exercise, so *Teach* encourages readers to think sincerely about the complex aspects of a "good fit."

One overarching idea of the text can be summed up by this statement: "We teach who we are." By this, I mean that an individual's entire self is present in the classroom and who we are, what we believe, what we think about ourselves and our students are exposed through the dynamic processes of teaching and learning. By the time a student finishes this book, he or she should have a clearer personal sense of what it may mean to be a teacher.

An **Introduction to Education** course is the first occasion when students are asked to think critically about the field of education. Planning to become a teacher is a complex activity that requires both personal reflection and an understanding of how schools came to be the way they are today. Combining historical and contemporary perspectives, this text helps future teachers examine the ways in which society and culture shape schools and the ways in which schools are shaped by society and culture. How did we get to "now?" What changes has American public education undergone since its inception? Why do we need public schools, and how are they transforming to meet the needs of diverse populations of students?

Whether the initial course is titled **Foundations of Education** or **Becoming a Teacher** or simply an **Introduction to Teaching**, *Teach: Introduction to Education*, Fourth Edition, offers several features to engage students in personal reflection and critical thinking.

Pedagogical Features

The Chapter Introduction contains **Learning Outcomes** and the **InTASC Standards** relevant to that chapter's content. The end of the chapter brings the student back to the InTASC Standards and the Learning Outcomes while explicitly defining the **Key Terms** in an integrated **Chapter Review** section. Model answers for the questions at the back of each chapter are provided. **Journal Prompts** at the end of each chapter encourage the readers to continue writing about their journeys toward becoming teachers.

Each chapter features stories from teachers and classroom observations that bring authenticity to the chapter content, answering the question: "What does it look like?" . . . To be a classroom teacher? To develop a teaching style? To create curriculum? To engage students in their own thinking? To create community? To become a professional?

Fourth Edition Content Features

This new edition of *Teach* explores topics that have emerged as major issues in contemporary education since the last edition, as well as foundational concepts that received new attention.

These topics include the STEM, STEAM, and maker movements; school choice and homeschooling; sexual orientation and gender identity; gun violence in school; the impact of backward design and authentic assessment in teaching; the enormous role that technology plays in teaching and learning, as well as the potential pitfalls of social media and smartphones; emphasis on student diversity; the process of building a professional portfolio; and the overall importance of personal wellness in teacher success.

New to SAGE, the fourth edition seeks to make the process of deciding to become a teacher and the philosophy of teaching and learning accessible and relevant to introductory education students.

Digital Resources

SSAGE Coursepacks

Instructor Resources

SAGE coursepacks and SAGE edge online resources are included FREE with this text. For a brief demo, contact your sales representative today.

SAGE coursepacks for instructors makes it easy to import our quality content into your school's learning management system (LMS)*. Intuitive and simple to use, it allows you to

Say NO to . . .

- required access codes
- learning a new system

Say YES to . . .

- using only the content you want and need
- high-quality assessment and multimedia exercises

***For use in:** Blackboard, Canvas, Brightspace by Desire-2Learn (D2L), and Moodle

Don't use an LMS platform? No problem, you can still access many of the online resources for your text via SAGE edge.

With SAGE coursepacks, you get:

- quality textbook content delivered **directly into your LMS**;
- an **intuitive**, **simple format** that makes it easy to integrate the material into your course with minimal effort;
- **assessment tools** that foster review, practice, and critical thinking, including:
  - diagnostic chapter **pre-tests and post-tests** that identify opportunities for improvement, track student progress, and ensure mastery of key learning objectives
  - **test banks** built on Bloom's Taxonomy that provide a diverse range of test items with ExamView test generation
  - **activity and quiz options** that allow you to choose only the assignments and tests you want
  - **instructions** on how to use and integrate the comprehensive assessments and resources provided;

- **assignable SAGE Premium Video** (available via the interactive eBook version, linked through SAGE coursepacks) that is tied to learning objectives, and produced exclusively for this text to bring concepts to life, featuring:
  - **Engaging interviews with teachers and principals** sharing the biggest joys and challenges of being an educator, as well as their passion and enthusiasm for their students.
  - **Video Cases** that show footage from real classrooms demonstrating what a typical day is like in an elementary or a secondary school. You will see lead teachers and paraprofessionals working together in small groups with their students, as well as students learning together as a class and in smaller, differentiated groups.
  - **Corresponding multimedia assessment options** that automatically feed to your gradebook
  - Comprehensive, downloadable, easy-to-use *Media Guide in the Coursepack* for every video resource, listing the chapter to which the video content is tied, matching learning objective(s), a helpful description of the video content, and assessment questions
- **chapter-specific discussion questions** to help launch engaging classroom interaction while reinforcing important content;
- exclusive **SAGE journal articles** built into course materials and assessment tools, that tie influential research and scholarship to chapter concepts;
- editable, chapter-specific **PowerPoint® slides** that offer flexibility when creating multimedia lectures so you don't have to start from scratch;
- **sample course syllabi** with suggested models for structuring your course that give you options to customize your course to your exact needs;
- **lecture notes** that summarize key concepts on a chapter-by-chapter basis to help you with preparation for lectures and class discussions;
- **integrated links to the interactive eBook** that make it easy for students to maximize their study time with this "anywhere, anytime" mobile-friendly version of the text. It also offers access to more digital tools and resources, including SAGE Premium Video; and
- **select tables and figures** from the textbook.

Student Resources

edge.sagepub.com/koch4e

SAGE edge for students enhances learning, it's easy to use, and offers:

- an **open-access site** that makes it easy for students to maximize their study time, anywhere, anytime;
- **video and multimedia resources** that bring concepts to life, are tied to learning objectives, and make learning easier;
- **eFlashcards** that strengthen understanding of key terms and concepts;
- **eQuizzes** that allow students to practice and assess how much they've learned and where they need to focus their attention;

- **exclusive access to influential** SAGE journal articles that tie important research and scholarship to chapter concepts to strengthen learning.

Interactive eBook

Teach: Introduction to Education, Fourth Edition, is also available as an **Interactive eBook** that can be packaged with the text for just $5 or purchased separately. The Interactive eBook offers hyperlinks to original videos, including **video cases** that feature **real classroom footage** and engaging **teacher interviews** showing readers how to implement strategies from the book into their own future classrooms. Users will also have immediate access to study tools such as highlighting, bookmarking, note-taking/sharing, and more!

• Acknowledgments •

Teach 4e is the result of the kind of contemporary collaboration that could only be possible in a digitally connected world. Communication with contributors and researchers via the Internet, blogs, Twitter feeds, and podcasts resulted in rich and diverse sources of information for this text. Interviews with former Hofstra students who followed their dreams and became wonderful teachers—Amanda Prinz, Winnelle Outerbridge, Jessica Powers, Kathryn Farley, Meredith Landau, Jaime Barron, and Sharyn Wanderman—were complemented by interviews with my new Maryland teacher colleagues—Ben Tarr, Cheryl O'Malley, and Helene Schuster. Your stories add authenticity to the work, and your willingness to share the joys and pitfalls of teaching is both kind and generous.

A large group of reviewers examined the third edition and offered excellent guidance for *Teach 4e*. They include:

Curby Alexander, Texas Christian University

Dr. Carmen Garcia-Cáceres, University of Texas Rio Grande Valley

Casey Hamilton, Owensboro Community & Technical College

Kathleen Holt, Nashua Community College

Gregory Jennings, EdD, Lehman College, City University of New York

Jennifer Jones, MEd, Muskegon Community College

Dr. Katherin Garland, Santa Fe College

Alfred P. Longo, PhD, Ocean County College

Peggy Perkins Auman, Florida A&M University

Dr. Lisa Repaskey, Norfolk State University

Robert J. Walker, EdD, Southwest Tennessee Community College

Many thanks to all of these expert commentators.

My sincere appreciation goes to individuals at SAGE, starting with Reid Hester, who encouraged me to move forward with *Teach 4e*, and Steve Scoble, Jennifer Jovin and Elizabeth You, whose expert advice sealed the deal. Clearly, the final text emerged cohesively due to the superb assistance of the development editor, Kathryn Abbott, to whom I am forever grateful, and to the wise guidance of Diane Wainwright, the copy editor. My granddaughters Sydney and Kayley Tarantino continue to inspire me with their understanding of the possibilities for teaching and learning in a digital age, and finally, *Teach 4e* is dedicated to my husband, Bob Koch, who has always made it possible for me to pursue my dreams. Thanks, Bobby.

• About the Author •

Anna Elliot Photography

Janice Koch is Professor Emerita of Science Education at Hofstra University, Long Island, New York. She developed and taught science education courses to elementary, middle, and secondary preservice and in-service teachers. Additionally, she taught courses addressing introduction to education, action research, qualitative research, and gender issues in the classroom. Dr. Koch shares her passion for teaching and learning through presentations as well as through her introduction to education text *Teach*, Fourth Edition (SAGE, 2020). Her acclaimed textbook *Science Stories*, Sixth Edition (Cengage, 2018), has been used by thousands of preservice and in-service educators interested in creating meaningful science experiences for their students. Dr. Koch was named one of the Top Fifty Women on Long Island by *Long Island Business News* in 2004 and 2005. She and her husband currently reside in central Maryland, where she consults on education projects across the country and internationally and evaluates grant-funded science education initiatives. She recently served on the Committee for Precollege Engineering Education for the National Academies of Sciences, Engineering, and Medicine (2016–2018).

Thinking About Teaching

Making the Decision

iStock/FatCamera

Becoming a Teacher

Looking Forward and Backward at the Same Time

Everyone who remembers his [or her] own education remembers teachers, not methods and techniques. The teacher is the heart of the educational system.

—Sidney Hook, American philosopher (student of John Dewey), 1902–1989

Learning Outcomes

After reading this chapter, you should be able to:

1-1 Reflect on your own educational history and how it can affect the type of teacher you become. Examine the importance of reflection, metacognition, and "knowing yourself."

1-2 Examine the "goodness of fit" between your own personal qualities and the demands of teaching.

1-3 Explain the effect that a committed teacher has on the climate and culture within a school.

1-4 Consider how the era of testing and standardization in the 21st century has affected the way contemporary schools function.

InTASC Standards

• Standard 3: Learning Environments

• Standard 9: Professional Learning and Ethical Practice

This book invites you on a personal journey of reflection about education—your own education, the education of people you know, and the education of children who will become the future of the United States. It is a journey of self-exploration, during which you will look inside your mind and heart and consider what it takes, emotionally and intellectually, to become a teacher who experiences joy and satisfaction through service to others.

The world of professional education is rapidly changing as digital technology offers many options for accessing and analyzing information. We now have a formal, more standard way to evaluate an individual's "readiness to teach." For many years, people have been seeking a fair and standard way to evaluate the potential effectiveness of a new teacher. It is a tricky process because teaching and learning are personal human activities that reflect the inner worlds of the students and teachers. *Teach 4e* will help you to think about good teaching practices and consider what they may look like in the classroom. Beyond those practices, there is much more to discover, including who *you* are, your hopes and dreams, and your goals for your students.

Any plan to improve educational outcomes is dependent on the teachers who carry it out and on the abilities of those attracted to the field. In this book, you will have the opportunity to explore some of the attributes that can help to make you a successful classroom teacher.

We will examine the specific challenges of becoming a teacher in today's social and political context, including testing, standards, and the effect of digital technology on the lives of young people and on your own life.

Although much about teaching and learning remains the same year after year, access to digital technology has significantly changed the ways students communicate, learn, and spend their time inside and outside of school. As we prepare to enter the third decade of the 21st century, we must consider these compelling truths about our world.

• The world is rapidly changing and is a far different place than it was only 10 years ago.

• The global economy and the technological innovations of the past several decades demand a well-educated citizenry.

• The best teachers grow and change with rapidly shifting social and cultural conditions, and thereby become lifelong learners.

• Online education is a significant presence in K–12 schools all over the country.

• Digital media occupies a great deal of time for students of all ages.

• Every single student has the ability to learn. Becoming a teacher means accepting the daily responsibility to help all students learn at whatever level and place in their lives they may be.

• Education provides students with the opportunity to become productive and contributing members of society.

• Teachers make a difference. The quality of the teacher in the classroom is one of the most important influences on student achievement.

• Preparing to teach involves personal reflection and a commitment to understanding yourself and the world around you.

• You will need to demonstrate through your written work and classroom performance videos that you are ready to teach.

While this book is about schools and schooling, teachers and teaching, learners and the process of learning, it is also about you. What do you already know about classrooms, and how can you apply that knowledge to the complex experience of being a classroom teacher? Your answers to these questions will play a big role in deciding the kind of teacher you will become. Research has shown that out of all the factors that contribute to a student's school day, the single most important one in improving students' performance is the effectiveness of the teacher. Yes, the teacher makes all the difference.

You have within you everything you need to become the kind of teacher you want to be. You will be challenged to identify the attitudes, skills, and dispositions that teaching requires. You will need to make a commitment to becoming a lifelong learner—that is, expanding your ideas by what you learn from your students, your research, and your own personal growth. Donald Schön (1983), an educational researcher, used the term **reflective practitioner** to refer to a teacher who consistently and consciously modifies his or her own teaching practice based on the active consideration of events in his or her classroom. That expression has stood the test of time, and reflection is essential for being an effective teacher. You are invited to conceptualize teaching as a personal activity requiring a large capacity for reflective thought and deliberate action and experimentation.

Teaching, which requires a heightened sense of self and a commitment to the social good, demands nothing less of its professionals than an ongoing examination of their authentic motives for teaching. Hence, in addition to *knowledge* about schools, curriculum, and instruction, this text provides a *venue* through which you can actively consider your skills, attitudes, and dispositions as they relate to becoming a teacher.

We begin by examining your interest in education. This chapter will encourage you to reflect on your own educational background as you explore the possibility of forging a career as a teacher.

Looking Backward: Talking About Teaching

I recently asked a number of new teachers what made them decide to enter teaching; some of them remarked that they had always loved school. School was, for them, the happiest place to be. But several others shared not-so-glorious

stories about their experiences. They decided to go into teaching to make a difference, to teach others in ways they wish they themselves had been taught. Still others had no specific personal calling to teach. They "fell into" teaching because they needed a job. And some are trying to figure out if teaching is for them. Whichever of these categories you feel you may fit, with this book you can discover if teaching is for you.

Laura and Sharyn pursued teaching careers because they loved school and loved learning. Laura explained that from her earliest years in school, she was excited when the school year began and sad when it ended. School was her happiest place, so she decided to pursue a career that would keep her there. Sharyn described similar feelings:

She remembered how, as a child, she could not wait for summer camp to be over because she wanted to go back to school. In high school, she was part of a peer tutoring program and also privately tutored friends and classmates. When they did well, she was actually happier than when she did well because she knew she had helped her friends to succeed. Sharyn's love for school and learning, combined with the joy she felt when her friends (whom she tutored) succeeded, led her to teaching. Sharyn wanted to enable children to love learning as much as she did.

A third teacher, Derrick, told me that most of his teachers were female. Not until sixth grade did he experience his first male teacher—the music teacher. He gained an appreciation of music from this teacher and started to imagine that he might teach as well. He played school with his younger brother and began to consider a career in education. Later, a male history teacher encouraged him to study that subject, and he majored in history in college while also pursuing a professional program in elementary education. A kindergarten teacher today, Derrick is firmly convinced that men are needed in early-childhood education so children can see that men are able caretakers. We will meet another male early-childhood teacher in Chapter 2.

Are you like Laura, Sharyn, or Derrick in your conviction that teaching is a career you want to pursue? Or are you more ambivalent? The "Writing & Reflection" activity will help you think about ways in which your educational past, and your thoughts and feelings about it, may influence your future career.

Your Educational Autobiography

What was school like for you? What kind of a student were you? When you think of teaching, which teacher or teachers do you conjure up?

You may think questions like these are irrelevant at this stage of your life. But examining your early experiences as a student is an important task:

Who you are as a person, the kinds of experiences you had inside and outside of school, your values, beliefs and aspirations shape what you will be as

---

reflective practitioner A teacher who consistently reflects on classroom events (both successes and problems) and modifies teaching practices accordingly.

WRITING & REFLECTION
DRAW YOURSELF AS A TEACHER

These samples show how three teacher candidates responded to the challenge to draw a teacher. What ideas about teaching do the drawings suggest?

Draw a picture of yourself teaching a lesson. You do not have to be an artist; stick figures are fine. Just imagine yourself in a classroom. Be sure to include the students! This is a way to explore your images of teaching. Close the book while you work. When you finish your drawing, return to this section.

As you analyze your drawing, you may want to reflect on the following questions:

- How is your classroom arranged?
- Are desks in rows? Or are tables grouped around the room?
- What are you doing? What are your students doing?
- Are you standing in front? In the middle? To the side?
- Are students raising their hands?
- Judging from your drawing, what mental models do you have of yourself as a teacher?

a teacher and how you will teach and how you will respond to the changing contexts of teaching. (Bullough & Gitlin, 2001, p. 45)

Thinking about your own story and then telling it is an important step in looking backward.

An **educational autobiography** is your story of your life as a student. It has no definite length but usually responds to the following questions:

- What do you think of when you think of school?
- Where did you attend school?
- When you walked in the building, did you have a sense of comfort? Fear? Anxiety?
- Close your eyes and imagine you are back in elementary, middle, or high school. What was school like for you? Do you remember what school *smells* like? *Sounds* like?
- Try to imagine specific teachers. What grades did they teach? Who were your friends in those grades?

My story begins with kindergarten:

I remember starting kindergarten at the age of 4 years and 6 months. Arbitrary calendar cutoff dates, typical of many public school districts, allowed me to enter school well before my fifth birthday. Neighbors would say, "She made the year." That referred to being allowed to commence kindergarten prior to turning 5. Other children, born 4 weeks later, had "missed the year" and began kindergarten after their fifth birthday. They would be the oldest in the grade, whereas I was the youngest.

I remember being frightened and throwing up every day for the first 2 months of kindergarten. But I also recall my kindergarten teachers' accepting and welcoming me each day, regardless of my physiological reaction to my separation from home. I was a "young" 4-and-a-half-year-old and would probably have been better served by missing the year. How patient and kind my two kindergarten teachers were! They saw me coming and intuitively knew that I was not ready for school. After helping me get over being sick each morning (they had a pail ready), they guided me gently to my seat. Their understanding that I had to become comfortable at my own pace enabled me to make an adjustment without shame and embarrassment.

educational autobiography Your own educational history, told by you.

I shall always remember their acceptance of me and my lack of readiness. How lucky I was to have these two teachers as I acclimated to being away from home.

Being a Teacher Is Like . . .

"Being a teacher feels like being a dentist—we are always pulling teeth," a new teacher remarked to me recently. "Ouch," I responded. "Is it that hard?"

"Well," she replied, "when they don't give me what I am looking for, I feel like that."

Aha, I think—some comparison! One of the most important misconceptions about teaching is that it is a solitary activity—something you do *to have control over someone else*. In fact, teaching and learning is an interaction, a conversation, a collaborative process involving you, the teacher, and all of your students. Teaching is about the students, *their* needs, not *your* needs or even your needs for them. The teacher who feels like a dentist is focusing on what his or her needs are, not on the needs of the students.

It is true that sometimes we wish students would respond in certain ways and they just do not. Yet there are much better similes than pulling teeth. Much of the time teaching is like:

- **Being a tour guide.** According to one teacher, a good tour guide takes travelers to new places, interprets experiences and sites, helps travelers understand and appreciate these new experiences, and develops a group atmosphere to maximize positive experiences for the travelers. A good tour guide has general goals in mind but is flexible and allows for exploration of ideas that arise from the group. Indeed, there are many times when teaching is like being a tour guide. The teacher sets the itinerary and takes the students through the lessons to many new places.

iStock/minemero

- **Being a sailor.** Sometimes when you go sailing, you think you are going to reach a certain island. You set out for that destination, but you find it does not have a dock. The dock is simply not there. So you need to have an alternative plan. On other days, you have a destination in mind, but the wind is blowing in the wrong direction and the sailboat will not go there. Yes, on many days, teaching is like sailing, and the teacher changes course in midstream as he or she determines a better direction and a more feasible destination.

iStock/katerinchik73

- **Being a sculptor.** Sculptors are fond of saying that they do not "make" their art; they uncover what is already hidden in the material. Similarly, teachers uncover the ideas emerging in the minds of their students.

Neda Krstic

- **Climbing a hill.** Another teacher explains that teaching is a constant process of ascending an incline. Every once in a while you stop, take a breather, make sure everyone is comfortable, and then you start climbing again. That sounds like you need a lot of strength.

iStock/zeljkosantrac

WRITING & REFLECTION
TEACHING IS LIKE . . .

Think of one or more comparisons for teaching.

If you need some leads, visit the website "Metaphorically Speaking" from the Annenberg Media Learner Interactive

Workshops   (http://www.learner.org/channel/workshops/nextmove/metaphor/). You may come up with several similes or metaphors that seem apt. As you choose them, explain why you think each is a good description of teaching.

The "Writing & Reflection" activity will help you come up with your own simile or metaphor for teaching. There is an important reason for exploring these comparisons. It gets you started on developing your personal philosophy of teaching statement. A **philosophy of teaching statement** outlines your ideas about teaching and learning, sets out techniques for being reflective about your practice, and describes how you may teach. It may also include your goals for yourself as a teacher. If you decide to pursue a career in teaching, your philosophy of teaching statement could form an important part of your teaching portfolio. It can also be a baseline philosophical platform that changes over time with experience.

Your teaching philosophy should be backed up by evidence from research. For many decades, educators have studied how people learn and have compiled evidence about successful teaching strategies. As you read this text, you will encounter some of that research; the more you learn about it, the better prepared you will be to state your own teaching philosophy. But it is never too early to begin this kind of thinking. Take a few moments to think about your own teachers.

A Favorite Teacher

Does one teacher stand out in your mind as having influenced you in a positive way? How did this teacher make an impact, and what was the result of his or her connection to you? Answering these questions is another good way to reflect on your educational past. When I think about these questions, I remember junior high school.

I had a seventh-grade teacher, Mrs. Fisher, in JHS 117 in the Bronx in New York City. I was, as you read in the early part of my educational autobiography, really young for my grade; I was 11 years old. Mrs. Fisher was my science teacher, and, in those days, much of general science revolved around learning how the internal combustion engine of an automobile worked.

I really liked science, but I was shy, young, and from a poor neighborhood. I had little self-confidence. Mrs. Fisher took me aside one day and said, "You know, Janice, you are very

good in science; you should go to the Bronx High School of Science." This high school is one of the specialized schools in New York City requiring that students pass an entrance exam. Mrs. Fisher gave me the application and helped me complete it.

I passed the exam, was admitted, and began attending the Bronx High School of Science at the age of 12. My experience at this distinctive high school changed the course of my future education and career. Years later, I went to visit Mrs. Fisher and thanked her for having taken an interest in me. I determined that one day I, too, would make a difference for students. Very often, teachers do not even know how they affect the future decisions of their students. That is why Christa McAuliffe, the former teacher turned astronaut who perished in the Space Shuttle Challenger disaster in 1986, said famously, "I touch the future—I teach."

What Qualities Make a Good Teacher?

After reflecting on your favorite teacher, you may want to compare the attributes of this teacher with a list of some general qualities of good teachers. (See "Qualities of Good Teachers," p. 8). This list is not the final word on good teacher qualities, but it is a start. I call it the "5 Cs." How do these qualities match up with the ones your favorite teacher had?

In making this comparison, think about to what extent you possess these qualities. As we proceed, we will often return to the concept of **goodness of fit**. This term refers to how good a match there may be between your personal qualities and the demands of teaching.

Do not seek a perfect match between yourself and the characteristics listed. You are always growing and changing as a person, and you certainly may develop qualities you do not possess now. When you begin to think about a career in teaching, one of your responsibilities is to analyze your own strengths and weaknesses. Realizing your strengths allows you to use them to the fullest potential, whereas identifying your weaknesses allows you to work toward improving or overcoming them.

---

philosophy of teaching statement A description of your ideas about teaching and learning, and how those ideas will influence your practice. It should be based on your knowledge of educational research.

goodness of fit A term generally used in descriptive statistics to describe the match between a theory and a particular set of observations; in this book, it means the match between a teacher candidate's personal attributes, values, and disposition and the demands of teaching.

QUALITIES OF GOOD TEACHERS: "5 Cs"

A good teacher needs to be:

Committed   Good teachers have a commitment to their own ongoing education as well as the learning experiences of the young people in their charge. They are committed to fostering a love of learning in their students.

Caring   Teachers demonstrate their hopes for their students through the ways they nurture their development, encouraging students to achieve and supporting them as they reach new heights of understanding. They also demonstrate their "caring" by how prepared they are as they begin the school day.

Courageous   It requires courage to maintain a commitment over time, persisting in working on behalf of every student, regardless of ability.

Conscious   Good teachers are consistently aware of their interactions with their students. They consciously function to ensure respectful and meaningful discourse. They do not casually "shoot from the hip" when engaging with their students. They are deliberate and considered.

iStock/fstop123

Centered   Good teachers have a centered presence in the classroom. They command the students' attention by their own personal comfort with being at the center of responsibility. They communicate, through their body language and speech, their own readiness to work with their students.

Looking Forward: The Profession

Now it is time to begin looking forward. What is special about teaching as a career? What do you need to know about the profession you are considering?

An Essential Profession

How we think about and voice the purpose of school matters. . . . It affects the way we think about students—all students—about intelligence, achievement, human development, teaching and learning, opportunity and obligation. (Rose, 2009, p. 169)

In a U.S. Department of Education report, *Promising Practices: New Ways to Improve Teacher Quality* (1998), teaching is referred to as "the essential profession, the one that makes all other professions possible." What do you think that means? The report further declares that without well-qualified, caring, and committed teachers, neither improved curricula and assessments nor safe schools—not even the highest standards in the world—will ensure that our children are prepared for the challenges and opportunities in this century. Despite being more than 20 years old, this report has stood the test of time. Teaching is the essential profession. More than ever

before in our history, education will make the difference between those who prosper in the new economy and those who are left behind. Teaching shapes education and therefore shapes the future of the United States—molding the skills of the future workforce and laying the foundation for good citizenship and full participation in community and civic life.

Hence, it is the teacher who will bring to life the ideals, attitudes, learning experiences, and joy that are possible in a classroom. The curriculum, which we will explore later in this text, is a lifeless document in itself. It is the classroom teacher who enables the curriculum materials to have personal meaning for each learner.

Does this sound like a tall order? It is! Because what teachers know and are able to do have such a profound impact on the future of education, you need to understand how people learn. You need to become familiar with different contexts for teaching and the diversity of students in schools.

We would not expect that a future doctor would be able to examine a patient or perform surgery with just a few months' training. Yet we often expect students to become teachers after a short period of in-classroom training. This is why many teacher education programs (and yours may be one) require early field experiences, during which you observe and participate in the life of a classroom at the grade level you are thinking about teaching.

The National Education Association

The **National Education Association (NEA)** is the nation's largest professional employee organization. It has over 3 million members who work in educational settings from preschools to universities. With affiliate organizations in all 50 states and in more than 14,000 U.S. communities, the NEA provides local services such as workshops and collective bargaining for teachers. On state and national scales, it acts as a lobbying group for educational issues.

Chapter 2 will have much more to say about professional organizations for teachers. I bring up the NEA here because, as far back as 1929, members adopted a code of ethics for the profession. The preamble to the NEA Code of Ethics (1975) begins, "The educator, believing in the worth and dignity of each human being, recognizes the supreme importance of the pursuit of truth, devotion to excellence, and the nurture of democratic principles." This statement refers to a teacher's commitment to all of his or her students. A teacher's authentic desire to make a connection with every student and to consider each individual's needs is the essence of good teaching.

This statement's meaning probably requires even more careful thought today than it did in the past. We are living in an age of a digital technology revolution when the amount of information available to teachers and their students is exploding, accessible on devices that we carry in our pockets. Teachers must encourage students to embrace the value of examining multiple viewpoints on a topic but also teach them how to evaluate the validity of information. Hence, our commitment might better be stated as recognizing the importance of *multiple* truths and *multiple expressions* of excellence. This phrase also reminds us to honor democratic principles such as individual expression, capitalizing on special student interests, and expanding students' abilities to explore and critique multiple ideas and values.

The NEA Code of Ethics includes principles of commitment to the student and to the profession. It includes the responsibility to adhere to the highest ethical standards: "Your ethical responsibility as a teacher goes beyond telling the truth. Your responsibility is to place the needs of students at the center of your work and to give them priority over your own needs."

Hence, your constant question should be, "What is in the best interests of my students?" This is important as you consider a career in teaching. Many people enter the profession and discover that it is difficult to be as generous of spirit as the profession demands. That would not make you a bad person, but you need to consider how it relates to the goodness of fit between this profession and your personal attributes.

National Education Association (NEA) The largest organization of teachers and other education professionals, headquartered in Washington, DC.

An Organized Profession

Overall, teaching is a highly organized profession. In addition to the NEA, the **American Federation of Teachers (AFT)**, created in 1916 and affiliated with the U.S. labor movement, has more than 1.6 million members. Both the NEA and the AFT provide legal services and collective bargaining representation as well as a network of support for teachers, including professional development resources for your growth as a teacher. These large groups also wield a great deal of political influence on behalf of educators and schools.

When you enter the teaching profession, you may decide to join one or both of these organizations. We will visit them again in this book's final chapter, but it is not too early to think about becoming a member.

Starting Early

The **National Association for the Education of Young Children (NAEYC)** is the nation's largest early-learning professional organization. Early-childhood education is the most critical stage for preparing future learners. The NAEYC has standards for creating the first step in the "cradle-to-career" educational pipeline. High-quality early-learning programs are the foundation for future success in schools. The NAEYC focuses on the quality of education for all children, birth through age 8. A look at the position statement on student diversity developed by the NAEYC (see "Honoring Diversity: Position Statement") provides insight into the ways in which teaching very young children could never be considered an afterthought! We will explore the role of early education in leveling the playing field for young children of poverty in Chapter 6.

iStock/kali9

American Federation of Teachers (AFT) An international union, affiliated with the American Federation of Labor and Congress of Industrial Organizations, representing teachers and other school personnel as well as many college faculty and staff members, health care workers, and public employees.

National Association for the Education of Young Children (NAEYC) This professional organization is dedicated to improving the quality of education for all children, birth to age 8.

HONORING DIVERSITY: POSITION STATEMENT

Young children and their families reflect a great and rapidly increasing diversity of language and culture. The NAEYC recommendations emphasize that early-childhood programs are responsible for creating a welcoming environment that respects diversity, supports children's ties to their families and community, and promotes both second language acquisition and preservation of children's home languages and cultural identities. Linguistic and cultural diversity is an asset, not a deficit, for young children.

Recommendations for working with families

- *Actively involve families in the early-learning program.* Links between school, home, and community are important for all young children, but forging them can be challenging when families and program staff differ in culture and language. Ties to the community, respectful relationships with families, and encouragement of active, culturally meaningful family involvement are essential.

- *Help all families realize the cognitive advantages of a child knowing more than one language, and provide them with strategies to support, maintain, and preserve home-language learning.* Families may think that speaking to their children only in English will help them learn the language faster. But home-language preservation benefits children's cognitive development, and families with limited English proficiency provide stronger language models when they emphasize their home language.

- *Convince families that their home's cultural values and norms are honored.* Continuity between home and the early-childhood setting supports children's social, emotional, cognitive, and language development. Though not always identical, practices at home and in school should be complementary.

Recommendations for working with young children

- *Ensure that children remain cognitively, linguistically, and emotionally connected to their home language and culture.*

Children's positive development requires maintaining close ties to their family and community. If home language and culture are supported, children, families, and communities stay securely connected.

- *Encourage home language and literacy development, knowing that this contributes to children's ability to acquire English language proficiency.* Research confirms that bilingualism is an asset and an educational achievement. When children become proficient and literate in their home language, they transfer those skills to a second language.

- *Help develop essential concepts in the children's first language and within cultural contexts that they understand.* Although some children can seem superficially fluent in their second language, most children find it easier to learn new, complex concepts in a familiar language and cultural framework. Once established, these concepts readily transfer into a second language and contribute to later academic mastery.

Respect for diversity must become part of every classroom teacher's agenda, regardless of grade level and subject matter, and of whether the teacher looks and sounds like his or her students.

Honoring diversity means accepting that we are all products of our own culture, our own biases, and our own beliefs. You must constantly ask: "Who are my students? What are their lives like? What are their stories? . . . and knowing these things, how can I help them learn?" This is all part of respecting the learner and ultimately respecting ourselves as learners. Chapter 5 addresses the issue of the wide diversity of students in today's schools and its implications for teaching and learning. If we think of diversity as an opportunity, we will grow from the challenge and become better teachers.

A National Board

In 1987, the **National Board for Professional Teaching Standards (NBPTS)** was created to set forth a vision for what accomplished teachers might "look like." These principles were developed in response to the report *A Nation Prepared: Teachers for the 21st Century* (Carnegie Forum on Education and the Economy, 1986). National Board certification was designed to develop, retain, and recognize accomplished teachers and to generate ongoing improvement in

schools nationwide. It is the most respected professional certification available in K–12 education. Created by teachers for teachers, these standards represent a consensus among educators about what accomplished teachers should know and be able to do. Board certification is available in 25 areas spanning 16 disciplines from pre-K through 12th grade (http://www.nbpts.org/national-board-certification/overview/). Besides being an advocacy organization, the NBPTS offers a national system to certify teachers who meet these standards.

The NBPTS intends this entirely voluntary certification to be a symbol of professional teaching excellence (National Board for Professional Teaching Standards, 2002).

National Board for Professional Teaching Standards (NBPTS) A nonprofit organization that aims to advance the quality of teaching by developing professional standards for teachers.

State licensing systems for teachers set entry-level standards, but NBPTS certification requires more advanced standards. There are now over 112,000 National Board-certified teachers in all 50 states. This represents over 3% of all teachers. In Chapter 10, we will review the standards set forth by the NBPTS as well as some of the components of the certification test. For now, the board and its work is yet another indication of the professionalism of teaching and the exciting prospects you have in entering the field.

More Than a Profession

We have been talking about teaching as a profession, but is that all it is? Carl Jung, the noted Swiss psychiatrist, said:

> An understanding heart is everything in a teacher. One looks back with appreciation at the brilliant teachers, but with gratitude to those who touched our human feeling. The curriculum is so much necessary raw material, but warmth is the vital element for the growing plant and for the soul of the child. (McGuire, 1954, para. 249)

So much is said about the skills and knowledge that are needed for teaching. The unspoken requirement, however, has to do with your disposition—your own ability to understand your students and to connect with them in ways that help them become better learners.

More than in most other professions, your personality and your belief in yourself shine through the techniques and strategies you employ. Your authentic self—that part of you that wants to make a contribution to the social good—is evident in the way you address the students, in your smile, in your level of preparedness for class, in the questions you ask, and in the respect you demonstrate for students as individuals. As you work with this text, be sure to explore your innermost hopes and dreams, and keep asking yourself, "Is teaching really for me?"

The Workplace: School Climate and School Culture

The day-to-day workings of a school influence how you enact your philosophy of teaching. Schools are constantly in flux, depending on student enrollment, collaboration among colleagues, pressures from the local community, and the vision of the school leader.

iStock/monkeybusinessimages

▲ Some classroom climates can be experienced even by a casual observer.

CAN YOU FEEL THE SCHOOL CLIMATE?

Frequently, you can tell if a school's climate is nurturing by the feeling you get in the halls—if the principal and other administrators are readily visible, and if teachers smile and greet students by name. In such a school, students are treated as individuals.

At the other extreme, in a school with an authoritarian climate, the halls are very quiet, there are strict "no talking" rules, doors are closed tight, and there is a feeling of tension in the air.

Teaching practices, student and teacher diversity, and the relationships among administrators, teachers, parents, and students all contribute to school climate.

Although no single, universally accepted definition of school culture has been established, there is general agreement that it involves deep patterns of values, beliefs, and traditions formed over the course of the school's history (Deal & Peterson, 1999). A school culture may have, for instance, a reputation for being very academic. My high school did. The culture of my high school could be described as academically driven, college preparatory, nonathletic, and cerebral. We

were thought of as geeks because we attended this serious-minded high school whose culture had been forged since its inception. Other high schools in my area had a culture that was more social, athletic, and active in the community, though also academic.

A school's culture is evident in its shared values, heroes, rituals, ceremonies, stories, and cultural networks. For example, if a school's leaders believe that motivation and academic achievement are a definitive part of the school's culture, they communicate and celebrate those values in as many ways as possible. A strong school culture flourishes with a clear set of values and norms that actively guide the way the school functions. In my high school, students were made to feel proud of the academic productivity of their classmates. Achievement was rewarded in the school newspaper and in organized assemblies.

When you think back to the ways in which the schools you attended functioned, how would you describe the school culture of your elementary, middle, and high schools? What did the schools stand for? How was that communicated?

As you think about applying a teacher's professional commitments and values in a particular school setting, there are two terms you should know: **school climate and school culture.** These phrases refer to "the sum of the values, cultures, safety practices, and organizational structures within a school that cause it to function and react in particular ways" (McBrien & Brandt, 1997, p. 87).

Often, the two terms, school climate and school culture, are used interchangeably, but some educators make a distinction between them: *school climate* refers to the way students experience the school, and *school culture* means the way teachers and administrators interact and collaborate.

Still other educators think about school climate as the general social atmosphere or environment in a school. This is my preferred way of using the term. The social environment in this sense includes the relationships among students, between students and teachers, among teachers themselves, and between teachers and administrators. Students experience their environment differently depending on the rules and protocols set up by school administrators and teachers. School climate also includes the "orderliness of the environment, the clarity of the rules, and the strictness of the teachers in enforcing the rules" (Moos, 1979, p. 96).

Think back to your educational autobiography. According to the definition of school climate as the general social atmosphere, how would you describe the climate of your elementary school, middle school, and high school? A school climate may be described as nurturing, authoritarian, or somewhere in between. For example, I experienced my high school as simultaneously nurturing and strict, caring and rigorous. We can also ask whether a school has a healthy climate, one in which students are made aware of expectations for their behavior toward one another and their teachers. In your own elementary school, middle school, and high school, was the student body diverse in terms of ethnicity, race, and social class, and if so, was there evidence of prejudice or racism? How was that expressed? What did school officials do to make students feel like valued members of the educational community?

An Era of Testing and Standardization

In 2002, the federal law No Child Left Behind (NCLB) was passed. Among other provisions, it required public schools to test every student in Grades 3 through 8 in reading and mathematics. It is safe to say that the 13 years that followed its passage are considered the **era of testing** and standardization in education.

school climate and school culture The values, cultures, practices, and organization of a school.

In December 2015, the federal Every Student Succeeds Act (ESSA) standardized tests in each state to measure basic skills and rote learning. Many of you reading this text may have taken these same tests in your precollege education. These tests are often referred to as *standards-based assessments*, referring to assessments that compare student accomplishment to preestablished achievement goals rather than to the achievement of other students. The standard is supposed to be absolute, independent of the students who meet it. By contrast, norm-referenced tests describe what students can do relative to other students. The fact that a student scores at the 60th percentile in mathematics in a norm-referenced test, for example, tells us only that she fares as well as or better than 60% of her peers—not how many mathematical skills she has mastered.

Education standards in content areas are designed to define what students should know and be able to do in that area of learning. The standards-based assessments measure students' progress based on their test performance. Teachers all over the country have been trained to help students meet the expectations of these tests, and this has strongly influenced the daily life of the classroom.

The ESSA replaced the NCLB Act while maintaining many provisions of the NCLB. ESSA provides for more flexibility in standardized testing to be determined by the states. It is important to note that both laws were reauthorizations of the 1965 Elementary and Secondary Education Act (ESEA), which asserted that full educational opportunity should be our nation's top priority. As you will see in Chapter 3, education is federally funded and locally implemented. ESSA goes a long way in providing states with more local control than did NCLB. It remains unclear what effects this has had on standardized testing. While the subject of many disparaging views, NCLB highlighted educational inequality in this country, known as the *achievement gap*.

Concluding Thoughts

Although teaching is an important and essential profession, ideas about it are often oversimplified. Our memories of our teachers are sometimes selective and misleading. However, the interpersonal nature of teaching demands that those interested in the profession take stock of their own attributes and dispositions, their personal school experiences, and their future goals for themselves as teachers. It is never too soon to start reflecting on your decision to become a teacher.

era of testing The period of time since the passage in 2001 of the federal No Child Left Behind Act that mandated standardized testing in mathematics and language arts in Grades 3 through 8.

CHAPTER REVIEW

Key Terms

American Federation of Teachers (AFT) (p. 9)

educational autobiography (p. 5)

era of testing (p. 12)

goodness of fit (p. 7)

National Association for the Education of Young Children (NAEYC) (p. 9)

National Board for Professional Teaching Standards (NBPTS) (p. 10)

National Education Association (NEA) (p. 9)

philosophy of teaching statement (p. 7)

reflective practitioner (p. 4)

school climate and school culture (p. 12)

Review the Learning Outcomes

Review each section of the chapter and answer the following:

LO 1-1 What does your own educational history imply for your future as a teacher?

LO 1-2 How do you assess your goodness of fit between your personal qualities and the demands of teaching?

LO 1-3 Give an example of the effect a committed teacher may have on the school climate.

LO 1-4 What do you think is the lasting effect of the era of testing?

InTASC Standards

Review the InTASC Standards for the chapter and explain how the chapter addressed each one.

Standard 3: Learning Environment

Standard 9: Professional Learning and Ethical Practice

Journal Prompt

Compare the qualities of a good teacher as described by the 5Cs with your own personal qualities. Are there some you do not have currently but could work to develop?

SAGE edge™

Get the tools you need to sharpen your study skills. SAGE edge offers a robust online environment featuring an impressive array of free tools and resources.

Access practice quizzes, eFlashcards, video, and multimedia at **edge.sagepub.com/koch4e**.

Purestock/Getty Images

Teaching Stories

Storytelling is the most powerful way to put ideas into the world today.

—Robert McAfee Brown, American theologian and teacher, 1920–2001

Learning Outcomes

After reading this chapter, you should be able to:

2-1 Describe what the expression "We teach who we are!" means.

2-2 Think about how the hidden curriculum affects the climate in the classroom.

2-3 Explore the support systems that are in place for new teachers.

2-4 Compare the lifelong learning needs of teachers with those in other professions.

2-5 Start your own teaching story as you explore teaching as a career.

InTASC Standards

- Standard 3: Learning Environments
- Standard 6: Assessment
- Standard 7: Planning for Instruction
- Standard 9: Learning Environments

Through the stories of new and experienced teachers, this chapter provides a glimpse into the ways teachers from grades pre-K–12 make their decisions to enter the field and what they consider the most exciting and challenging aspects of their work. Their stories are designed to help you explore what Parker Palmer (2017) calls the "inner landscape of a teacher's life."

Being a teacher requires an emotional and intellectual commitment. In a typical school day, teachers can experience excitement and frustration, pleasure and angst, great leaps of joy as well as sadness. How ready you are to navigate these emotions—while at the same time staying focused on your goals for the day—is something only you can know. The stories in this chapter may remind you of yourself or of a teacher you have had.

Taking the Roll Call for Students and Teachers

About 56 million students are enrolled in American public and private elementary and secondary schools with over 50 million students in public schools. An estimated 5.3 million students attend private schools. Serving these students are 3.6 million teachers, which includes over 400,000 private school teachers. In public schools, between 1985 and 2015, there was a 30% increase in elementary enrollment (pre-K through Grade 8), compared with a 17% increase in secondary enrollment (Grades 9–12). Part of the relatively fast growth in public elementary school enrollment resulted from the expansion of pre-K enrollment (U.S. Department of Education, 2017a).

The majority of public school teachers in the U.S. workforce are more than 30 years of age, with an average age of 42. About 80% are White, which is a decline from 90% in 2001; 77% are female (U.S. Department of Education, 2017b).

Given the increasing diversity of students in the United States, many educators believe that U.S. schools have an urgent need for young teachers from varied ethnic backgrounds. Efforts to diversify the nation's teaching workforce have not kept up with the changing landscape of our students. For example, it is important that more men enter the profession, since researchers have asserted that male role models are significant figures in the classroom. Black men are the most underrepresented demographic in the teaching workforce (Mitchell, 2016). Studies are exploring what it takes to recruit and keep minority male teachers in the classroom (Bristol, 2015). Many non-White males see teaching as a woman's profession, especially at the pre-K and elementary levels where the absence of males, especially non-White males, is most pronounced. We know that more than half of all teachers, public and private, are between 30 and 49 years of age, while only 15% are under age 30 (Figure 2.1). This speaks to the large number of younger teachers that leave the profession. It also speaks to the importance of emphasizing how rewarding a teaching career is and how most teachers realize satisfaction over a lifetime of teaching. It is also important to dispel teacher stereotypes. In addition, notice that over 55% of teachers have attained a master's degree or higher, signaling the importance of lifelong learning as they continue in their careers.

Early-Childhood Education

There are many more early-childhood teachers today than there were just a few years ago, paralleling the rise of pre-K classes in public and private schools. In Chapter 1, we described the National Association for the Education of Young People (NAEYC), a group that works tirelessly on improving the education of our youngest students.

A national association dedicated to the early education of children highlights the significance of an auspicious beginning for a child's future learning.

You may be wondering why so much attention is given to preschool and kindergarten through second grade. Preschool, pre-K, and kindergarten play a vital role in the development of children. What they learn and experience in their early years shapes their views of themselves and the world. Early-learning programs, enrolling children as young as 3 years old, are seen as the key to closing achievement gaps, which we will examine later. Special sensitivities and skills are required for early-childhood teaching, and they are embodied by the following teacher.

BEN. Ben is a relatively new preschool teacher, working for his second year at a private preschool in a suburban community on the East Coast. He is well thought of by

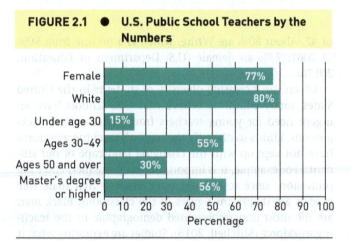

FIGURE 2.1 ● U.S. Public School Teachers by the Numbers

Category	Percentage
Female	77%
White	80%
Under age 30	15%
Ages 30–49	55%
Ages 50 and over	30%
Master's degree or higher	56%

Source: U.S. Department of Education. (2016a). *Digest of Education Statistics* (Table 105.40). https://nces.ed.gov/pubs2016/2016014.pdf

iStock/DragonImages

▲ Preschool, pre-K, and kindergarten play a vital role in the development of children. What they learn and experience in their early years shapes their views of themselves and the world. Early-learning programs, enrolling children as young as 3 years old, are seen as the key to closing achievement gaps.

his peers and adored by his students, and he is fond of saying "everything is a work in progress, including me." I experience Ben as a very calm and even-tempered person, and I could picture him being very patient with his young charges. Ben feels the stigma on preschool teaching for women and men is unwarranted. He explains that we need excellent preschool teachers to make sure that our kids are growing up well. He explains that it is important work, and you can feel like you are making a significant difference. His current group of students includes 2- and 3-year-olds, and I was interested in learning how he became a teacher of small children.

Like many teachers with whom I have spoken, Ben "fell into" preschool teaching. After being unsure of his college major, he took some education classes and eventually majored in English and philosophy. He explains:

"I always knew I wanted to teach; however, I thought I would want to teach older students. I have always liked and got along very well with my young cousins, so when a good friend, who had been teaching at this preschool and really enjoying it, suggested to me that I may like teaching preschool students, I gave it a try. The rest is history. I definitely learned on the job through professional development courses and by being coached by my peer teachers, and I discovered that working with young children is something I am good at."

When asked about the upsides of preschool teaching, he remarked:

"Understanding the impact you can make on very young children is really an important reward. I love knowing that the children are having a good time and that they are happy to see me; sometimes kids don't want to leave. Happy kids are those who are learning!"

He explained that his goals include promoting the children's social development:

"I want them to understand that their words are powerful and that they can use their words to communicate with each other. Watching the children improve in that skill is very rewarding. I also love to watch them build skills for themselves, so I am careful not to do too much for them and to encourage them to do it themselves . . . whether it be putting on their shoes or opening their lunches. I try not to do these tasks for them, and I am getting better at this every day. I show the children how to do a task and encourage them to do it themselves. It is so important to set a young child on a path where they can feel good about themselves . . . that feeling of 'look what I can do.'"

When asked what was most stressful about his work, Ben responded by explaining how difficult it was at the beginning not to do things for the children.

"I found myself learning from my students . . . the way they develop, and the challenges they are facing. It was really difficult at first not to do things for the children, but that does not help them learn for themselves."

Instead, Ben spends time patiently holding out the expectations that they can perform the task on their own with a bit of guidance.

"You have to be so consistent with young children and know how important your language is. They are teaching me a lot every single day. I tell them that their words are the most important thing they have. I feel like I plant little seeds."

Often, early-childhood educators are dismissed by society as glorified babysitters. This is incorrect and damaging to the profession and to an understanding of the crucial role that early learning plays in the development of healthy children and productive students. There is consistent controversy over the role of play in early-learning environments. Watching young children at play reminds us of the social skills the students develop through play, such as empathy, impulse control, capacity for sharing, communicating, and problem solving. Play-based activities also enhance children's capacity to think creatively, make choices, explore their environment, and develop prewriting and sequencing skills. Learning is an interactive, social experience that requires communication between the learners and their peers as well as their teachers. Perhaps the most dominant misconception about early-childhood teaching is that it is not as work-intensive as teaching in the higher grades. In fact, preparing a curriculum and activities for young children requires many hours of research and careful planning. Preschool teachers often work in teams, collaborating on a wide range of early-childhood issues. Ben shares that:

"Watching more experienced teachers work and having conversations with them has been so helpful. Everything that my peers do is in the interests of their kids. Even if you do not understand it at first, when you learn their reasoning, you know their goals are to help the children grow."

Like the teachers you will read about in the following section, Ben receives support from his colleagues and from taking professional development courses.

Deciding to Become a Teacher

In my entire life as a student, I remember only twice being given the opportunity to come up with my own ideas, a fact I consider typical and terrible.

—Eleanor Duckworth, educational researcher (1991)

The Bureau of Labor Statistics' description of "Teaching for a Living" begins with the following: "If you dream of inspiring the minds of the future, consider teaching" (Vilorio, 2016). Over the years, I have often asked elementary, middle, and high school teachers from all backgrounds to talk about themselves and their attitudes toward the profession. We begin with what some of them said about their reasons for becoming teachers. Notice how, for some teachers, both new and experienced, teaching was a calling. For others, they had twists and turns in their careers before winding up in the classroom. Think about their stories as you begin your own journey.

KATHRYN.   Kathryn is a high school biology and chemistry teacher, teaching Grades 9 and 10 in a suburban northeastern school district. She teaches in two different schools in the same district and goes back and forth between them. Her students adore her, and she works them really hard. She majored in the sciences in college and took a minor in secondary education. She just always knew that, as much as she loves scientific research, she always wanted to be a teacher:

"When I was in elementary school, I loved being able to try new things and make new discoveries. I think I was initially taken with the idea of daily exploration in any way, shape, or form, and that trend continued well into middle and high school. Even simple things seemed magical in a classroom; tadpoles transformed in front of us; dissecting frogs became a lesson in the operating room; learning poetry turned me into John Donne. When considering college options, I knew my heart belonged in teaching. I spent much of my high school career forcing myself to master material, with the most effective method being through explanations to my peers. I had heard the saying multiple times, that if you want to prove you know a subject, try teaching it to someone else. Being in school exposed me to the teaching profession, and I thrived in an environment that challenged me to adapt socially, intellectually, and emotionally on a daily basis. I knew that not every job had the potential to do that."

HELENE.   Helene is a wildly popular French teacher, and for the last 7 years has taught five classes of seventh and eighth graders as part of the world languages department of a suburban middle school in the mid-Atlantic. Born and raised mostly in France, Helene's decision to become a teacher was not easy for her, even though most of her family in France are teachers. Helene majored and then worked in business for several years before deciding to get her master's degree in education and become certified to teach Grades K–8. She had been surrounded in her early life by people who loved teaching. She wanted to instill in young people an appreciation for another language and its culture. She is known for creating a warm and caring atmosphere in her classroom. Here's how she responded when asked how she found her way to teaching:

"I entered a 10-month intensive graduate program that included two student teaching placements, and I loved them both. I knew I was making the right decision. I was one of those people who became a teacher to make a difference. I wanted to do something good. I started at the elementary level and loved it, but as I got older, I realized 'why not teach French?' It is my native language! It was a challenge to prepare myself for teaching French, especially because I am a native speaker. I was an experienced educator at this point, but I was doing something brand-new to me. I want to create a very warm and caring atmosphere in my classroom, and if you make a mistake, I will not single you out, I will hold your hand and walk you through it. The most exciting thing about my work is my relationships with students. It is at the root of my work and determines the pleasure I get out of the process. When students feel like they know you and trust you and that you care, they will do anything for you."

iStock/asiseeit

JESSICA. Jessica is an English teacher and literacy coordinator in a high school on a military base in the Midwest. She has been teaching for 15 years. As an undergraduate, she majored in dance, her first love. This is how she answers the question about deciding to become a teacher:

"I had always wanted to be a teacher. When I was growing up, I loved to play school with the children I babysat, and I would give the neighborhood children free dance lessons. After college, I decided that I didn't want to be a dancer full time, so I turned to my other love—English. From the very first day of my very first graduate class in education, I knew I had chosen the right career.

"I attribute my interest in teaching to several things: (1) a lifelong love of learning; (2) I had always loved going to school, even when I wasn't the best student (I did better in school as I got older); and (3) the fact that my mother is also a teacher, and I grew up watching her grade papers and plan her instruction."

AMANDA. Amanda is a third-grade teacher in the rural Northeast. When I first entered her classroom, I was struck by how quiet it was. She apologized profusely for the silence, remarking that the students were usually noisier and more actively engaged in groups, but this time they were just finishing independent reading. She promised that soon I would see the real class! So often we think of good classes as silent, but learning often happens in social exchanges with others, as we will see in later chapters. When asked why she entered teaching, Amanda said:

"Teaching has always been my calling. Ever since my first week of kindergarten, I knew that teaching would be my chosen path. That first day, I came home exclaiming to my mom, 'I want to be a teacher just like Mrs. Seguin!' I spent the rest of my elementary school days playing teacher with my sister, my friends, and even my stuffed animals when no one was available. I had grade books, lesson plans, and homemade worksheets, and I made

signs for my door that indicated my room was now 'Miss Riggs's 1st grade class.'

"Even though I have always been drawn to the profession, it wasn't until my first year of college when I was taking an education course that I began to fully understand why I wanted to be a part of education. My dad was never what one might call a reader or a writer. The only book that I saw him read was the Bible, and I remember him asking me for help in spelling different words starting in second grade. Yet it was my dad who showed me the responsibility of being an educator. I was talking with him about a literacy lesson that I needed to prepare for class. I shared the many techniques that I had learned and how I was going to have the kids first participate in a hands-on activity and then draw the knowledge out from the activity. My father changed my outlook on education forever when he said, 'I would have learned how to read and write if my teachers had taught like you.' It was then that I realized I wanted to be a teacher to reach those kids who couldn't learn through traditional teaching methods. I wanted to find a way so that every student 'clicked' with literacy and gained the skills to make his or her life one of continuous learning."

CHERYL. Cheryl has been teaching elementary school for 19 years and is currently a sought-after and beloved teacher in a K–5 elementary school on the east coast. Formerly a third-grade teacher, this is her first year teaching second grade, and she is enjoying the challenge. According to Cheryl, staying in one grade for too long can make you stale. She loves working with a new team of colleagues and a new curriculum. While Cheryl works in an affluent community during the school year, she teaches during the summer in a high-needs area where the challenges and rewards are very different. Cheryl's path to becoming a classroom teacher went like this:

"Going into teaching was a comfort level for me. As the oldest of five children, we were always around a lot of children, and I had a high level of comfort and confidence with children. At family gatherings, I was always the leader. I studied early-childhood education when I went to college and then when I moved to another state I went back to school for another certification for older grades. I would say I fell into teaching because of the comfort level and because, when I was volunteering, I realized how much I enjoyed working with students. As a young mother, I volunteered in my children's elementary school and was approached by the principal to consider being a full-time teacher in that school. I had not thought of making the commitment at that time; however, I was encouraged to get certified and join the full-time teaching force. I'm so glad I did."

iStock/Fabrique Imagique

▲
Teachers are important role models for their students.

When speaking with Cheryl, one gets the impression that her "falling into teaching" was a natural extension of her life and her education. As we can see, this is not always the case. Often when teachers are asked why they decided to enter the profession, they say, "I love children" or "I love kids." These answers echo the findings of many formal studies. Another burning reason for deciding to become a teacher is an individual's love of learning. The most successful teachers I know—like the ones featured in this chapter—typically talk about how they "loved learning." That is not to say they do not also love children, but teaching is a complex activity. In the words of educational researcher Jackie Grennon Brooks (2002):

> Common thinking is that teaching is simple. But teaching isn't simple. It's a highly sophisticated intellectual activity that requires, among other things, a centered presence in the classroom, good negotiation skills, understandings of pedagogy and psychology that inform one another, and sensitivity to sociological factors in learning. (p. 11)

When beginning education students talk about entering teaching because they love kids, I learn from talking with them that they have been babysitters and camp counselors, and that they have enjoyed these responsibilities. That is a fine start, but these informal experiences with children or adolescents are different from the more structured experiences found in classrooms and the demands of teaching. At this point in your education, you may have already visited one or more classrooms and observed teaching in action, so you are aware of the vast differences between the formal and informal settings in which we interact with youngsters.

In addition to loving learning, people pursuing teaching careers often also loved school. Notice especially what Kathryn said about the inspiration provided by daily exploration and experimentation.

Sometimes, a future teacher will tell me that he or she finds the profession appealing because they like the hours! One visit to the Bureau of Labor Statistics reveals the following: For many teachers, the workday starts early and ends late. Job duties vary by subject and grade level, but teaching involves class preparation, instruction time, and after-school duties. The idea of teaching as a 9 to 3 job is a myth.

Another major reason secondary teacher candidates cited for becoming educators was prior experience as a high school tutor or peer teacher. Some teacher candidates were motivated to teach because of positive experiences in informal teaching settings, and some had early religious training that affected their desire to serve others and teach.

What about Helene's story? She started working in business, as some of you may have, and then realized she wanted to make a difference for young people. Not everyone who enters the field has had a lifelong calling to teach. Yet life as a teacher becomes fulfilling when there is a good match between the person and the demands of the profession. This is what I referred to as goodness of fit in Chapter 1.

Excitement and Challenges in Teaching

*Every September, every teacher proceeds
into foreign territories.*
—Maxine Hong Kingston, distinguished
writer and professor

When teachers are asked about the most exciting aspects of their work, invariably their answers relate to student learning. In this section, we explore what some teachers say really excites them about their work, and then we examine some difficult challenges.

What Are the Most Exciting Aspects of Teaching?

KATHRYN. "When I started teaching, I lived for the light bulb moments—the times when difficult concepts finally

WRITING & REFLECTION
"I LIKE THE HOURS"

Sam wakes up one morning and says, "I want to be a teacher." When asked why, Sam answers, "I like the hours."

This is an uninspiring reason, and it is misguided as well. Did you know that teachers work much longer than the traditional 9:00-to-3:00 day? Look at the following data the National Education Association (NEA, 2006) gathered from its teacher members:

Twenty-first-century teachers

- spend an average of 50 hours per week on all teaching duties,

- teach an average of 21 pupils in a class at the elementary level and 28 pupils per class at the secondary level,

- spend an average of $443 per year of their own money to meet the needs of their students, and

- enter the teaching profession to help shape the next generation.

clicked for a student. I liked being challenged to think of explanations and analogies that were outside of the box. As much as you plan and try to perfect your lesson, there will always be something that can totally derail a class. People are unpredictable, and the spontaneous moments show both the students' and the teacher's true colors. A lot of the profession is having the flexibility to handle whatever situation arises. I love being able to say that not a day goes by where I do the exact same thing. Good teachers change their lessons, try new techniques, master skills that work, but nothing is ever the same—guaranteeing that every day will be exciting.

"I don't like the clock. The students in my building have a unique set of challenges, and I do the best I can to let them know they are safe and supported in my classroom. When students know you care, they are willing to go the extra mile for their teacher, and that's what makes my job so exciting. To have your 'work' thank you is probably the most rewarding feeling ever."

AMANDA. "To me, the process of teaching and learning is exciting—the look on a student's face when he or she finally gets it, watching a student move from confusion to understanding, fielding a question you did not expect and do not know the answer to. It has been my greatest joy to see that student who struggled so much in an area work hard and become successful.

"There are many times when I struggle with presenting difficult material so that all students can grasp the 'big idea' of the lesson. I can go through four or five activities in my room, and sometimes there are a handful of kids who just cannot make sense of the material. Finally finding a way to reach those kids—now that is exciting.

"The classroom is a complex roller-coaster ride in the dark; you never know what will happen next. From scheduling

iStock/Rawpixel

changes to student needs, environmental factors (try teaching about fractions in 90-degree weather!), and even your own moods, no plan is ever left in its original state. An educator must roll with the needs of his or her students, and those needs are ever changing, every day. I find that exciting."

JESSICA. "The most exciting aspects of being a teacher are the possibilities that come with each new day. I teach adolescents, and they truly are different people every day. Watching them change and grow from the first day of the school year to the last is like watching a transformation right in front of your own eyes, and it is very exciting and challenging."

HELENE. "What fills me up is when I see increased self confidence in the students and when the students feel comfortable using the language and taking risks. I am most surprised by how much I care about the kids. I get choked up about it because as a student, I had a lot of negative experiences. I want the students to enjoy learning and enjoy being in school; if you enjoy learning, you will persist through it."

CHERYL. "I love the 'ah-ha' moment where you can watch kids connect the dots and have them recognize what they are really good at. Then they can start liking themselves and show pride in their accomplishments. My favorite part of the day is when the kids are so excited to get into the classroom, and when I hear the bell ring and when those kids walk in the door, I feel their excitement. They are happy to be in my room. They tell me their news since last we were together: 'I painted my room last night.' 'Today's my father's birthday.' They know I care."

Rewards of a Teaching Life

The following observations about teaching provide an overview of these teachers' beliefs based on their experiences and their hopes for the profession as they continue. You can think of these observations as the "teaching ideas behind their stories."

- For these teachers, the idea of meeting new students every year and, in Jessica's case, feeling like there are new students almost daily, is a stimulating aspect of being a teacher. Each day is different, requiring a sharp and attentive adult presence in the classroom. These teachers enjoy the challenge.

- Kathryn loves that every day is a new challenge and that nothing is ever the same.

- Amanda notes that the process of teaching is more exciting than the outcomes. Like Amanda, many teachers try different approaches to content material to make sure they reach the various types of learners in their classes.

- Kathryn, Amanda, Helene, Cheryl, and Jessica talk about the excitement of reaching the children and recognizing that they "got it" as it related to new knowledge construction.

- These teachers, typical of most, work actively on their teaching preparations and constantly challenge themselves to come up with novel ways to engage students in their own learning. They remind me that "to teach is to learn." Kathryn tells us that she really understands a concept when she has to decide how to teach it.

What Are the Most Difficult Challenges for Teachers?

KATHRYN. "I've always prided myself on staying organized and on top of all responsibilities. Sometimes it's incredibly easy, and other times you don't know how you will make it through the day. There are just so many facets to being a good teacher that require all of your attention, that multitasking alone isn't possible. The paperwork, the grading, the extra help, the lesson planning, the

phone calls, the make-up work, the list goes on and on, and it all adds up to an incredible amount of time. Finding time to complete everything to my personal level of satisfaction is hard. Not every new teacher is prepared for that when they walk in the door—I know I wasn't. I still give up Saturdays and end up having 13-hour Thursdays, but every minute is worth it when I know my students are becoming productive members of society and developing skills that will serve them throughout their life. I know that planning is so important for the success of the lesson.

"At first, I was intimidated by my colleagues and was afraid to ask for help. Your fellow teachers are your greatest allies. Any sports team will work better when they rely on each other, and teachers of any discipline learn that together they make better lessons. Each person has a unique set of talents, and every student deserves access to that. I have found that, in collaborating, we have motivational, engaging, exciting lessons that reach all levels of learners."

AMANDA. "I find that the most difficult challenge is staying focused on my purpose. I am not in the room to raise test scores, to be a child's best friend. I am there to help students go beyond their potential and gain skill sets needed for a successful, learning life. Many distractions are found in the school environment—often created by those who are well meaning. Stick to what you know is best for your students despite what others around you might think. Planning is everything . . . it helps keep you focused on your goals for the kids.

"One year, my room was across the hall from a teacher whom you might refer to as burned out. Every morning, she arrived at the same time as the kids. By the time the children began to enter her room, my classroom was busy with morning learning activities. At least four times a week, our classroom was disrupted with her rants of 'Why do Mrs. P's students get right to work and you are out here talking! I am tired of my class not being ready for the day!' These outbursts not only damaged her class but mine as well.

"A good educator knows how to instruct students about expected behaviors and not shout about bad behaviors. No matter how frustrated, disappointed, or exhausted I become, I am here as a teacher and a learner, and learning happens mostly by my example—a good example or a poor one."

CHERYL. "Teaching, like children, is not 'boxy.' Every day is different, and you need to make your own decisions in your own classroom. Now there are unannounced 'walk-throughs' all the time by administration because there is a movement for uniformity that does not match the challenges of teaching a diverse population. Teachers

TABLE 2.1 ● Recognizing and Dealing with Teacher Burnout

Signs of Burnout	What Teachers Can Do	What Schools Can Do
Your expectations for becoming a teacher and your experience are in conflict.	Consult with other teachers about your feelings and such matters as curriculum planning.	Create networks for new teachers and set up regular group meetings.
You do not feel like going to work.	Maintain a teacher journal in which you record your experiences and feelings.	Provide adequate resources and facilities to support teachers.
You have difficulty concentrating and feel inadequate in your role as a teacher.	Join new-teacher networks at your school or at the district level. Share your experiences, and keep journaling.	Provide clear job descriptions and expectations for new teachers.
You feel overwhelmed by the paperwork and the workload.	Find a mentor or seek the one to whom you have been assigned. Talk about your feelings!	Establish and maintain open communication between the school administration and the teachers.
You withdraw from your colleagues or enter into conflicts with them.	You may be emotionally exhausted. Find a professional to talk with.	Allow for and encourage professional development activities that help new teachers find mentors and become part of networks.

Sources: Adapted from Kyriacou (2001) and Wood & McCarthy (2002).

have to be strong and be advocates for yourself and your students."

Cheryl talks about having the students sit on large yoga balls instead of chairs, and recently she wrote a paper to make a case for the students sitting in this way. The county in which she worked wanted her to go back to chairs; however, her paper convinced the higher administration that sitting on these balls has many benefits for the children's posture, attentiveness, and readiness for learning.

Teaching, Learning, and Burnout

By a "learning life," Amanda refers to a desire to know more and to have the skills to acquire new knowledge when the need and desire arises. Amanda herself has a "learning life," and, by example and through practice, she engages her students in what it means to be a learner. Previously in the chapter, the quote from Jackie Grennon Brooks introduced the concept of the teacher as a "centered presence" in the classroom. Amanda's understanding of her role in the classroom and her goals for her students helps her establish this centered presence. She is prepared and capable, and has high expectations for her students. When Amanda says that learning happens by example, she means that she models to her students—demonstrates through her own behavior—what it looks like to be a learner. She learns about the content areas she teaches through her own research; she learns about her students through the interactions she has with them; and she learns about herself as she strives to refine her practice and to discover what works best for her students.

Amanda's teacher neighbor appears to be "burned out," meaning that she has lost the motivation to excel in her work and is no longer able to be an effective teacher. **Teacher burnout**, a reaction to prolonged high stress, commonly results either in withdrawing and caring less, or in working harder, often mechanically, to the point of exhaustion (Farber, 1991). As in any other field, burnout can have serious consequences for the health and happiness of teachers, their students, and the families with which they interact. There are many causes of teacher burnout, the most common being working conditions that are unsupportive and stressful interactions with parents and students. New teachers may experience burnout when the work of teaching requires a different set of skills from what they had anticipated. Teachers who have been in the profession longer and have not taken advantage of opportunities to renew their skills through formal and informal professional development may also experience burnout.

Table 2.1 lists some symptoms of burnout and steps you can take to combat it. One of the most important protections from burnout is being reflective. Remember what Chapter 1 said about being a reflective practitioner. Often, a teaching journal—an idea presented in the "Writing & Reflection" activity and the "Journal Prompts" at the end of each chapter—is helpful in this respect. Writing in the journal is a way to monitor your work and your emotional availability for the tasks ahead of you.

teacher burnout The condition of teachers who have lost their motivation, desire, sense of purpose, and energy for being effective practitioners.

Often connected to the idea of burnout are teacher complaints about their salaries. Many educators believe that the feminization of the teaching profession—the decline in the percentage of male teachers—has helped reduce the pressure on administrators and school boards to authorize better pay and benefits for teachers. Of course, salaries for teachers differ depending on geographic location and grade level; preschool teachers make less than their colleagues at the elementary level, and elementary school teachers earn less than do those who teach at secondary schools. On average, annual salaries are highest for secondary teachers, at $57,200 per year.

Other opportunities are available for teachers who specialize in meeting the needs of students with a range of learning and physical disabilities. These teachers are often called *special education teachers*, and they are uniquely prepared to help students who have special needs. As well, teachers may become reading specialists, working with small groups of students to enhance literacy instruction in several classes each day, typically in an elementary school. Other teachers pursue gifted education, spearheading programs in schools that are designed to meet the needs of students considered performing well above their grade level. These special areas of concentration are discussed in later chapters.

Teachers' salaries have, in fact, risen considerably over the past few decades. While salaries vary from state to state, the median salaries for all K–12 teachers are presented in Table 2.2.

TABLE 2.2 ● All K–12 Teachers Median Salary by Job	
High School Teacher	$48,106
Middle School Teacher	$46,054
Special Education Teacher, Preschool, Kindergarten, or Elementary School	$45,290
Special Education Teacher, Secondary School	$49,275

Source: Payscale.com. (n.d.). *Average salary for all K–12 teachers.* https://www.payscale.com/research/US/All_K-12_Teachers/Salary

Challenges and Opportunities

When asked to discuss the challenges in their professional lives as teachers, responses overwhelmingly focused on the demands from the school community, outside of meeting the needs of the students. Jessica sums it up here:

JESSICA. "One of the most difficult challenges for teachers stems from paperwork! I had no idea going into the profession how much paperwork there is to manage. I assumed that lesson plans, student handouts, and student work would be all the paperwork I'd come into contact with. In addition to those items, there are constant requests for information from the office, the nurse, the psychologists, special education teachers, parents, administrators, and even

WRITING & REFLECTION
BEGIN A TEACHING JOURNAL

Start now to keep a professional journal for yourself. If you have not had a lot of practice journaling, starting a reflective journal can be daunting. You may want to begin by inserting the writing activities from Chapter 1: drawing yourself as a teacher and your metaphor or simile for teaching, as well as your educational autobiography and a memory of a favorite teacher. You can keep your journal in a notebook, a blank book, a binder, or digitally on your computer or online—any method that is most comfortable and inspiring to you.

Being a reflective teacher is a theme we will return to again and again in this text. Reflective teachers take careful note of how their teaching practice is going and modify their methods accordingly. Because you are just embarking on teaching, your reflective journal should include how you are experiencing being an education student and what you are learning about teaching and yourself.

You can continue to fill your journal as you read this book, using as inspiration both the guided "Writing & Reflection" activities found in each chapter as well as your own thoughts

and ideas on questions and topics presented. As you journal, try to let your thoughts flow, without trying to edit them or get them down perfectly, and see where they take you. Your true feelings are more likely to surface this way.

Here are a few questions to help you begin your teaching journal:

- How are you experiencing the introductory education course you are taking?

- What are you discovering about the teaching profession that you did not know previously? Are there any surprises?

- At this point, how do you feel about a career in teaching?

Remember: You are on your own journey of growth and change, and the journal is a good record-keeping device for this process. Getting into the habit of journaling now can serve you well into your future career as a teacher.

people in the community that must be dealt with promptly and regularly. The amount of paperwork required for a classroom observation, or a field trip, or a school play, can be mind boggling.

"These things shouldn't dissuade people from becoming teachers. You learn how to deal with them effectively and appropriately soon after you begin teaching. They represent difficulties I didn't know about before I entered teaching, but the benefits of this career far outweigh the challenges in the workplace."

Jessica's comment about paperwork excluded some other areas in the daily life of the classroom where paper needs to be managed. These include attendance reports, progress reports for each student, and evidence of student work. Elementary school teachers often keep work folders for each student, whereas in the middle and upper grades, student work is often handled using computer software programs. Science teachers usually have lengthy lab reports to evaluate, and language arts and social studies teachers evaluate analytical essays, term reports, book responses, and creative writing. Fortunately, digital technology, when available, makes handling data for especially large numbers of students much more manageable. We will visit those systems in Chapter 7.

Dealing with parents is part of a teacher's responsibility. We serve the children, but they are not ours. Jessica is conflicted about her communication with parents. Of course, parents are affected by what happens at their child's school and in their child's classroom. Communication between teachers and parents is important, and it is fostered through school practices that we will explore later in this text. These practices include a class web page, e-mail communication, as well as letters home. The "paperwork" responsibilities are often "electronic communication" responsibilities. Not only can parents influence decisions made about their child's education at school, but they can also contribute to the governance of the school through a parent-teacher association or similar group. It is always a good idea to reach out to parents and invite them to become part of your classroom community as helpers and contributors. In some school districts, parents are a frequent presence in classrooms. In other communities, parents are not available as often because of work responsibilities, but it is still important to invite them to contribute whenever possible. In other communities, parents are not a frequent presence either at school or electronically. In many poorer communities, parents are working outside the home to make ends meet. The availability of electronic communication by cell phone is a help in these communities where teachers wish the parents had more time to be engaged and students rely heavily on teachers and schools for a wide range of needs.

Many people experience schools as "little villages," where the principal is the mayor and other individuals have varying amounts of importance or privilege. In all jobs, the politics of the environment can affect each of the workers. It is a good idea to learn about the expectations and norms of the school environment in which you will be working. You may already have had jobs where the politics of the environment affected your work. Although workplace politics may annoy or sometimes discourage you, keep in mind how important it is that schools function as learning communities where all the professionals share a core set of common goals.

A major challenge for teachers at all levels is the preparation required to engage students in meaningful learning experiences. Many people, like Sam earlier in this chapter, are unaware of the number of hours beyond the school day that teachers spend in preparation. Teachers can never be *over*prepared. The term *curriculum*, as we will explore later in this text, refers to a plan of studies that includes the ways in which the instructional content is organized and presented at each grade level. Even if you have studied a subject area extensively, you may need to deepen your knowledge of certain topics in the curriculum. Students know when a teacher is prepared for the school day. It is evident in the materials the teacher has assembled and the activities the teacher is ready to implement. It contributes to Brooks's centered presence in the classroom.

Teaching and Vision

Research has found that all teachers carry in their head a vision of what they want to be as a teacher (Hammerness, 2006). That is, all teachers have their own sense of what a classroom should "look like" and how it should function. Yet these visions of teaching are as variable as are the individuals who choose to teach.

Our beliefs and images concerning teaching are often difficult to enact; there is often a disconnect between what we imagine and what we can practice. For example, when I walked into a second-grade classroom early one morning, the teacher had the children in the center of the room and was engaging them in hand motions and movement routines to a popular rock song blasting from her iPad. The children were loving it! When the activity was done, Ms. Outerbridge said, "OK, girls and boys, we are now ready to work!" When I asked her about this activity, she said that (like Jessica) she had been a dancer, and her life in dance had taught her that releasing the energy in our bodies was an important way to stimulate the thinking in our minds. She worried that when her students came to class they were too docile, having already learned by Grade 2 how to "be quiet." She wanted them to be active in their bodies so they could be active thinkers about the topics of study.

"How wonderful!" I thought. I knew, however, that try as I might, I could never get myself or my youngsters to learn and then enact this intricate movement routine. I do not have that set of skills. I admired Ms. Outerbridge's vision but could not enact it. It is in this way that who we are comes to bear upon what we do with children and how we engage them in learning—hence, the expression "we teach who we are."

Throughout your journey to become a teacher, you will be asked about your personal vision. It is a goal of teacher preparation programs that you develop a personal educational philosophy informed not only by the scholars and research you have learned about in your program but also by your own beliefs, metaphors, personal vision, and values. The combination of self-knowledge and scholarly knowledge will assist you in developing your own philosophy. You started to do this in Chapter 1 when you described your personal simile or metaphor for teaching.

The mantra that "we teach who we are" permeates this text. Ms. Outerbridge is a dancer; that background has served her as a learner, and she shares her passion with her second graders. Similarly, in the story that follows, my life as a scientist found its way into a third-grade classroom not long ago.

Every week, I was visiting a local elementary school classroom and exploring different topics in physical science with them. One weekend before a visit, I was in another state celebrating the seventh birthday of my first granddaughter. Her mother, my daughter, discovered that the batteries in her digital camera appeared to be dead and asked if I had batteries in my camera that she could use. We made the switch; I handed the "dead" batteries to my husband, and my daughter was able to use her camera.

Some hours later, when we arrived back home after the party, my husband noticed that his right pocket was very warm—uncomfortably so. "What do you have in there?" I asked. "Just the batteries and my loose change," he replied. Delighted, I shrieked, "The batteries are not dead, and there is an electrical circuit in your pocket. It is generating all this heat!"

It is a family joke now that my thrill at finding "science in our daily life" seemed to overcome my empathy for his discomfort. However, I recognized that this was another opportunity to make the topic relevant to the third graders who were making circuits for an electricity unit. I told the story to them that week and stopped short of an explanation. "If my husband had the dead batteries and some loose coins in his pocket, why would it be warm? Can you draw a picture of the contents of his pocket?" Eagerly students drew coins and batteries and understood that the metal coins acted as a wire and conducted electricity.

This story illustrates how our personal lives meet our professional lives in the classroom. Your students will learn a lot about you, and you will also learn a lot about them.

▲ A wide variety of classroom activities is necessary to engage students' minds and bodies.

iStock/skynesher

Hidden Curriculum

The stories we tell students about our lives and experiences outside of school are one small part of what may be considered the **hidden curriculum**: what students learn as they participate in the act of going to school, being part of a classroom community, and relating to their peers and their teachers. The phrase *hidden curriculum* was coined by the sociologist Phillip Jackson (1968), who described ways in which schools become arenas for socialization and transmit messages to students about how to be in the world. Long before that, educational philosopher John Dewey (1916) explored the hidden curriculum in schools as he examined the social values inherent in the experience of school. Hence, the hidden curriculum includes how we interact with students, how we enact the rules of the school culture, and how we communicate our expectations for student achievement and demeanor and our own passion for teaching and learning.

By telling the batteries-in-the-pocket story to my young students, I gave them a glimpse of what it is like to be an adult with a curious, scientific mind (and a family eager to make fun of my propensities). Perhaps the story helped some students in the class feel that science is fun, interesting, and relevant to daily life—and that certainly matches my vision of what I want to do in the classroom.

Every day, through countless similar incidents, teachers contribute positively to their school's hidden curriculum. However, teachers can also affect the hidden curriculum in negative ways. If you and other teachers are bored and cynical, for instance, you convey those feelings to your students. No matter how dutifully you slog through the subject matter, students will sense that it does not interest you, and they will absorb that message.

If you call on boys more than girls, for example, the hidden curriculum of your classroom might include the idea that boys are somehow more important. In early studies of gender and schooling in the 1980s, there were many instances in which teachers called on boys more frequently than girls as a way of exercising "control" in the classroom (Sadker & Sadker, 1995; Sadker & Zittleman, 2009). The belief in the latter environment was that if you kept the boys engaged, they would not be apt to "act up." Today, we know that calling on boys and girls in equal numbers is of significant importance.

The hidden curriculum, not a part of public documents, includes messages that deal with attitudes, beliefs, values, and behavior. For example, when the No Child Left Behind Act was passed in 2002, regular assessment of mathematics and language arts prompted many elementary school administrators to allocate much more time to these subjects than to science, social studies, art, or music. The tacit message for children is that science is less important than math and reading, for example. The Every Student Succeeds Act passed in 2015 gives states more flexibility for administering

hidden curriculum What students learn, beyond the academic content, from the experience of attending school.

standardized tests and has the promise of encouraging more diversity in the school curriculum. The hidden curriculum transmits the cultural and social norms of the school (how things are done, what routines matter, what dress is acceptable, who counts and who does not!). When you visit schools and examine their routines and practices, ask yourself what matters to the leaders of this school. By exploring what is displayed in their showcases and on their walls, the hidden curriculum can be revealed.

Support for Teachers

When asked who gave them the most support in their teaching careers, Kathryn, Jessica, Helene, Cheryl, Ben, and Amanda all agreed that their colleagues were the strongest source of support. This matches research that asserts that teachers are the most successful when they are in connection with competent colleagues who are happy to mentor each other (Ebner, 2018). The teachers I interviewed mentioned other sources of support as well. As you read the following stories, think about how these teachers interacted with their colleagues and others in the school and the community.

Who Provides the Most Support to Teachers?

AMANDA. "I have found it supportive to listen to fellow teachers and the administrators, students, parents, and community members. You can learn a vast amount from conversations with others. In a crowded teachers' room, I am the one who is content to sit alone and listen in on others' conversations. As you listen, you can learn so much about the expectations, the culture, the negatives and the positives, and ways to connect to the school and community in which you teach. I find keeping a teaching journal and jotting down what I discover about the students and the school to be very helpful. I try to make entries at least two or three times a week."

▲
Working with colleagues to plan curriculum and class projects and to bounce ideas off one another is an important part of the teaching profession.

JESSICA. "In the first years of teaching, much of my support came from my fellow teachers in the building. They were the ones who knew the answers to difficult situations and who would give encouraging words. I have found that to be true even now that I am no longer a new teacher. Other educators can give you ideas, advice, and a sympathetic ear when needed, and this help can come from other new teachers as well as from veterans in the profession. I was assigned a mentor at school, and this teacher was very helpful in acclimating me to the routines and procedures that I needed to understand at the very beginning. As time went on, she became an important role model for me."

CHERYL. "For me, professional development is an opportunity to learn with my colleagues. I really like working with them; they are great sources of support. Collaborating with them, observing them, and asking them to observe me improves my practice. The team that I am on takes time to do this. It is really helpful to watch colleagues do lessons and to have them watch me. There is also mandatory professional development regardless of how many years you are teaching. We have meetings before and after work. In any group of teachers, someone will be really good at something that you are not good at. There is so much to learn."

Mentoring New Teachers

Many schools and school districts are adopting mentor teacher programs. Mentor teachers are specially trained to work with new teachers and support them in understanding the school culture, the curriculum, and the resources available to them as professionals. You may want to ask if there is a mentor program where you begin teaching. Mentoring has been a trend over the past 10 years as the teaching profession has recognized the need to develop a special transition period during which new teachers acclimate to their profession. This period as a whole is often called *induction*. Good mentors have a broad range of skills and are able to help new teachers apply their professional knowledge in the classroom. They are generally master teachers who have demonstrated a love of teaching and learning, and are eager to share their experiences with others.

Learning From New Teachers

Although it may feel like teachers new to the profession are always the learners, new research indicates that they contribute a great deal to the school environment. New teachers bring new ideas and perspectives as well as new energy to school departments and grade levels. While experienced teachers have the advantage over new teachers in many areas, new teachers often have a better understanding of the most recent research, best practices, and pedagogical or technological advances. Because teaching is often so all consuming, veteran teachers may not have time to keep up with the latest innovations or current educational research. When new teachers bring their personal expertise to a department, school, or district, it adds a lot to the school climate and curriculum (Johnson, 2018).

iStock/FatCamera

Teachers as Lifelong Learners

We are living in a rapidly changing global environment in which youngsters' and adults' lives are drastically different than they were even 10 years ago. We are all experiencing the information technology revolution, which has brought access to huge volumes of information—a degree of accessibility never before experienced in human history. This explosion of information, along with the continuous connectedness that we all feel as a result of Internet and cell phone technology, has changed the pace and progress of our daily lives.

In this ever-changing society, the activities that interest students today are necessarily different from the activities that interested you even just a few years ago. Teachers must constantly adapt and improve their skills as they respond to the recurring question: What works best in the classroom for these particular students at this period of time in our history?

Many educators today like to think of schools as **learning communities**, a term that emphasizes interaction and collaboration in the learning process. The phrase also conveys the idea that all the participants—teachers, students, and administrators—are always learning. Hence, teachers see their own continuing education as part of their work and their lives.

This need for ongoing **professional development**, as it is called, actually makes many people excited about entering teaching. These individuals understand that to teach is to learn. To improve our practice requires targeted efforts at our own growth as teachers and learners. Professional development can take many forms. We will learn more about the many ways teachers extend their education in a later chapter. For now, let's hear from Kathryn, Amanda, and Jessica to learn how they are doing it.

▲ Mentoring new teachers is a significant part of professional development in many schools.

learning communities A classroom, a cluster of classes, or a school organized so as to promote active engagement in learning, collaboration between teachers and students, and a sense that everyone involved shares the experience of being a learner.

professional development Teachers' lifelong effort to improve their skills and professional knowledge. Although professional development often includes advanced courses and workshops, much of your progress will depend on your own continued reading, reflection, and analysis.

How Do Teachers Continue Professional Development?

KATHRYN. "Professional development is easy for teachers who know they still have a lot to learn. The school I work in now consistently provides a variety of workshops focusing on literacy and technology. I attend a few seminars every year that are sponsored by a local science outreach institute. I've participated in a teacher program in Panama in association with the Smithsonian Institute to expose teachers to hands-on science. I've led workshops for my colleagues to show them how they can incorporate publications and inquiry-based projects into everyday lessons. It is challenging, it is time consuming, but when my students can apply skills because I took the time to learn them first, I know it's worth the effort."

AMANDA. "Alongside life experience, continued schooling is needed. Formal education presents important new ideas, strategies, and problems, and helps your mind grow in the same way that you want your students' minds to grow. In addition, formal education puts you in contact with professors who are experts in their fields and classmates who have a wealth of knowledge to add to your own. Being in a formal learning environment gives you a community of peers with whom you can bounce around ideas. Formal education is a wonderful resource for a teacher."

JESSICA. "I have taken courses on differentiated instruction, brain-based learning, and adolescent literacy. Whenever possible, I participate in local and national conferences, which enables me to meet teachers from all over the country. These conferences reaffirm my career choice and reinvigorate me to try new ideas with students. I belong to a number of professional organizations that offer regular publications to read and ways to network with other educators. My district sponsors online educational book studies, and I try to participate in at least one per school year; there is a wealth of helpful, thought-provoking information that can be gleaned from the experiences of other teachers. I occasionally present at conferences, which requires a new level of understanding and preparation, so this furthers my professional knowledge."

Benefits of Lifelong Learning

Teachers are expected to keep up with the latest developments in education. In many schools and districts, in fact, teachers are offered financial incentives to continue to learn through professional education courses at a college or university, or through professional development courses, often referred to as *in-service courses*, offered by the school district itself. These incentives are based on how many formal graduate school credits or professional development credits a teacher earns in a given academic year. Obviously, you'll appreciate the chance to earn a higher salary.

Yet as the stories you have just read illustrate, there are other incentives for taking professional development courses. Kathryn, Amanda, and Jessica think of themselves as lifelong learners. They take a genuine interest in expanding their minds and improving their teaching. In fact, all of them have reached the stage of doing their own research or making their own presentations—contributing to the sum of knowledge in the field.

Professional organizations can play a major role in expanding your development as a teacher. The NEA, the American Federation of Teachers, and the NAEYC, discussed in Chapter 1, offer teachers the opportunity to attend conferences, read and contribute to journals, and access professional resources. So do many other organizations; here is just a partial list.

- The National Science Teachers Association (NSTA)
- The National Council of Teachers of Mathematics (NCTM)
- The National Council of Teachers of English (NCTE)
- The National Council for the Social Studies (NCSS)

MAP 2.1 ● Participation in edTPA[1]

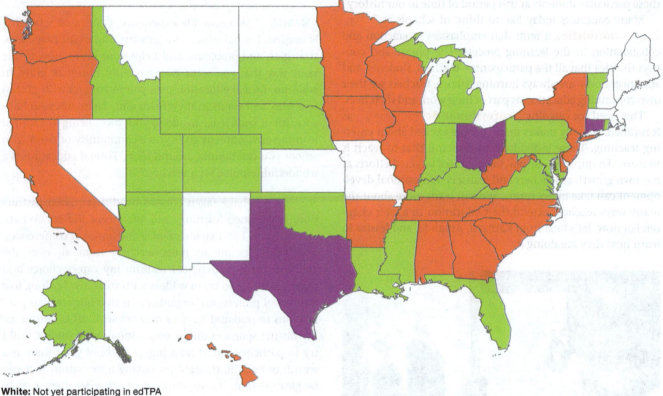

White: Not yet participating in edTPA

Orange: Policy in Place
In general, these states have statewide policies requiring a state-approved performance assessment as part of program completion or for state licensure and/or state program accreditation/review. In these states, edTPA also has been approved as a performance assessment for these purposes.

Purple: Taking Steps Toward Implementation
A performance assessment and/or edTPA are being considered at the state level for program completion or as a licensure requirement.

Green: State Participating in edTPA
At least one provider of teacher preparation—either traditional or alternative—is exploring or trying out edTPA.

Source: http://edtpa.aacte.org/state-policy (accessed February 2, 2018).

---

[1] Stanford University faculty and staff at the Stanford Center for Assessment, Learning, and Equity (SCALE) developed edTPA. They received substantive advice and feedback from teachers and teacher educators, and drew from experience gained from over 25 years of developing performance-based assessments of teaching, including the National Board for Professional Teaching Standards (NBPTS), the Interstate Teacher Assessment and Support Consortium (InTASC) Standards portfolio, and the Performance Assessment for California Teachers. The design and review teams included hundreds of university faculty, national subject-matter organization representatives (e.g., NCTM, NCTE, NSTA, etc.), and K–12 teachers. SCALE continues to gather and use input from the edTPA community to enhance and improve the assessment. Stanford University is the exclusive author and owner of edTPA. The edTPA trademarks are owned by the Board of Trustees of the Leland Stanford Junior University. Use of the edTPA trademarks is permitted only pursuant to the terms of a written license agreement.

- The National Association of Special Education Teachers (NASET)

- The National Association for Gifted Children (NAGC)

Many teaching resources are available at no cost online through these professional organizations. Professional development takes place in informal settings as well, and this is often the most important kind. In one local school district where I have worked, teachers are encouraged to take field trips to local geological formations—by themselves, without their students—even if they do not teach science in a formal way. Imagine you are an elementary school teacher in this district. How might that type of field trip contribute to your professional development? How might it help you interest your young students in the world around them?

edTPA

In Chapter 1, we indicated that preservice teachers will need to demonstrate through written work, artifacts, and classroom performance videos that they are ready to teach. This is part of a new preservice teacher assessment process, **edTPA**, which stands for "Educative Teacher Performance Assessment" and is mandated in many states (American Association of Colleges for Teacher Education, 2015). The evidence submitted in the edTPA is evaluated across five components of teaching practice:

- Planning

- Instruction

- Assessment

- Analyzing Teaching

- Academic Language

....

edTPA A new preservice teacher assessment process.

Currently, there are 768 Educator Preparation Programs in 40 states and the District of Columbia participating in edTPA. The participation map shows the prevalence of this assessment.

We will discuss the components of this assessment throughout the text, but for this chapter, I call your attention to the importance of planning. This means that good teachers plan supports, including a variety of tasks, materials, and scaffolding, tied to the specific learning objectives. Planning takes into account the needs of students with differing learning abilities. Teachers can never be overprepared!

Building a personal philosophy of teaching is an important starting point in your development as a teacher. Your teaching philosophy is a work in progress and will most likely change with time and exposure to new ideas about how people learn. In the next two chapters of this book, you will read about important educational philosophies that have influenced U.S. education. Your own thinking should evolve as you engage with these ideas. What remains constant is the fact that teaching is hard work and requires that you be reflective, ever conscious, and well prepared—that you be a centered presence in the classroom and ask yourself, what kind of teacher would I like to be?

Concluding Thoughts

Learning about other teachers' hopes, dreams, and experiences gives you a way to consider what teaching might be like for you. Teaching demands so much from the individual teacher. Our emotional sides have to be expressed to communicate a sense of warmth and congeniality, whereas our intellectual selves need to maintain a sense of order, continuity, and consistency. It is a complex endeavor, requiring self-reflection and good analytical skills. One cannot overemphasize the need for personal reflection and the desire to become a lifelong learner. Luckily, teachers receive support from organizations, mentors, preparatory institutions, and sometimes induction programs. As you consider the brief stories of other teachers, think about your own journey and your path toward becoming a teacher.

CHAPTER REVIEW

Key Terms

edTPA (p. 29)

hidden curriculum (p. 25)

learning communities (p. 27)

professional development (p. 27)

teacher burnout (p. 22)

Review the Learning Outcomes

Review each section of the chapter and answer the following:

LO 2-1 Give an example of what it means to "teach who we are."

LO 2-2 What is your idea of a hidden curriculum?

LO 2-3 Give an example of a support system for new teachers that you may like to avail yourself of.

LO 2-4 What other professions require lifelong learning in the way that teaching does?

LO 2-5 How does your own teaching story begin?

InTASC Standards

Review the InTASC Standards for the chapter and explain how the chapter addressed each one.

Standard 3: Learning Environments

Standard 6: Assessment

Standard 7: Planning for Instruction

Standard 9: Learning Environments

Journal Prompts

What made you decide to become a teacher?

How did your own experience of school influence your interest in teaching as a career choice?

$SAGE edge™

Get the tools you need to sharpen your study skills. SAGE edge offers a robust online environment featuring an impressive array of free tools and resources.

Access practice quizzes, eFlashcards, video, and multimedia at **edge.sagepub.com/koch4e**.

Educational Foundations

History and Instructional Practices

PART II

Bettmann/Getty Images

A History of Schooling in America

Having a history is a prerequisite to claiming a right to shape the future.

—Sara Evans, historian, University of Minnesota (1989)

Learning Outcomes

After reading this chapter, you should be able to:

3-1 Analyze the influence of the early pioneers of public education in the United States.

3-2 Explain the dominant philosophies that influenced education.

3-3 Discuss the impact of federal government legislation on the ways that public education has increased accountability in the 21st century.

3-4 Describe the transition from the No Child Left Behind Act to the Every Student Succeeds Act.

Teaching has a long and impassioned history in the United States. Knowing what and who came before us gives us a deeper understanding of our mission as we move forward. We teach in a contemporary context; the culture of that context, like the culture of an individual school, shapes our practice now more than ever in our nation's history. We are living at a time when private foundations and federal and state governments are designing solutions to problems that besiege public schooling in the United States. There are few who doubt that teachers make a huge difference—that it is better to be in a poorer school with a great teacher than a richer school with a terrible teacher. Still, amidst the fuss is the challenge of how to evaluate a "terrific" teacher and what "terrific," "successful," or "great" teachers look like. Reasonable doubts remain about effective school reform, and even more doubts about the best way to educate future teachers like you. In order to assess teacher candidates' readiness to teach, the edTPA, which was introduced in Chapter 2, was developed. The topics that this assessment ask you to become knowledgeable about are addressed by this text.

American schools are represented by wide varieties including a tapestry of experimental and traditional public schools, all designed to ensure a literate populace in a democratic society. Simultaneously, the digital revolution is transforming the meaning of teaching and learning as "delivery systems," providing online courses for precollege students. Many of you may have taken these online courses en route to earning your high school diploma. Teaching online may be a route you will want to take. There is so much information available online that it can challenge our thinking about what we need to know and be able to do as educated women and men. It also challenges our skills as teachers, since teaching and learning are two sides of the same coin. It is a dialectic and requires an exchange of ideas. Teaching is not "telling," and online teaching and learning is far more than a delivery system. Against this backdrop of rapid change and confusing options, this chapter provides an overview of the history of

education in the United States to give you a historical context for where we are today. What do you picture in your mind when you think of an elementary school? A middle school? A high school? Did any of you attend a junior high school? The history of U.S. public education reflects the changes that an emerging nation endures as it matures and ensures that all of its citizens become educated.

Learning about the evolution of public schools in our country reminds us that free societies require an educated populace, one where people understand their choices in a diverse society. Like many other complex histories, the history of education reveals the changing belief systems of the times. As the pendulum swings from more rigid governance of the schools to more flexible governance and back again, the main goal and hope is that all its citizens will have access to, and participate in, the process of becoming educated through a public school system designed to meet their needs.

An Introduction to the History of U.S. Public Education

We begin with a new nation emerging after the Revolutionary War in which the colonies won their independence and experienced a wave of immigration in the 19th century. Notice the following themes as we move into the 20th and 21st centuries:

- The meaning of education for a thriving democracy
- The effect of geographic location on access to education
- The roles that social capital, wealth, privilege, and poverty play in the success or failures of schools
- The transmission of values and beliefs through public education
- Changes over time in the roles played by local communities, the states, and the federal government

The Colonies

Colonial education in the 1600s began in the home when Puritans[1] established colonies in what is now the northeastern United States. In the early New England colonies, education was designed to further Puritan values and ensure that children were well versed in the Bible. The major thrust in early colonial education was the reading and understanding of scripture, so for many early colonists, religious education was synonymous with general education.

The primary responsibility for educating children was placed on the family. There is a different form of homeschooling today as many families are teaching their children at home using resources readily available over the Internet. We will discuss this resurgent trend later in this text, but you can see that it has deep roots.

Many New England families could also opt to send their children to **dame schools**, which offered education to children 6 to 8 years old. The dame school was like an informal day care center. Parents would leave their children in the home of a neighborhood woman several days a week. The woman would go about her chores while teaching the children their letters, numbers, and prayers. Religious teachings, as you can see, were routinely woven into the daily lives of children. These women usually accepted a small fee for each child, and instruction often took place in the kitchen. For the most part, this was the only form of schooling offered to girls because education was not considered important for their life's work. Can you imagine that?

Another form of education in the colonies was apprenticeship. After young boys finished the dame school, they were sometimes apprenticed to artisans to learn a trade. Serving an apprenticeship allowed boys to learn a craft they could carry into adulthood. Girls, on the other hand, were usually taught domestic skills at home and learned to stitch letters and sayings onto embroidered samplers. Theirs was a second-rate education compared with what was available for boys.

Latin Grammar Schools

Realizing they needed a way to educate leaders for their communities, the Puritan colonists established **Latin grammar schools**, the first of which opened in Boston in 1635. Here, the sons of the upper social classes studied Latin and Greek language and literature as well as the Bible.

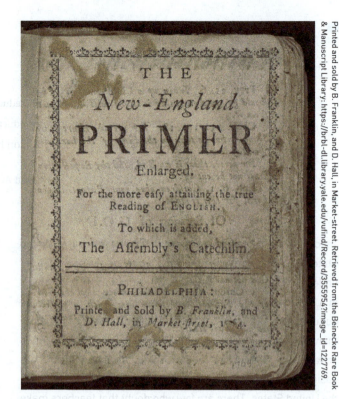

Printed and sold by B. Franklin, and D. Hall, in Market-street. Retrieved from the Beinecke Rare Book & Manuscript Library: https://brbl-dl.library.yale.edu/vufind/Record/3555954?image_id=1227769.

▲
The New England Primer was used to teach reading in the American colonies. It often included church teachings, scripture, and catechisms.

To further extend the boys' education, the Puritans founded Harvard College in 1636. To enter this college, boys had to pass an entrance exam that required reading and speaking Latin and Greek.

In 1647, Massachusetts passed a law requiring formal education. Known as the Old Deluder Satan Act, it mandated that every town of 50 households must appoint and pay a teacher of reading and writing, and every town of 100 households must provide a grammar school to prepare youths for university. With the passage of this law, new town schools were established for the youngest students, and Latin grammar schools for older students spread through Massachusetts. Thus began the first education act in this country that ensured there would be public schools where children would learn to read and write. The Old Deluder Satan Act was so named because the Puritans believed in the presence of evil in the form of Satan; if children studied the Scriptures, they would resist Satan's temptations. They believed that learning to read would thwart evil.

Ultimately, the Latin grammar school extended into the other New England colonies and to some extent into the mid-Atlantic colonies as well. These schools were run by an elected board of townspeople and financially supported by the families of the attendees. Under this system, after finishing dame school or town school, wealthy boys could attend a Latin grammar school to prepare for college and a leadership role in society. Girls who finished the dame school or town school would continue to study their letters at home while learning domestic chores. The Latin grammar school is considered one of the forerunners of the U.S. high school.

---

[1] The Puritans were Protestant dissenters in England who opposed many practices of the established church. When Charles I took the English throne in 1625, government persecution of Puritans increased. Giving up hope of reforming the English church, many Puritans emigrated, among them the early settlers of the Massachusetts Bay Colony (Boston Historical Society and Museum, 2010).

dame schools Some colonial women transformed their homes into schools where they taught reading, writing, and computation. These schools became known as dame schools.

Latin grammar school A type of school that flourished in the New England colonies in the 1600s and 1700s. It emphasized Latin and Greek to prepare young men for college.

WRITING & REFLECTION
SOCIAL CAPITAL

From the time of the early colonies to the present, Americans have frequently debated the relationship between schools and society and the best way for government to fulfill its responsibility to educate its citizens. Historically, various traditions and forms of schooling have been mediated by the political, economic, and cultural struggles of the people. This means that, for some people, access to education has been easier than for others.

The term *social capital* refers to connections among individuals that give them access to cultural and civic events and institutions. Hence, youngsters from families with social capital are familiar with libraries, museums, and travel. Moreover, parents with social capital know how to get the best education for their children. Social capital generally comes with wealth, privilege, and other marks of social status.

The concept of social capital helps us understand how social issues were addressed as U.S. schools developed. Clearly, our systems of education have become more inclusive; but in the first 150 years of nationhood, high-quality education was readily available only if you were rich, White, and male.

Do you remember my story about Mrs. Fisher from Chapter 1 (p. 7)? She encouraged me to apply to a special high school in my city. Information about special high schools was readily available to families with social capital, but my parents were working-class immigrants who did not fully understand how to negotiate the educational system in New York City. Fortunately, my teacher helped me through the process of applying to take the entrance exam.

The issue of social capital comes up often as we explore the history of schooling in the United States. There has always been pressure for schools to provide more and better services for an increasingly diverse array of students.

You had to be wealthy, White, and male to have access to the better forms of education in the early colonies. To what extent has this changed, and to what extent has it been perpetuated?

Geographical Differences in Colonial Education

Educational access in the early colonies was determined not only by wealth and privilege but by location. Where you lived had a great impact on the type of education that was available. Do you think that is true today?

In the northern colonies, largely settled by Puritans, people lived in towns and relatively close to one another. Town schools, which principally taught the Bible, became readily available after 1647. In the mid-Atlantic colonies, however, a wide range of European ethnic and religious groups established different types of schools, and various trades established apprenticeship programs. Local control was the norm. Though some Latin grammar schools existed, other private schools developed that were dedicated to job training and practical skills.

The southern colonies, where the population was more rural, had fewer schools during the colonial era. Wealthy plantation owners hired private tutors for their children. Many young gentlemen from these plantations were sent to Europe for their education.

The Late Colonial Period

By the late colonial era, in addition to the types of schools described so far, options for parents included the following:

- Schools managed by private associations, often devoted to the skills needed for a specific type of job

- Religious schools, sponsored by churches for their members; some churches also established charity schools for the urban poor

- Boarding schools

- A few private academies offering secondary education with a broader curriculum than the early Latin grammar schools

Several of these options required tuition, others were paid for by public funds, and some were funded by a combination of both.

Most girls received little schooling after the first few years. And if you were Native American or African American, you had practically no chance of formal education. The schools established for the poor typically required a family to sign a "pauper's oath," a public document that admitted your poverty. As a result, most poor children did not attend school. Consider how you would feel if, to send your child to school, you had to sign a pauper's oath. Many families chose to leave their children illiterate rather than suffer the shame of this type of public admission.

A New Nation and Its Early Pioneers of Education

In the late 1700s, after the colonies gained their independence from Great Britain, efforts were made to consolidate schools and mandate education throughout the new nation. Congress enacted the Land Ordinance Act of 1785 and the Northwest Ordinance of 1787. These measures set aside land for public schools. Subsequently, as sending children to school, rather than teaching them at home, grew in popularity, formal schools were started wherever space could be found.

Schoolhouses of that day were practical shelters: one room with benches and a stove. Desks and blackboards did not appear until many years later. No grades were given in the beginning, and one teacher worked with several age levels at the same time. Children simply learned at their own pace.

The Academy

Thomas Jefferson and Benjamin Franklin, among other founders of the new nation, believed that schools should move beyond the education of wealthy men for the ministry to a more broadly based education. In 1751, Franklin established a new kind of secondary school, one that would eventually replace the Latin grammar school—the academy. The Franklin Academy in Philadelphia offered a variety of subjects, ranging from science and mathematics to athletics, navigation, and bookkeeping. It was open to both girls and boys—if their parents could afford the tuition.

Soon after the Declaration of Independence was signed, other private academies were established, most of them limited to boys. These included most notably Phillips Academy in Andover, Massachusetts (1778), and Phillips Exeter Academy in Exeter, New Hampshire (1781). Academies changed the model for secondary schools by offering elective as well as required courses. It was still the case, however, that the common denominator for attendance was wealth.

Rise of the Common School

At the turn of the 19th century, education in the new nation was a hodgepodge of schools for basic reading and writing, and grammar schools or academies for college preparation and leadership. Many young people still learned through apprenticeships or private tutoring.

Jefferson, Franklin, and others believed that the new democracy required an educated citizenry for its survival. To work properly, they thought, a democracy needs informed citizens, as well as an educational system that allows people to succeed on the basis of their skills and dedication rather than inherited privilege.

These ideas gave rise to the movement for common schools—a system of tax-supported elementary schools. The common school is known today as the public elementary school. Horace Mann, an educational historian and reformer who championed the movement, saw common schools as promoting important civic virtues. He criticized private academies because they offered widely different curricula and perpetuated social differences between the privileged classes and ordinary citizens (Wisconsin Education Association Council, 2006).

From their beginnings in Massachusetts in the 1820s, common schools were gradually established in other New England, midwestern, western, and finally southern states. Their spread became more rapid after the Civil War.

Immigration played a key role in the thinking about public education. The 1830s and 1840s brought expansion in manufacturing and transportation. These decades also brought considerable immigration from Europe, especially in the Northeast. Immigrants were becoming an important part of the economy, and factory owners needed a trained, disciplined workforce. At the same time, as population grew in the cities, social tensions rose because of increased poverty, slums, and crime.

Prominent citizens worried about the morals of poor immigrant children and the influence their parents had on them. Many Protestant ministers looked at the rise of Catholic immigrant populations as a possible cause of social problems. Many people believed that schools could offer a way to address these concerns. By centralizing the control of public education, schools could be used to uplift the poor, spread dominant national values, and assimilate immigrant children into the English-speaking U.S. culture. State authorities, not immigrant parents, would be in control.

However, even though public schools were at this point nonsectarian, they were not necessarily nonreligious. Because common schools were seen as responsible, in part, for the moral development of children, it was believed that religion could not be completely separated from the schools. There was much debate about curriculum. Although the main thrust in common schools was the study of the "three Rs" (reading, 'riting, and 'rithmetic), history, and science, some schools had regular readings of the King James version of the Bible. Catholic immigrants objected vehemently, and many church parishes in the late 1800s began their own church schools, known as parochial schools. Not until many years later, in 1963, did the Supreme Court rule that prayers and Bible readings would no longer be allowed in public schools.

With tax-supported public education in place, more and more children attended school on a regular basis (see Figure 3.1). However, because of the large size of many immigrant families, parents often needed to send their children into the workforce to help out economically. These poor working families viewed education for their children as a luxury they could not afford. To ensure that children went to school and not to work, compulsory attendance laws came into existence. These laws were adopted by each individual state, beginning with Massachusetts in 1852 and ending with Alaska (then a U.S. territory) in 1929 (Information Please Database, 2006). Eventually, legislation restricting the employment of children in industrial settings was passed by the federal government.

Expansion of Public Schools

By the 1870s, there was broad attendance in U.S. public elementary schools, but a large gap in available educational

---

academy A type of private secondary school that arose in the late colonial period and came to dominate American secondary education until the establishment of public high schools. Academies had a more practical curriculum than Latin grammar schools did, and students typically could choose subjects appropriate to their later careers.

common schools A public, tax-supported elementary school. Begun in Massachusetts in the 1820s, common schools aimed to provide a common curriculum for children. Horace Mann, an advocate for the common school, is often considered the "father of the public school."

parochial schools A school operated by a religious group. Today, in the United States, the term most often refers to a school governed by the local Catholic parish or diocese.

FIGURE 3.1 ● Rising School Attendance, 1850–2010

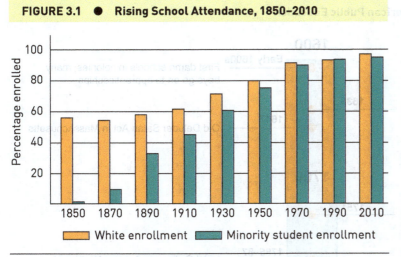

Source: Data (1850–1990) from Snyder, T. D., ed., *120 Years of American Education: A Statistical Portrait* (Washington, DC: National Center for Education Statistics, 1993) Table 2, p. 14.; (2010) Lauren Musu-Gillette et al, eds., *Status and Trends in the Education of Racial and Ethnic Groups* (Washington, DC: National Center for Education Statistics, 2016).

opportunities remained between those schools and universities. Only the wealthy continued their education at private preparatory schools for colleges and universities. Gradually, however, as society became more industrialized and laws were passed to discourage the hiring of teenage workers, parents came to view the high school as the pathway to better jobs for their children. Tax-supported public high schools slowly took hold and became the dominant form of secondary education by 1890.

The rise of the public high school led to the need for a bridge between elementary school and high school. In the early 1900s, the junior high school was established to bridge this gap, concentrating on the emotional and intellectual needs of students in Grades 7, 8, and 9. In the 1950s, some middle schools were established for Grades 5–8, and by the end of the 20th century, the middle school was gradually replacing the junior high school (Manning, 2000). The emphasis in middle school was on interdisciplinary learning and team teaching, in which groups of students had the same teachers in common.

The timeline in Figure 3.2 summarizes many of the events we have discussed. It is remarkable to consider how many more children were educated as the common school movement took hold and public secondary schools began to flourish. In many areas of the United States in the early 1800s, school lasted only about 75 to 80 days a year because the entire family was needed to work the farm. By the 1830s, only about half of all children attended school, and then only for a short period of time. But as the industrial revolution drew people to the cities for work and common schools flourished, more children began attending school, and by the end of the 1890s, more than 70% of children were receiving schooling. There was such a great need for schools between 1890 and 1914 that a new high school was

added every day in some part of the United States (Krug, 1964; Wisconsin Education Association Council, 2006).

Today we can celebrate the fact that, as our nation grew, more and more people attended public schools. This does not mean, however, that we have now achieved the goal of equal educational opportunity for everyone. Later in this text, as we compare the quality of education offered to students in poor urban and rural areas with the public education available in more affluent communities, you will see that challenges remain. Still, there is no question that more diverse students—including girls and women, people of color, and the poor—are graduating from high school today and going on to postsecondary education than ever before in this country.

Teacher Education and the Development of Normal Schools

You may be wondering who were the teachers in the rapidly expanding common school movement of the 19th century. Where did they come from, and what was their training?

Horace Mann, who spearheaded the common school movement, was also a major influence in teacher education. Founded shortly after the establishment of the first common schools, **normal schools** were 2-year institutions designed to prepare teachers through courses in the history and philosophy of education and methods of teaching. Normal schools were intended to improve the quality of the growing common school system by producing more qualified teachers. The first, called simply the Normal School, opened in 1839 in Lexington, Massachusetts.

By the end of the 1800s, normal schools had evolved into 4-year colleges dedicated to teacher education. Many universities that are well known today, such as the University of California, Los Angeles, were founded as normal schools.

Normal Schools and Female Teachers

Normal schools played a major role in bringing women into the teaching profession. In the early days of U.S. education, schoolmasters were almost always male. Women, who were mostly uneducated, were not considered suitable for the job, even though the prerequisite for teaching consisted of little more than having attended school yourself. It was assumed that women were incapable of maintaining the discipline necessary to teach effectively. On the rare occasion that a woman did secure a job, it was with young children only. As the country expanded, common schools multiplied rapidly, but women were still a minority of teachers.

normal schools A type of teacher-education institution begun in the 1830s; forerunner of the teachers' college.

FIGURE 3.2 ● Some Important Events in American Public Education

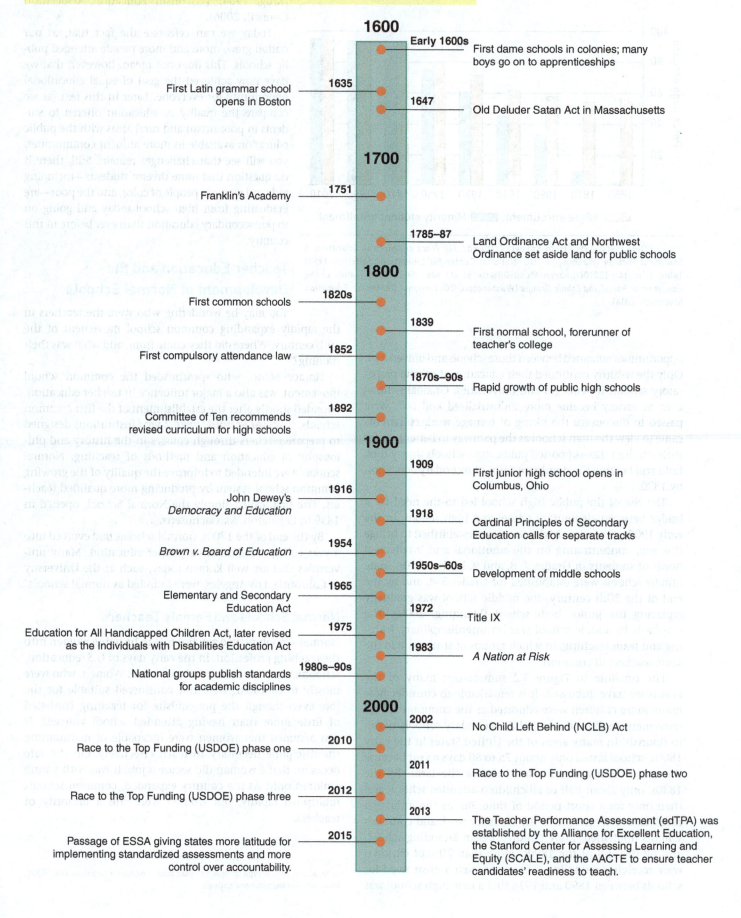

1600

Early 1600s — First dame schools in colonies; many boys go on to apprenticeships

1635 — First Latin grammar school opens in Boston

1647 — Old Deluder Satan Act in Massachusetts

1700

1751 — Franklin's Academy

1785–87 — Land Ordinance Act and Northwest Ordinance set aside land for public schools

1800

1820s — First common schools

1839 — First normal school, forerunner of teacher's college

1852 — First compulsory attendance law

1870s–90s — Rapid growth of public high schools

1892 — Committee of Ten recommends revised curriculum for high schools

1900

1909 — First junior high school opens in Columbus, Ohio

1916 — John Dewey's *Democracy and Education*

1918 — Cardinal Principles of Secondary Education calls for separate tracks

1954 — *Brown v. Board of Education*

1950s–60s — Development of middle schools

1965 — Elementary and Secondary Education Act

1972 — Title IX

1975 — Education for All Handicapped Children Act, later revised as the Individuals with Disabilities Education Act

1983 — *A Nation at Risk*

1980s–90s — National groups publish standards for academic disciplines

2000

2002 — No Child Left Behind (NCLB) Act

2010 — Race to the Top Funding (USDOE) phase one

2011 — Race to the Top Funding (USDOE) phase two

2012 — Race to the Top Funding (USDOE) phase three

2013 — The Teacher Performance Assessment (edTPA) was established by the Alliance for Excellent Education, the Stanford Center for Assessing Learning and Equity (SCALE), and the AACTE to ensure teacher candidates' readiness to teach.

2015 — Passage of ESSA giving states more latitude for implementing standardized assessments and more control over accountability.

Frances Benjamin Johnston/Library of Congress Prints and Photographs Division Washington, DC

Normal schools played a major role in bringing women into the teaching profession. Here is a class of Normal School students examining electromagnets around 1900 in Washington, DC.

Normal schools, however, welcomed female students and made elementary school teaching a career path for many women. By 1900, 71% of rural teachers were women (Hoffman, 1981).

Gender Roles in Teaching

Even as women became the majority of public school teachers, there were considerable constraints on women teachers, chief among them was that they were not allowed to marry. Indeed, spinsterhood was often associated with schoolteachers. It was believed that women would have divided loyalties if they were allowed to marry while being employed as teachers. (Can you imagine that happening now?) It was not until after World War II that married women were allowed to enter the teaching profession in most U.S. states. Examining gender stereotypes in schools is important—not only for teachers themselves but also for the models they present to students. For example, Ben in Chapter 2 is a model to little boys and girls of how men can provide caring and nurturing experiences to young children.

By the 1950s, the teaching profession, once dominated entirely by men, was female dominated. At the same time, men were still prominent in educational administration and in secondary school jobs in mathematics and science. Here again, a persistent pattern of discrimination through the late 20th century: Women were seen as best suited to teaching young children, whereas men were better able to teach math and science and run the school.

In recent years, women have gained greater access to careers in educational administration and as teachers of mathematics and science. At the same time, however, the overall percentage of men in teaching has declined significantly since the 1960s. Just as it is important to have women teaching math, it is vital to have men represented in early-childhood and elementary education. Breaking down gender divisions

in schools is important—not only for teachers themselves but also for the models they present to students. We will have more to say about gender and schooling later in this text.

The Tuskegee Normal School and the Education of African Americans

Even after the Civil War, Reconstruction, and the passage of the 13th, 14th, and 15th amendments that ended slavery, gave citizenship to former slaves, and granted voting rights to African American men, it took a long time for African Americans to achieve equal access to a quality education. Some would argue that appropriate education remains unavailable to minority students today. As we will see in later chapters, our diverse culture and society pose many challenges and opportunities for teachers and students alike. In this respect, we can find inspiration in the story of Booker T. Washington, an African American teacher, who in 1881 became the first head of what was then called the Tuskegee Normal School for Colored Teachers in Tuskegee, Alabama. Later renamed the Tuskegee Institute, the institution today is Tuskegee University.

Under the leadership of Washington, the Tuskegee Normal School prepared African American teachers to be self-reliant and to acquire practical vocational skills, not only in teaching but also in agriculture and other occupations. By the early 20th century, the African American scholar and advocate W. E. B. Du Bois, a graduate of Harvard College and a well-known intellectual, was criticizing Washington's emphasis on vocational training at Tuskegee. Du Bois insisted that formal education in an academically rich course of study was necessary for African American people to truly advance. Regardless of these critiques, however, Washington did a great deal to advance the education of African Americans and their representation in the teaching profession.

Drawing African Americans and other minorities into the teaching force remains an issue today. African Americans make up more than 15% of U.S. public school students; so do Hispanics. Yet only about 7% of teachers are African American, and 8% are Hispanic. About one third of U.S. public schools have no teachers of color on the faculty (U.S. Department of Education, 2016b). To improve this situation, state departments of education and many colleges and universities are offering financial incentives to minority students for becoming teachers. An example of such a

WRITING & REFLECTION
YOUR SCHOOL'S HISTORY

What is the history of the college or university where you are studying? When did teacher education programs emerge in your institution?

program, in existence since 1985, is the Minority Teacher Recruitment Project at the University of Louisville (http://louisville.edu/education/research/centers/mtrp/).

The Swinging Pendulum: Dominant Philosophies Influencing Education

The struggle to change or reform educational practices is as old as organized public schooling. From common school days to present times, the content and processes of education have been under continuous scrutiny. Schools, like other public institutions, are products of their times politically, socially, and economically. Schools both reflect and influence the societal events of their day.

We are all a part of what we are trying to change. As teachers and future teachers, we seek a profession dedicated to student learning. As citizens, we know that, as Thomas Jefferson observed, it is impossible for a nation to be both free and ignorant. But we are people of diverse regions, ethnicities, and social and economic backgrounds, and to be successful educators we need to make sense of (1) who we are in the world and (2) what conditions we believe are important for learning to occur.

At different periods in our history, different philosophies have dominated our thinking about teaching and learning, and about the manner in which education should proceed. In this section, we look at several competing philosophies that have shaped efforts to reform U.S. schools since late in the 19th century.

Many classrooms today are hybrids of several of these philosophies of education. As you read this section, think about what is happening in schools today and how the current phase of U.S. public education will be viewed by others 50 years from now. During this recent era of standardization and testing, which of these philosophies appears to dominate?

The High School Curriculum

From the end of the Civil War to the late 1800s, the high school curriculum kept expanding as the demand for new courses grew. There was no preset pattern for how the courses being offered should develop; hence, the high school curriculum retained old subjects such as languages and mathematics, and added new ones as demand arose. These new subjects included botany, physiology, anatomy, physics, and astronomy. For those students not interested in pursuing a college education, courses such as commercial arithmetic, banking, business correspondence, stenography, and typewriting were added.

By the late 1800s, opinions about the purpose of high school were sharply divided. Some believed high school should groom students for college. Others thought high school should prepare students for more practical endeavors, serving those who saw high school as the termination of their formal education.

In 1892, the National Education Association (NEA) addressed this issue by appointing the Committee of Ten, which consisted of 10 scholars led by Harvard University President Charles Eliot, to determine the proper curriculum for high schools. The Committee of Ten recommended 8 years of elementary school and 4 years of high school, and proposed a curriculum that was common to both college-bound and terminal students. The new curriculum featured fewer subjects, each of which would be studied for a longer period of time. The courses included foreign languages, history, mathematics, science, and English. Although these subjects offered an alternative to classical Latin and Greek courses, this was a rigorous academic curriculum, and the dominant belief was that the same subjects would be equally beneficial to continuing and terminal students.

In 1918, the NEA partly reversed course when its Commission on the Reorganization of Secondary Education issued a report called *Cardinal Principles of Secondary Education*. In this report, the commission recommended a differentiated curriculum for the comprehensive high school, offering four different tracks: college preparatory, commercial, industrial, and general academic. The commercial course of study included bookkeeping, shorthand, and typing. The industrial track included preparatory courses for domestic, agricultural, and trade endeavors.

Although high school curricula varied considerably during the rest of the 20th century, some of the ideas set forth by the Committee of Ten and the *Cardinal Principles* continued to be dominant. The core courses—English, foreign language, science, mathematics, and history (which later evolved into social studies)—persisted in the comprehensive high school curriculum. So did the notion that high school should follow a **tracking** system, offering different courses or tracks for students with different academic aspirations.

The Emergence of Essentialism

As you can see from the debate over the high school curriculum, educators in the early 20th century were developing strong opinions about the proper sort of education for contemporary society. In the 1930s, the educator William Bagley coined the term **essentialism** for a philosophy that had a strong impact then and continues to be influential today. According to this view, certain core kinds of knowledge are essential to a person's life in society. Essentialists believe that everyone can and should learn these key elements and, therefore, that the schools' primary mission is to teach them.

When you hear about teaching the basics or about rigorous training in the three Rs, you are listening to an essentialist view of education. The essentials are generally embodied in the standard, time-honored subjects; in other words, essentialists

---

tracking The practice of placing students in different classes or courses based on achievement test scores or on perceived differences in abilities. Tracks can be identified by ability (high, average, or low) or by the kind of preparation they provide (academic, general, or vocational).

essentialism An educational philosophy holding that the purpose of education is to learn specific knowledge provided by core academic disciplines such as mathematics, science, literature, and history. Teachers must impart the key elements of these subjects so that all students have access to this basic or "essential" knowledge.

believe that students should take courses in algebra and history, not in ceramics and interpretive dance. In stressing that the curriculum should remain consistent, essentialists tend to assume that a common culture should exist for all Americans. Their vision of the classroom is teacher centered: Teachers are the dominant figures, transferring their knowledge and wisdom for the good of the students. An essentialist classroom is one in which the teacher knows best. Students listen to their teacher and learn what is taught.

To many educators in the early 20th century, essentialism made good common sense. It was soon challenged, however, by the progressivism of thinkers like John Dewey.

Progressivism and John Dewey

What the best and wisest parent
wants for his own child, that must the
community want for all its children.

—John Dewey (1907)

Probably the most influential educator of the 20th century, John Dewey (1859–1952) was an educational philosopher and a professor at the University of Chicago and Columbia University in New York. He participated in a variety of political causes, such as women's rights and the unionization of teachers, and he contributed frequently to popular magazines and journals in which he connected social action in democracy with educational principles.

In Dewey's view, students should be active participants in their own learning; they learn by doing, and their interests must be a driving force behind curriculum and classroom experiences. His educational philosophy has been referred to as **progressivism** and as *pragmatism*. It was progressive because it gave more responsibility to students and pragmatic (practical) because it embedded teaching and learning in the context of daily living. This approach contradicted the strict, top-down, authoritarian model of education that had thrived from colonial times into the 19th century and that continued to be reflected in essentialist approaches.

Dewey thought that schools should help children learn how to live and work cooperatively with others. Consequently, he believed that students needed to participate in decisions that affected their learning and that they should be guided by academically autonomous teachers—that is, teachers who were not bound by rigid rules about what and how to teach and who were able to build on students' strengths and talents. Dewey and his followers viewed the school as a laboratory in which the purpose of the curriculum was to integrate education with real-life experiences, and a child's curiosity defined the process of learning just as much as the subject matter being taught.

Dewey, and the progressive movement in education that he helped found, had a profound influence on educational thought in the United States. Progressives advocated

John Dewey (1859–1952) was an educational philosopher and reformer associated with the philosophy of pragmatism and the progressive movement.

a vibrant school setting with a curriculum that followed the interests and needs of students, encouraged active learning and problem solving, fostered deep understanding of concepts through experimentation, and supported assessment of students through close observation by well-prepared and caring teachers.

Dewey's progressivism fell out of favor, however, when it was deemed necessary that the United States foster stricter teaching methods during the Cold War following World War II. The Soviet Union's launch of the satellite Sputnik in 1957—making that nation the first in space—became a symbol of what U.S. public education had failed to achieve. Progressivism lost ground as U.S. educators shifted again toward a more authoritarian approach and a strict adherence to lecture and rote learning. A new wave of essentialism took over, and schools focused on the task of preparing students for the technological and engineering challenges of the time.

Educational progressivism revived in the 1960s as the "child-centered" movement gained popularity in the United States. In the years since, various groups of educators have revisited the ideas of Dewey and his followers, and revised them to address the changing needs of schools, children, and society. The philosophical influence of progressive ideas in education can be seen today in multiage approaches to instruction, experiential education, problem-based learning, engineering design, and student-centered instruction.

progressivism An educational philosophy that stresses active learning through problem solving, projects, and hands-on experiences.

Enduring Ideas: The Influence of Perennialism

An educational philosophy related to essentialism, **perennialism** stresses the belief that all knowledge or wisdom has been accumulated over time and is represented by the great works of literature and art as well as religious texts. This educational philosophy found a strong expression in the 1980s with the *Paideia Proposal* by Mortimer Adler. In this influential call for school reform, Adler proposed one universal curriculum for elementary and secondary students, allowing for no electives. Everyone would take the same courses, and the curriculum would reflect the enduring ideas found in the works of history's finest thinkers and writers.

Like essentialism, perennialism holds that one type of education is good for all students. It differs from essentialism by placing greater emphasis on classic works of literature, history, art, and philosophy (including works of the ancient Greeks and Romans), and on the teaching of values and moral character. Essentialism can include practical, vocation-oriented courses—a class in computer skills, for instance—but perennialism leaves little room for such frivolity.

The perennialist approach has found a home at several U.S. colleges, such as St. John's College in Maryland and in the state of New Mexico, and its influence shows in the core curricula at some larger universities, including the University of Chicago and Columbia University. Threads of the perennialist philosophy are present in many parochial schools as well. Whenever you hear about a program centered on "great ideas" or "great books," it most likely reflects perennialist ideas.

Adler emphasized the Socratic Method, a type of teaching based on extensive discussion with students. In this respect, he was somewhat less teacher centered than many essentialists. His perennialism does, however, leave little room for flexibility in the curriculum and little opportunity to reflect the changing demographics of our times.

Radical Reform Philosophies: Social Reconstructionism, Critical Theory, and Existentialism

Alongside essentialism, progressivism, and perennialism, the 20th century gave rise to some radical reform philosophies that proposed a fundamental rethinking of the nature of schooling. Among these are social reconstructionism, critical theory, and existentialism.

Social reconstructionism is an educational philosophy that emphasizes social justice and a curriculum promoting social reform. Responding to the vast inequities in society and recognizing the plight of the poor, social reconstructionists believe that schools must produce an agenda for social change. Linked with social reconstructionism is critical theory or critical pedagogy, which stresses that students

should learn to challenge oppression. In this view, education should tackle the real-world problems of hunger, violence, poverty, and inequality. Clearly, students are at the center of this curriculum with teachers advocating involvement in social reform. The focus of critical theorists and social reconstructionists is the transformation of systems of oppression through education to improve the human condition.

Among critical theorists, Paulo Freire (1921–1997), a Brazilian whose experiences living in poverty led him to champion education and literacy as the vehicle for social change, has had a particularly profound impact on the thinking of many educators. His most influential work was *Pedagogy of the Oppressed*, published in English in 1970.

Another philosophy that proposes fundamental changes in education is existentialism, which posits student-centered learning as the ideal. Rooted in the thinking of 19th-century philosophers like Søren Kierkegaard, existentialism gained popular notice in the mid-20th century through the works of Jean Paul Sartre and others. According to this philosophy, the only authoritative truth lies within the individual. Existentialism is defined by what it rejects—namely, the existence of any source of objective truth other than the individual person, who must seek the meaning of his or her own existence.

Applied to education, existentialism proposes that students make all decisions about their choice of subject matter and activities as they seek to make meaning of their place in the world. This philosophy has not had as profound an impact on U.S. schools as the other philosophies described in this chapter have, but you can find elements of it in classrooms where teachers insist that students make their own decisions about what is important for them to know. The best-known model of existentialism is Summerhill, a school founded in England by A. S. Neill in 1921. Clearly, students are at the center of this curriculum.

Table 3.1 summarizes some key features of the educational philosophies we have discussed.

Aesthetics and Maxine Greene

We want to expand the range of literacy, offering the young new ways of symbolizing, new ways of structuring their experience, so they can see more, hear more, make more connections, embark on unfamiliar adventures into meaning.

—Maxine Greene (2001)

In this era of global interdependence and multicultural diversity, educators continue to develop their ideas about the purposes of education and the best ways to reform schools. One influential contemporary thinker is the late Maxine Greene, a U.S. philosopher, social activist, and teacher who was an active scholar and educator at Teachers College, Columbia University, from 1965 until her death in 2014. She believed that the role of education is to create meaning in the lives of students and teachers through an interaction between knowledge and experience with the world.

Greene's educational philosophy was rooted in Dewey's ideas about art and aesthetics. Dewey's democratic view of education suggested that when children are able to

---

perennialism An educational philosophy that emphasizes enduring ideas conveyed through the study of great works of literature and art. Perennialists believe in a single core curriculum for everyone.

TABLE 3.1 ● Key Elements of Five Education Philosophies

Philosophy	Focus of Study	Teacher's Role
Essentialism	Core knowledge that students need to be educated citizens; this knowledge is embodied in traditional academic disciplines such as history and mathematics	Teachers are the central figures in the classroom, transferring their knowledge to students
Perennialism	Enduring ideas found in the great works of literature and art	Teachers engage in extended dialogue with students, discussing and reasoning about the great ideas
Progressivism	Integration of study with real-life experiences through active learning, problem solving, and experimentation	Teachers structure the learning activities and encourage students to explore the ideas that arise; teachers can vary the curriculum to match the needs and interests of students
Social reconstructionism/ critical theory	Schooling promotes social and political reform by focusing on social problems and the need for change	Teachers guide students to think critically about social injustice and challenge oppression
Existentialism	Students choose their own course of study as part of their effort to figure out their place in the world and the meaning of their lives	Teachers support students in exploring their own interests

approach problem solving artistically and imaginatively, they grow socially and culturally through their shared experiences, insights, and understandings. Therefore, the arts are an essential part of the human experience.

Building on Dewey, Greene contributed to the growth of a paradigm known as **aesthetic education**. She believed that the goal of education is to help students realize that they are responsible not merely for their own individual experiences, but they also need to have a deep connection to, and responsibility for, other human beings who share this world. Her philosophy asked us to consider how being able to express oneself in a number of different "languages"—including imagery, music, and dance—helps us make meaning of ideas (Greene, 1995). Greene (1978) also believed that education must lead students and teachers to the discovery of their own truths and that the arts promote a type of consciousness or "wide-awakeness" in service to this process. She stressed the importance of shared perspectives in looking at the world and a respect for differences in experience.

In connection with her work at the Lincoln Center Institute for the Arts in Education in New York City, of which she was a founding member, Greene began the Maxine Greene Foundation for Social Imagination, the Arts, and Education, which prepares teachers to guide students in merging artistic expression with social justice. Its tenets focus on equity issues, quality of experiences in school, and the uses of imagination as a means of breaking down the barriers of diversity that children encounter in their daily lives. This perspective values the personal liberty of children and

celebrates the imagination for its ability to open a child's mind to different possibilities and alternative solutions. An underlying assumption is that the humanities can serve as a catalyst enabling teachers and students to explore ideas more deeply and be more critically engaged with the world.

How do Maxine Greene's ideas work in an actual classroom? Consider this story:

In a sixth-grade class, Ms. Nelson is interested in her students' capacity for careful observation. She is a great admirer of many types of artists, and decorating her room are poster reproductions of famous paintings. The students move their chairs to position themselves by the poster of van Gogh's *The Starry Night* (see image, p. 44), and Ms. Nelson asks, "What do you think van Gogh was thinking about when he painted this?"

"Circles," one student responds. Another says "dreams," and still another student offers "motion." Then Ms. Nelson asks, "What do *you* think of when you look at this painting?" Students respond with phrases like "wind blowing," "scary dreams," "day and night," and "church spires." The students really seem to like the painting, and Ms. Nelson urges them on. She asks, "What is the organizing principle behind this painting?" (This is a question she asks often when the class looks at collections of objects: what principle did the collector use to gather these objects together?)

The students decide that van Gogh was looking for images that used circles and pointy spires. Those were his organizing principles.

Asked about her goals for *The Starry Night* lesson, Ms. Nelson explains, "I am interested in getting students ready to make careful observations. We are doing a science unit on mystery powders, and I want them to think about properties that

....

aesthetic education Traditionally, this term referred merely to education in the fine arts, such as painting and music. In the broader view of Maxine Greene and other recent philosophers, however, it means education that enables students to use artistic forms and imagination to approach all fields of learning, including the sciences, and to share their perspectives with others.

Digital Image © The Museum of Modern Art/
Licensed by SCALA/Art Resource, NY

▲
Vincent Van Gogh's *The Starry Night* (1889) is one of the most well-known paintings in modern culture. Ms. Nelson (see p. 43) uses it to prepare students to make careful observations, reflecting the philosophy of Maxine Greene.

objects have in common." Can you explain how this lesson represents Maxine Greene's philosophy of integrating the arts into education?

The progressive philosophies of Dewey and Greene share a number of fundamental views:

- Making connections with social issues should be central to school curricula.

- The arts are creative tools that can expose children to new perspectives and new ways of communicating.

- Learning is an experiential process. Students learn by interacting with material in intellectual and sometimes manipulative ways; that is what "learning by doing" means.

- All forms of education should emphasize learning by **inquiry**—a process in which students ask meaningful questions and then seek their own answers.

Greene believed that people who choose to become teachers should ideally be "those who have learned the importance of becoming reflective enough to think about their own thinking and become conscious of their own consciousness" (Greene, 1995, p. 13). What do you think that means?

In today's era of standardization and testing, there are frequent obstacles to the progressive philosophies of Dewey and Greene as teachers prepare students for high-stakes testing. As a teacher, finding ways to prepare your

....
inquiry A multifaceted activity that involves making observations, posing questions about the subject matter, and conducting research or investigations to develop answers. Inquiry is common to scientific learning but also relevant to other fields.

WRITING & REFLECTION
AESTHETIC EDUCATION

In what ways, if any, do you think schools shortchange students by not offering extensive experiences in the creative arts? Did you have specific aesthetic experiences that influenced your schooling?

students for tests while incorporating creativity and curiosity in your lessons is an important and meaningful goal.

Educational Reform: Funding, Priorities, and Standards

Although education of the citizenry was important to the founders of the United States, there is no mention of education for all in the Constitution. Hence, schooling became the domain and responsibility of the states, which left most of the control of schools to local communities.

Thus, U.S. schools have traditionally been run by local school boards, and the bulk of the money they need has been raised through local taxes, especially property taxes. Many critics have argued that the reliance on local property taxes is unfair because it means that wealthier districts can raise more money for schools than poorer districts can. Yet Americans have long been reluctant to give up local funding and the control that goes with it.

As we noted previously, however, the Soviet Union's launch of Sputnik in 1957 prompted a rethinking of U.S. educational priorities. Federal and state governments increasingly began to intervene in educational matters, setting priorities and (at least sometimes) providing funds to make sure those priorities were met. The overall result of these changes is that local school districts receive federal money to implement reform movements in their districts. Although local schools are happy to receive government money, they are not always pleased that the funds come with strings attached, reducing local control over the way schools operate.

The following sections introduce you to several ways in which government legislation, publications, and court cases have changed the course of U.S. public education.

Separate but Equal?

As noted previously in this chapter, African Americans—most of whom were enslaved—were denied the right to an education when the United States was new and evolving. Even after the Civil War, schools for African Americans were slow to develop. Where they did emerge, they were separate schools, only for Black children. In 1896, the U.S. Supreme Court ruled in *Plessy v. Ferguson* that "separate but equal" public facilities for different races were legal. The reality, of course, was that the schools serving African Americans were not equal. They did not share equally in the resources available for public schooling; in most locations, they had fewer tax dollars and inferior conditions.

The situation came to a head in 1954 with the case of *Brown v. Board of Education of Topeka, Kansas*. In this landmark case, the U.S. Supreme Court ruled unanimously that separate schools for Whites and Blacks were inherently unequal because the effects of such separate schooling are likely to be different. Because of this inequality, the court ruled, schools could not remain segregated.

Initially, the *Brown* decision had the most impact in the South, where schools were segregated by law (de jure segregation). Many northern schools were segregated informally because of segregated living patterns for Whites and Blacks (de facto segregation). Over the following decades, many school systems and various court cases dealt with the challenge of eliminating de facto segregation with mixed success. The efforts toward integration had a significant impact, but there was much turmoil and resistance. Numerous educators argue that de facto segregation still exists today in many areas, especially in suburban United States.

Federal legislation, including the Civil Rights Act (1964), reinforced the importance of creating educational opportunities for all Americans regardless of race, gender, or ethnicity. The Bilingual Education Acts of 1968 and 1974 provided supplemental funding for school districts to establish programs for large numbers of children with limited English-language ability. Similarly, the Equal Educational Opportunities Act of 1974 provided specific definitions of what constituted denial of equal educational opportunity. These included "failure to take the appropriate action to overcome language barriers that impede equal participation by all students in an instructional program."

The Elementary and Secondary Education Act

The most extensive federal financing of schools in the United States was made possible in 1965 when Congress passed the Elementary and Secondary Education Act (ESEA). This legislation was seen as part of President Lyndon Johnson's War on Poverty because it ensured that federal assistance would be sent to the poorest schools and communities in the nation. Its immediate impact was to provide $1 billion to improve the education of students from families living below the poverty line.

Every 5 years since its enactment, ESEA has been reauthorized; it is the single largest source of federal support for K–12 education. The federal government distributes the funds to the states, and the states identify the schools and districts to receive the funds. This legislation, particularly the section known as **Title I**, has led to many important programs that fall into the general category of compensatory education—educational services designed specifically to create better opportunities for students with disadvantages, such as those from high-poverty neighborhoods. Examples include the following:

Thomas J. O'Halloran/Library of Congress Prints and Photographs Division Washington, DC

▲ It was not until 1954, when the Supreme Court ruled that separate schools for Whites and Blacks were inherently unequal, that schools began racial integration.

- Early-childhood education: Head Start, the most well-known national early-childhood program, helps prepare preschool children for school, focusing not just on academic skills but also on nutrition, health, and family environment.

- Tutoring and other supplemental academic instruction

- After-school centers

- Computer labs for poor schools

- Dropout prevention services

- Job training

- Parental education

- Professional development for teachers

Two major revisions of the ESEA of 1965 occurred in this century. The **No Child Left Behind (NCLB) Act** of 2002 revised the ESEA and called for states to develop content-area standards and annual testing of math and reading in Grades 3 to 8. Schools with poor test results face the possibility of being closed. This revision also gives parents greater choice about where their children go to school. In 2015, the NCLB Act of 2002 was replaced by the **Every Student Succeeds Act (ESSA)**. ESSA gives states more flexibility, but it also asks a lot of them. Further discussion of ESSA can be found toward the end of this chapter.

Brown v. Board of Education of Topeka, Kansas A 1954 case in which the U.S. Supreme Court outlawed segregation in public education.

Title I The section of federal education law that provides funds for compensatory education.

No Child Left Behind (NCLB) Act Revised the ESEA and called for states to develop content-area standards and annual testing of math and reading in Grades 3 to 8.

Every Student Succeeds Act (ESSA) Gives states and local districts more flexibility in how they raise standards and undertake essential reforms to improve student achievement and teacher effectiveness.

Title IX

Title IX, part of the Education Amendments of 1972, is a federal law that prohibits discrimination on the basis of sex in any federally funded education program or activity. The main objective of Title IX is to avoid the use of federal money to support sexually discriminatory practices.

Title IX was modeled on Title VI of the Civil Rights Act of 1964 that prohibits discrimination based on race, color, and national origin. However, unlike Title VI, which applies to all federal financial assistance, Title IX is limited to *education* programs or activities that receive federal financial assistance.

Title IX protects the rights of both males and females from prekindergarten through graduate school in sports, financial aid, employment, counseling, and school regulations and policies. One impact of Title IX has been on girls' sports activities and facilities; it requires that schools provide equal opportunities, funding, and facilities for boys' and girls' teams. Unfortunately, Title IX enforcement has been fairly lax, so it is not unusual to find schools in apparent violation of part of the regulation.

What has been your own experience of the effect of gender on educational opportunities? Many studies have explored the ways in which some girls and boys experience school differently. Many students, for example, who have attended single-sex private schools have had positive experiences. In fact, some public schools, for a wide range of reasons, have offered single-sex classes as well. In one public school I encountered, an all-girls physics class was thought to be a good way to engage more young women in physics. Success was measured by the achievement of the young women in the class. Similarly, in Queensland, Australia, several high schools are experimenting with all-boys English literature and writing classes. They also are meeting with successful outcomes in terms of achievement. Do these examples show that "separate but equal" can be a useful principle when it comes to segregation by sex? There is a great deal of controversy surrounding this issue, and the prevailing sentiment is in favor of quality coeducation where the rights and opportunities for both genders are protected. Those opposed to single-sex environments fear that they have the potential to degrade into a lesser education for girls as happened with segregated schools for students of color.

Two other sections of the 1964 Civil Rights Act relate to education as well, and they can be used in conjunction with Title IX to challenge discriminatory practices:

- Title IV authorizes federal assistance to prohibit discrimination in education on the basis of sex, race, and national origin.

- Title VII prohibits sex discrimination and other types of employment discrimination both in and outside of education contexts (Klein, Ortman, & Friedman, 2002).

A Nation at Risk

In 1983, the National Commission on Excellence in Education, a group of scholars and educators convened by the U.S. Department of Education, issued a report in the form of an open letter to the U.S. people. Called *A Nation at Risk: The Imperative for Educational Reform*, this document showed deep concern about the educational system in the United States:

> Our society and its educational institutions seem to have lost sight of the basic purposes of schooling, and of the high expectations and disciplined effort needed to attain them. This report, the result of 18 months of study, seeks to generate reform of our educational system in fundamental ways and to renew the Nation's commitment to schools and colleges of high quality throughout the length and breadth of our land. (National Commission on Excellence in Education, 1983, p. 1)

The report called for tougher standards for graduation, increases in the required number of mathematics and science courses, higher college entrance requirements, and a return to what was called "academic basics." It also defined "computer skills" as a new basic.

The report further recommended an increase in the amount of homework given, a longer school day, more rigorous requirements for teachers, and updated textbooks. *A Nation at Risk* inaugurated a new period of academic rigor, with increased attention to skills and standards, and less emphasis on progressive concerns such as schools' role in building social understanding. The "at risk" wording implied that the United States would lose its global competitive edge if the reforms were not carried out. Even though these recommendations came from the federal government, they were implemented (or sometimes ignored) in different ways at the local, state, and district levels.

The Individuals With Disabilities Education Act

In 1975, Congress passed the Education for All Handicapped Children Act (Public Law 94-142) to ensure that all children with disabilities could receive free, appropriate public education, just like other children. This law was revised in 1990, in 1997, and most recently in 2004. It is now known as the **Individuals with Disabilities Education Act**.

What is so important about this act? Before 1975, there was no organized, equitable way of addressing the needs of disabled students in the public school system. Often they were marginalized, taught in separate classrooms, and provided with watered-down curricula.

As a result of the federal legislation, however, strong efforts have been made to include students with disabilities in regular

....

Title IX Part of the federal Education Amendments of 1972, Title IX states that "No person in the United States shall, on the basis of sex, be excluded from participation in, be denied the benefits of, or be subjected to discrimination under any education program or activity receiving Federal financial assistance."

....

A Nation at Risk: The Imperative for Educational Reform A 1983 federal report that found U.S. schools in serious trouble and inaugurated a new wave of school reform focused on academic basics and higher standards for student achievement.

Individuals with Disabilities Education Act The federal law that guarantees that all children with disabilities receive free, appropriate public education.

Tracy A. Woodward/The Washington Post/Getty Images

▲ Strong efforts are made to include students with disabilities in regular classrooms.

classrooms. This reform, known as **inclusion**, has been implemented to greater or lesser degrees in different school districts. In some classrooms, students with learning disabilities are integrated with general education students as much as possible. In other classrooms, students with special educational needs are included in the general education classroom some of the time; this arrangement is called *partial inclusion*. Some districts have a self-contained class as well for students with special needs (who are often called *special education students*). Often, depending on the needs of the student population, all three models exist in the same school district. Reform movements on behalf of children with disabilities have dominated special education programs for the past 30 years. Much educational research suggests that inclusion benefits both special education students and students from the general population. We will return to the subject of inclusion in Chapter 6.

Standards-Based Reform

As a response to *A Nation at Risk* and similar publications that followed, groups of scholars from content area associations developed standards for their disciplines, beginning with the National Council of Teachers of Mathematics. The first version of *Principles and Standards for School Mathematics* appeared in 1989. Language arts, science, social studies, and foreign languages followed in the 1990s, developing standards for what children at each grade level from prekindergarten to Grade 12 should know and be able to do in each of the content areas. States were asked to prepare content standards based on these national guidelines and to create assessments to match the standards.

Hence, the era in which we are presently living—and in which you are preparing to teach—is dominated by standards-based school reform and assessments. Many of you went to school as the standards-based movement was getting under way. Standards in the academic area were developed by professional organizations in concert with scholars and teachers in the field. Standards-based educational reform refers to clear, measurable academic standards for all school students in all academic areas.

inclusion The practice of educating students with disabilities in regular classrooms alongside nondisabled students.

NCLB and ESSA

National standards and the testing that assesses whether students are meeting those standards is a policy issue that has supporters and critics. This movement, supported in part by NCLB, is a model of considerable rigor, accountability, and strict benchmarks for student learning. Supporters of the movement contend that this reform movement encourages schools to set higher standards for their students and to find ways in which their students can meet those standards. Critics insist that curriculum needs to be connected to the students' lived experiences and that standards will stifle innovation and creativity in the classroom.

NCLB (signed by President George W. Bush in January 2002) was the most dramatic federal education legislation since ESEA. Although NCLB was a reauthorization and revision of ESEA, it went beyond the previous act in several important ways. It increased funding for less-wealthy school districts and emphasized higher achievement for financially poor and minority students. It also introduced new measures for holding schools accountable for students' progress. Most controversially, NCLB set new rules for standardized testing, requiring that students in Grades 3 through 8 be tested every year in mathematics and reading. This requirement had important implications for the way the curriculum was developed and implemented in many elementary schools across the country.

Because of the initial push for statewide standardized tests in mathematics and reading, elementary students in the first decade of this century received less instruction in science and social studies. For many educators, the promise of the NCLB legislation became a massive testing movement, and there has not been substantial research to demonstrate that these standards-based assessments actually improved student learning. The controversy centers on the notion that there was so much at stake from one standardized assessment in either mathematics or language arts. It is important to remember, however, that NCLB asked public schools to be accountable for the progress their students make in these areas. Prior to NCLB, this level of accountability had not existed. This was very significant for American public education because it resulted in using data to reveal the achievement gap between White middle class and poor minority communities.

In 2012, President Barack Obama's administration recommended overhauling NCLB, and many of its features changed, including its name. The Every Student Succeeds Act, passed in December 2015, gives states and local districts more flexibility in how they raise standards and undertake essential reforms to improve student achievement and teacher effectiveness. This flexibility means that a state can determine the assessment measures for student performance, and they do not have to rely on a single type of testing. They can use multiple measures to assess student learning while still maintaining a high level of accountability. The accountability requirements of NCLB promoted standardized testing that fostered a "one-size-fits-all" formula for achievement and accountability. Many educators believe that this approach cannot work successfully in a society as diverse as ours. Based on standards set by NCLB, more schools were listed as failing in 2011 than in 2010.

Many feel that the computations required to meet passing standards do not reflect the genuine progress made in many of these so-called failing districts and schools.

Since ESSA's implementation, states and districts have sought multiple ways of gauging students' performance while trying to maintain the safeguards for historically overlooked groups of students that NCLB exposed through its assessment requirement. Instead of relying solely on test results to measure school performance, states and local districts must use a combination of measures including graduation rates and achievement in advanced coursework. States must also develop plans for how to intervene in their lowest-performing schools and those where long-overlooked groups of learners—such as students of color, English language learners, and children with disabilities—are not performing competently (Klein, 2016).

Under ESSA, each state has to submit accountability plans; however, with the current federal administration, it is unclear how these plans will be assessed. For example, a new federal thrust toward school choice and directing federal monies toward helping students in private, charter, and home schools may change portions of ESSA. We will discuss school choice in Chapter 6.

The flexibility of local control still predominates in some places, as the following story demonstrates:

Ms. Bennett is the principal of a public elementary school in Maryland, where children in Grades 1 through 5 explore a different human-made artifact each year. The first grade studies bridges, the second grade studies elevators, the third grade investigates escalators, the fourth grade focuses on airplanes, and fifth-grade students explore the automobile. These various products of engineering design form themes that are addressed during the entire school year, regardless of what other topics are studied in that year.

How did this unusual curriculum come about? Few elementary schools have a mandate to teach students about such inventions in a formal way. When you meet Ms. Bennett, however, you learn that she entered the field of education after several years as a civil engineer. One of the first women in her college class to excel in civil engineering, she brought her passion for the work to her elementary school students. As a principal, Ms. Bennett enlisted her faculty's help to make learning about engineering design part of the school's curriculum. Many believe that the rigid testing that has dominated public education in the first decades of the 21st century has caused the more creative aspects of the curriculum to take a backseat to preparation for the exams.

Common Core State Standards

The **Common Core State Standards** (CCSS) Initiative is a state-led effort coordinated by the National Governors Association Center for Best Practices and the Council of Chief State School Officers (CCSSO) to develop a clear and consistent framework to prepare students for college and the workforce through the collaboration with teachers, school administrators, and experts. The standards are designed to provide teachers and parents with a common understanding of what students are expected to learn. Consistent standards will provide appropriate benchmarks for all students, regardless of where they live. These standards define the knowledge and skills students should have within their K–12 education careers so that they will graduate from high school able to succeed in entry-level, credit-bearing academic college courses and in workforce training programs (CCSS, n.d.). These standards have been adopted by 42 states, the District of Columbia, four territories, and the Department of Defense Education Activity (CCSS, n.d.). States not adopting the CCSS are Alaska, Minnesota, Nebraska, Oklahoma, Texas, Indiana, Virginia, and South Carolina. Many reasons inform their decisions not to adopt the CCSS, including lack of resources for teacher professional development and the desire to maintain control over local standards for teaching and learning mathematics and language arts.

In 2009, the first official public draft of the college- and career-readiness standards in English language arts (ELA) and mathematics were released. Care was taken to ensure that these standards in mathematics and English could be used broadly for every state in the country and are designed to influence the development of high-quality curricula in each state. For teachers and students, using curriculum aligned with the CCSS is challenging; in ELA, for example, CCSS asks both teachers and students to spend more time instructionally on nonfiction texts. The CCSS fosters the development of students' skills at citing evidence in what they read for claims they make about its meaning. This involves close reading of texts, enabling students to critically examine the meanings of informational narratives. Similarly, the CCSS in mathematics asks students and teachers to examine the processes and number sense behind mathematical computations in ways that promote deep understanding of mathematical functions. The standards have been met with some resistance, as they represent new approaches to teaching and learning in ELA and mathematics. The CCSS are a significant part of statewide initiatives for educational reform. Improvements in public schooling require experimentation and innovation in the design of the school. As we will see in later chapters, this has led to a proliferation of charter schools, supported by public funds and existing under a special state charter with its own set of standards.

Concluding Thoughts

As you think about the history of U.S. public education, consider all the factors that contribute to the structure and design of schooling today. In addition to geography, acts

Common Core State Standards A state-led effort coordinated by the National Governors Association Center for Best Practices and the Council of Chief State School Officers (CCSSO) to develop a clear and consistent framework to prepare students for college and the workforce through the collaboration with teachers, school administrators, and experts.

of Congress, immigration, and educational movements, we now have international events, global challenges, an increased focus on accountability, and advanced digital technologies shaping and reshaping the landscape of public education.

Today we are faced with unprecedented cultural, ethnic, and racial diversity in our schools. Further, as young people spend more time online—texting, tweeting, snapchatting, instagramming, and seeking information—the nature of teaching and learning in the classroom is undergoing a transformation, reflecting these modes of communication. Although there are many local and national academic standards, *there is no standard student!* In this respect, we live in an unusual period in U.S. education. Yet our long educational history and the philosophies and debates that have emerged during that time continue to influence our choices.

CHAPTER REVIEW

Key Terms

A Nation at Risk: The Imperative for Educational Reform (p. 46)
academy (p. 36)
aesthetic education (p. 43)
Brown v. Board of Education of Topeka, Kansas (p. 45)
Common Core State Standards (p. 48)
common schools (p. 36)

dame schools (p. 34)
essentialism (p. 40)
Every Student Succeeds Act (ESSA) (p. 45)
inclusion (p. 47)
Individuals with Disabilities Education Act (p. 46)
inquiry (p. 44)
Latin grammar school (p. 34)

No Child Left Behind (NCLB) Act (p. 45)
normal schools (p. 37)
parochial schools (p. 36)
perennialism (p. 42)
progressivism (p. 41)
Title I (p. 45)
Title IX (p. 45)
tracking (p. 40)

Review the Learning Outcomes

Review each section of the chapter and answer the following:

LO 3-1 With which early pioneer in education do you identify? Why?

LO 3-2 Which of the dominant educational philosophies are we experiencing now? What is your evidence?

LO 3-3 How was the federal government instrumental in promoting standardized testing? What if states did not conform?

LO 3-4 In what ways is ESSA similar to NCLB? In what ways is it different?

Journal Prompts

How did you experience standardized testing when you were a young student? Were you a good test taker, or did testing make you nervous? Were there tests you enjoyed taking?

Get the tools you need to sharpen your study skills. SAGE edge offers a robust online environment featuring an impressive array of free tools and resources.

Access practice quizzes, eFlashcards, video, and multimedia at **edge.sagepub.com/koch4e**.

iStock/svetikd

What Does It Mean to Teach and to Learn?

If a doctor, lawyer, or dentist had 40 people in his office at one time, all of whom had different needs, and some of whom did not want to be there and were *causing trouble*, and the doctor, lawyer, or dentist, without assistance, had to treat them all with professional excellence for nine months, then he [or she] might have some conception of the classroom teacher's job.

—Donald D. Quinn

Learning Outcomes

After reading this chapter, you should be able to:

4-1 Explain the common myth that "anyone can teach."

4-2 Identify examples of the academic language associated with teacher education.

4-3 Compare learning theories, and examine how neuroscience has influenced current theories about how people learn.

4-4 Articulate the benefits of backward design for planning instruction.

4-5 Examine how curriculum is developed and the influence of the Common Core State Standards on mathematics and English curricula.

4-6 Analyze the statement: "We can teach our students, but we cannot learn for them."

4-7 Explain how understanding how your students learn and what their lives are like might influence your role as their teacher.

InTASC Standards

• Standard 1: Learner Development

• Standard 3: Learning Environments

• Standard 7: Planning for Instruction

What does Donald Quinn mean when he speaks of "different needs"? As you consider a teaching career, you will frequently hear the terms *pedagogy* and *instruction*. These terms are part of the language of the profession, what edTPA refers to as "academic language." This chapter will examine their meanings in the context of teaching and learning.

In this chapter, we also examine the meaning of teaching and learning through an exploration of learning theories. Currently, the field of neuroscience—the study of the structure, function, development, and physiology of the brain and the nervous system—is at the forefront of understanding how people perceive and interact with the external world. Other important approaches have also contributed to the way educators think about learning today. We will explore what we teach—the school's curriculum—as well as how the content of a school's curriculum is shaped by not only national standards but also by states, local school districts, local school boards, school curriculum committees, and teachers themselves.

Can Anyone Teach?

Most people have spent much of their lives as students in classrooms. Add up the years of schooling you have had up to this time—the number is certainly considerable, is it not? Because people have been in classrooms for so much of their lives, there exists a common myth that anyone can teach.

As a new teacher just starting out, I confided my nervousness about my first day of teaching to a friend, and he said to me, "Teaching is easy. You just stand up there and talk—and

you like to talk." For me, that was the first of several experiences with people who think they know what being a teacher is about. The idea that "teaching is talking" is the most significant misconception.

As you are probably discovering for yourself, teaching and learning are complex activities. They are far from easy and automatic. As we explore the ways a teacher fosters learning, you will see that there is a lot to know about the principles behind what a teacher does. Remember, too, that the process is a dialectic—it requires communication with your students, and it demands that you be an active listener, not just a talker. (My friend was right, however: I do like to talk.) As you will see, teaching is not "telling," and, in addition to what you have to *know* to be able to teach, there are many things you have to *do* to create the opportunities for students to learn. Perhaps one of the most important first steps is learning about your students—who they are and what their lives are like. People are different in so many ways. Your students will represent the broad diversity of the human condition; they will differ in how they learn, where they come from, their native language, their learning styles, and their prior life experiences.

Pedagogy and Instruction

In Chapter 2, we discussed how who we are comes to bear on what we do with our students and how we engage them in learning. In fact, who we are has everything to do with how we teach.

Pedagogy is commonly thought of today as the art or science of being a teacher. I like to think of this modern interpretation as the art and science of being a teacher. What makes pedagogy an art? It is a personal creative expression of oneself. I am reminded of the French philosopher and essayist Joseph Joubert (1754–1824, 2005), who said, "To teach is to learn something twice." As a teacher, you explore ways to create a lesson that will help your students understand something you already understand; this is like learning the concept again!

Yet pedagogy is more than an art. It is also a science because it relies on careful observations of (1) students' dispositions, (2) students' prior knowledge, and (3) students' responses to the activities and questions in which they are engaged. Scientists have helped us understand more clearly how students learn and how we can best promote that learning. Cognitive science is a multidisciplinary field that focuses on how information is represented, processed, and transformed as we learn something. How then does instruction differ from pedagogy?

In formal terms, **pedagogy** can be thought of as the belief system and the orientation that you bring to your instructional practice. **Instruction** emerges from pedagogy on a daily basis. It is the subtext beneath the instruction you provide in your classroom. For example, if you believe that you need to understand students' ideas and beliefs to help them gain new understanding, then that is part of your pedagogy. Your instructional decisions will emerge from that pedagogy. As teachers gain new ideas about how people learn, their pedagogical stance can shift in response to those ideas.

People often use the terms *instructional methods* and *pedagogy* interchangeably, but understanding the difference helps teachers reflect on their practice. Pedagogy is the **personal teaching philosophy** that gets expressed through instructional practice. It informs all the methods of instruction and decision making in the classroom. Keeping the meaning of the terms separate is important because it reminds us to revisit our personal teaching philosophy every time we plan for instruction.

Many special subject area teachers—such as math, science, social studies, language arts, and foreign-language teachers—believe that they need solely to be experts in their particular areas. However, even if you are a subject area expert, becoming an expert teacher in your subject area requires special professional understanding. Teachers must integrate, transform, and represent subject matter knowledge in ways that are understandable to students (Toh, Ho, Chew, & Riley, 2003). This special type of knowledge is referred to as **pedagogical content knowledge (PCK)**. Being subject specific, PCK refers to the ways particular subject matter material is best represented and communicated to make it accessible to students (Shulman, 1987, p. 4).

Probably the most important description of teaching and learning is that it is an exchange of ideas, a constant flow between you and your students that helps them further clarify their thinking. Making new knowledge your own is really complex, and neuroscientists are providing new insights into how that happens in the brain. For example, prior knowledge is important—it is the "hook" that a new idea latches onto. Sometimes, that new idea gets expressed using academic language, which is somewhat different from everyday language.

Academic language is the vocabulary words of the discipline that students need to learn and use to participate and engage in meaningful ways in the content area. It includes the oral, visual, and written language used for academic purposes. It represents the means by which students develop and express content understandings. For studying how to become an effective teacher, the academic language of the profession may include terms like *pedagogy, instruction, curriculum, pedagogical content knowledge, teaching philosophy, learning theories, assessment, rubrics*, and many more. As we continue in this chapter, other terms will be useful for you. You will also need to consider the academic language of your future classroom, which depends on your subject, grade level, knowledge of the field, and how best to teach it.

Now that we have clarified some of our terms, let us look at what some major investigators of the past century have discovered about the learning process. As you will see, their work has led to competing theories about the way learning occurs.

How People Learn

How does learning occur? The growth of the field of psychology in the 20th century, and recent advances in neuroscience in the 21st, have formed the foundation for learning theories that are reflected to a greater or lesser extent in schools across the country. **Learning theories** are formal ideas about how people learn. Today, the most significant shift in our thinking about the nature of learning has important implications for teaching. For a long time, teachers functioned on the implicit assumption that knowledge can be transferred intact from the mind of the teacher to the mind of the learner. We now understand that this is not how people learn, but what is a teacher to do to foster student learning? We examine traditional theories that look at the conditions described by psychologists and others that are considered optimal for learning, keeping in mind that "learning is not a spectator sport" (Koedinger, Kim, Zhuxin Jia, McLaughlin, & Bier, 2015).

---

pedagogy The art and science of teaching; all that you know and believe about teaching.

instruction The act or process of teaching; the way your pedagogy becomes enacted in practice.

personal teaching philosophy An individual's own pedagogy informed by his or her own beliefs and understanding of how students learn best. A teacher's personal philosophy outs itself through the instructional strategies employed with the students.

pedagogical content knowledge (PCK) The understanding of how particular topics, problems, or issues can be adapted and presented to match the diverse interests and abilities of learners.

academic language The language of the discipline that students need to learn and use to participate and engage in meaningful ways in the content area.

learning theory An explanation of how learning typically occurs and about conditions that favor learning.

FIGURE 4.1 ● Bloom's Taxonomy

Adapted from Vanderbilt University Center for Teaching, https://cft.vanderbilt.edu/guides-sub-pages/blooms-taxonomy/#1956, licensed under CC BY 4.0 https://creativecommons.org/licenses/by/4.0/

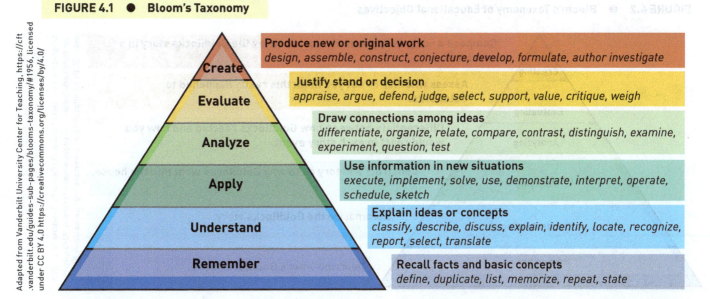

Create — **Produce new or original work**
design, assemble, construct, conjecture, develop, formulate, author investigate

Evaluate — **Justify stand or decision**
appraise, argue, defend, judge, select, support, value, critique, weigh

Analyze — **Draw connections among ideas**
differentiate, organize, relate, compare, contrast, distinguish, examine, experiment, question, test

Apply — **Use information in new situations**
execute, implement, solve, use, demonstrate, interpret, operate, schedule, sketch

Understand — **Explain ideas or concepts**
classify, describe, discuss, explain, identify, locate, recognize, report, select, translate

Remember — **Recall facts and basic concepts**
define, duplicate, list, memorize, repeat, state

Bloom's Taxonomy of Educational Objectives

In the 1950s, a committee of college and university examiners, led by the psychologist Benjamin Bloom, identified a taxonomy (classification system) of skills, or **educational objectives**, in three domains: the cognitive, the affective, and the psychomotor. The objectives in the **cognitive domain** of **Bloom's Taxonomy** represent a natural progression of behaviors that are important in learning. It was the committee's hope that teachers and curriculum developers would use these educational objectives as they developed curriculum and strategies for helping students to learn.

Bloom arranged the educational objectives into a hierarchy based on the idea that a simple behavior, integrated with other simple behaviors, forms a more complex behavior (Bloom, Englehart, Furst, Hill, & Krathwohl, 1956). The six major categories of objectives, from simplest to most complex, are **knowledge, comprehension, application, analysis, synthesis, and evaluation**. In the 1990s, Lorin Anderson, a student of Bloom's, revised the taxonomy to reflect the demands of 21st-century learning. Anderson revised and restated the objectives as verbs, not nouns (see Figure 4.1).

In addition, the synthesis level, referred to as *creating,* was deemed the highest level of cognitive function, trading places with evaluation.

educational objectives Goals identified with specific teaching and learning activities.

cognitive domain The objectives in the cognitive domain of Bloom's Taxonomy represent a natural progression of mental behaviors that are important in learning.

Bloom's Taxonomy: a classification system of educational objectives developed by psychologist Benjamin Bloom in the 1950s. The taxonomy has three domains: the cognitive, affective, and psychomotor. The cognitive domain was revised in the 1990s to represent a hierarchy of behaviors that include remembering, understanding, applying, analyzing, evaluating, and creating.

Knowledge, Comprehension, Application, Analysis, Synthesis, and Evaluation Bloom's original classes of learning behaviors. They were slightly reorganized and renamed with verbs in the 1990s.

- **Remembering:** Can the student recall or remember the information?

- **Understanding:** Can the student explain ideas or concepts?

- **Applying:** Can the student use the information in a new way?

- **Analyzing:** Can the student distinguish between the different parts?

- **Evaluating:** Can the student justify a stand or decision?

- **Creating:** Can the student create a new product or point of view?

You may wonder what it would look like to teach students at the various levels of Bloom's Taxonomy. This is a relevant question as we examine contemporary learning theories and the ways in which we assess students today. *Remembering* is the base of the hierarchical pyramid (see Figure 4.2). Some of the behaviors it requires are for students to recall, define, memorize, list, or repeat. As the learner moves to the next level of understanding, the prior knowledge of the first level is essential. This is true as we progress from each simpler level of cognitive function to the more complex level. Hence, *understanding* asks the student to describe, classify, discuss, and explain. By the time the learner progresses to the application level or *applying* the knowledge in a new way as the new version states, the learner can choose, use, demonstrate, interpret, solve, and write. At the *analyzing* level, learners compare, contrast, appraise, criticize, differentiate, question, and test the idea.

By the *evaluating* level, the learner is able to argue, defend, judge, and select; and by the level of *creating,* the learner can make new meaning and assemble, construct, design, formulate, develop, and write.

FIGURE 4.2 ● Bloom's Taxonomy of Educational Objectives

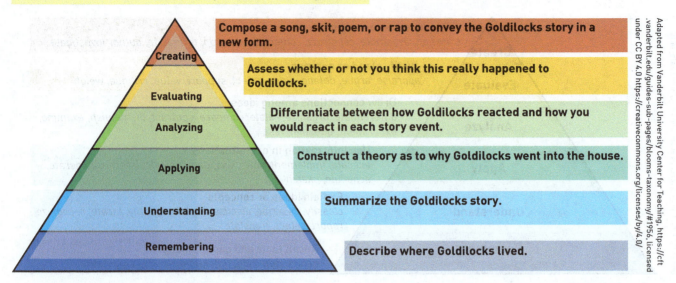

Adapted from Vanderbilt University Center for Teaching, https://cft.vanderbilt.edu/guides-sub-pages/blooms-taxonomy/#1956, licensed under CC 4.0 https://creativecommons.org/licenses/by/4.0/

As you explore the learning theories described in this chapter, examine the ways in which we now understand from neuroscience that learners are indeed active participants in their own concept construction.

Behaviorism: A Teacher-Centered Approach

In the mid-1900s, Harvard psychologist B. F. Skinner pioneered a theory of how people learn that still has followers today. Skinner's theory of *operant conditioning* viewed learning as a response to external stimuli in the environment. For Skinner, learning was a product that could be promoted by teachers who provided the right incentives and motivation. This general approach came to be known as **behaviorism**. Behaviorists believe that all learning is shaped by the stimuli in the environment, and that free will plays no role in the process.

Using the behaviorist approach, teachers structured their lessons around clear objectives that stated what students would be able to do by the end of the lesson. The desired behaviors were regulated by carefully planned reinforcements and punishments. The external rewards could include good grades, increased privileges, or a special smile from the teacher. Students were seen as passive participants in the classroom who responded to the teacher's direct rewards and punishments.

Behaviorist ideas still form a backdrop for many techniques used to establish classroom discipline. For instance, teachers rely on behaviorist principles when they set up specific rewards for good behavior. Behaviorism asserts that students will modify their behavior in response to consistent delivery of rewards and punishments.

Yet there are many critics of behaviorist techniques today. Some argue that behaviorist teachers exercise too much control over their students, with the result that students tend to learn facts rather than deep concepts. Others remind teachers that rewards and punishments do not help students develop their own internal mechanisms for doing quality work and that students eventually lose interest in what they are essentially being "bribed" to do (Kohn, 1999). Today, in some areas, students are being paid to complete high school. Money for grades is an experimental approach to stimulate lower-achieving students. It is, as you can imagine, quite controversial, and most parents do not agree with cash-based incentives for achievement.

Cognitive Learning Theories: The Role of the Learner

As behaviorists focused solely on students' observable behaviors as the indicators of learning, many educators and psychologists began to resist this view and suggested that the learner was not a passive recipient of new concepts but rather played a more active role in the learning process. **Cognitive learning theories** emerged to describe students' mental development. Cognitive learning theorists wanted to understand the ways in which the mind worked to discover and model the thought processes that occur during learning. Early cognitive learning theorists studied children for hours and hours to try to understand what they were thinking. Later cognitive learning theorists used brain scans to gain insight into how the mind works when we are learning something new.

A key figure in cognitive learning theory was the Swiss scholar and scientist Jean Piaget, who began conducting interviews and research studies with children in the 1920s. From these investigations, he developed his stages

---

behaviorism The theory that learning takes place in response to reinforcements (for instance, rewards or punishments) from the outside environment.

cognitive learning theories Explanations of the mental processes that occur during learning.

of cognitive development. According to Piaget, at certain times in a child's intellectual growth, different mental structures begin to emerge. He believed that most children between birth and 2 years of age are in the sensorimotor stage, in which learning occurs mainly through sensory impressions and movement. The child learns that he or she is separate from the environment and that aspects of the environment—parents or a favorite toy—continue to exist even though they may be outside the reach of his or her senses.

Later, between ages 2 and 7, children begin to learn words and other symbols (the preoperational stage). In this stage, a child's thinking is influenced by fantasy (the way the child would like things to be), and he or she assumes that others see situations from his or her viewpoint. The child takes in information and then changes it in his or her mind to fit his or her ideas.

In the next stage, from ages 7 to 11, the child develops the ability to generalize concepts from concrete experiences (the concrete operational stage). In this stage, the child makes rational judgments about concrete or observable phenomena, which in the past he or she needed to manipulate physically to understand.

Finally, at ages 11 and older, the child develops the ability to manipulate abstractions (the formal operational stage). In this stage, the learner no longer requires concrete objects to make rational judgments.

Piaget argued that at each of these stages of maturation, a child is ready for a different type of learning. The discrete boundaries of Piaget's stages of development came under scrutiny as researchers learned that children can be in several stages at once and that the stages cannot easily be linked to predetermined ages. In other words, as significant as Piaget's work is, we now understand that there are not clear demarcations of mental development from one stage to the next. As the learner progresses from one stage to the next, there is an overlap. For example, many children handle concrete operations earlier in their lives than Piaget thought.

At each stage, Piaget decided, knowledge is not passively received but is actively built up by the learner through a process of invention or creation, not reception. This gives a great deal of responsibility to the learner.

Jerome Bruner (1960, 1966), another cognitive learning theorist, took Piaget's ideas a step further by arguing that at any stage of cognitive development, teachers should allow children to discover ideas for themselves. A leading supporter of Piaget's work, Bruner suggested that at any given stage of cognitive development, teaching should proceed in a way that allows children to discover ideas for themselves. His work became known as discovery learning. Bruner differed from Piaget in one important respect. Whereas Piaget believed that readiness for a particular type of learning depended on a child's stage of cognitive development, Bruner noticed that children are always ready to learn a concept at some level. Realizing this, Bruner (1960) emphasized the importance of returning to curriculum topics at various

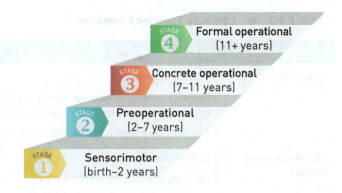

Piaget's Stages of Development.

ages, revisiting them at different stages of the child's development. This produces a spiraling of curriculum topics, as the same broad topics are revisited at higher grade levels. This practice has become an important part of curriculum planning. Discovery learning remains influential today and has much in common with constructivism, which we will come to in a moment.

Social Cognitive Theories: The Role of Social Interactions

Piaget's work was criticized for not taking into account the learner's social contexts. After all, when children develop their understanding of the world, they do not do so in a social or cultural vacuum. Some of Piaget's critics developed forms of social learning theory. Over time, these became **social cognitive learning theories**, which take into account both the learner's own mental processes and the social environment in which the learning occurs.

The Russian psychologist Lev Vygotsky (1962) showed how social contexts influence the ideas that people develop. As one example, the teacher and students in a classroom use language that is socially and culturally accepted in that specific environment. The ideas that children develop in the classroom conform to these socially accepted usages and meanings. When students work in groups and read each other's writing in order to critique it, for example, one student says of the other's work, "This is so cool." The meaning is that this student peer really liked the story, and the comment is readily understood. Clearly, different cultures, neighborhoods, and parts of the world would have different ways of expressing the same meaning. Because students do not learn in a cultural vacuum, studying how people learn requires consideration of the context.

Many social cognitivists stress the importance of modeling. For instance, if you were teaching young students how to add columns of numbers, you would probably model the process of exchanging 10 ones for one 10. According to social cognitivists, students would learn, in part, by observing you. They would then learn more by doing a similar

social cognitive learning theories Explanations that describe how learning involves interactions between the learner and the social environment.

TABLE 4.1 ● Learning Theories Compared

Learning Theory	Key Elements
Behaviorism	• Teacher-centered • Students respond to external stimuli and learn the correct responses through rewards and punishments, eventually internalizing rewards and punishments • Teachers are in absolute control through the stimuli they present in the classroom
Cognitive learning theories	• Learner-centered • Learning is active, not merely passive • Symbolic mental constructions in the minds of learners help them process information
Social cognitive learning theories	• Learner-centered • Internal mental processes are important, but we also learn through experiences shared with others; learning is as much social as it is individual
Constructivism	• Learner-centered • We all construct our own perspective of the world, based on individual experiences and personal schemes, which are internal knowledge structures • A person adjusts his or her mental model to incorporate new experiences and make sense of new information

problem themselves, and they would be further served by using manipulative materials and working on exchanging units with their peers in a group.

Thinking about modeling reminds us that teachers are not the only important social influence on learning. Parents, other adults, siblings, and peers have major effects on a child's intellectual development as well. A young person learns a great deal by observing various other people, communicating with them, and solving problems with them.

Constructivism: Student-Centered Learning

Piaget, Bruner, Vygotsky, and others paved the way for understanding in greater depth how people learn. The accumulated research has shown that the essence of learning is the constant effort to assimilate new information. For real learning to occur, you also have to make that information your own so that it becomes significant to you as you use it for your own purposes. These ideas form the basis of a group of learning theories called **constructivism**. The constructivist approach builds on cognitive and social cognitive theories but goes further by considering how new information becomes meaningful to the learner.

The Essence of Constructivism: Building Mental Schemes

Constructivism is the learning theory that most closely relates to what we currently understand about how people

....

constructivism A group of theories about knowledge and learning whose basic tenet is that all knowledge is constructed by synthesizing new ideas with prior knowledge. Constructivism holds that knowledge is not passively received; rather, it is actively built by the learner as he or she experiences the world.

learn. Learners interact with people, objects, and ideas to construct their understanding of what is happening around them. They are active participants in the act of learning.

At the heart of this learning theory is the concept of "mental schemes." A mental scheme is a sort of organizer in the brain. As the result of all your experiences during your lifetime, you have formed these organizing structures in your mind that help you make sense of the world. When you encounter new information, you try to fit it into your existing schemes. Sometimes it fits easily, but when it does not fit, you have to revise your existing mental scheme. In the next photo, Charlie Brown forces Linus to rethink his mental scheme about how long it takes to study to become a doctor. This changes Linus's thinking. When new information fails to match your existing schemes—when it does not fit your picture of the world—you have a choice. You can ignore the new information—in a sense, reject it. In that case, we can say that no new learning has occurred. Or you can remake your set of schemes to accommodate the new data—a process of truly making new information your own. That is what happens when we learn something.

Mental Schemes at Work

The following story illustrates mental schemes at work. It is the story of *my own personal* mental scheme for how mail was delivered where I grew up.

"I grew up in an inner-city apartment building with six floors and 20 apartments on each floor. When I was 6 years old, I was allowed to use the small key to open the mailbox assigned to my family and 'take out the mail.' This was my daily job after school.

Charles Schulz, Peanuts, owned by Andrews McMeel Syndication.

▲
The Role of Mental Schemes in Learning

In this *Peanuts* cartoon, Linus learns from Charlie Brown that his ambition to become a doctor requires 8 extra years of school. Being admired is not sufficient compensation for this, and Linus revises his mental scheme.

"I had my own personal theory about mail delivery. I imagined that, when the envelope was dropped in the public mailbox on the corner, a tube carried it through underground chutes to its destination in my little mailbox. Even at the age of 6, however, I was troubled by not being able to explain how the letter knew how to get to my mailbox.

"One day, when walking with my mother, I bent down to look under the mailbox on the corner. "What are you looking for?" she asked. "I was wondering where the tubes were," I responded. "What tubes?" she asked, and I then proceeded to share my theory. Nodding, she said that she could not explain right then how the mail got to the mailbox but she would arrange a way for me to find out.

"Shortly thereafter, I was home ill from school, in the care of my grandmother. My mother called from work and asked Grandma to take me down to the mailboxes at the precise time that Artie, our mailman, would arrive. She bundled me up and I was able to witness the mailman, with his special key, open the portal to all of the mailboxes in the building. One box at a time, he inserted the mail in the various boxes.

"He allowed me to help him, thrilled with my curiosity about how mail 'knows' where to go. He also invited me and my family to the local post office for a view of how the postal workers sort the mail for the various neighborhood routes.

"I shall never forget this experience. It demonstrates, for me, what it means to reorganize my mental schemes as I set about understanding more of my external world.

"It would have been easy for my mother to say, 'No, Janice, mail does not travel through tubes in the ground.' Instead, she honored my theory, found it quite interesting, and arranged for me to have an experience that would challenge my beliefs about underground tubes and mail delivery. By observing how the mailman opened all the mailboxes simultaneously with his large master key, I saw people as an intricate part of the mail delivery process. I began to expand my thinking and accommodate this new experience into my mental scheme."

Authentic instruction begins with close attention to students' existing ideas, knowledge, skills, and attitudes. Just

as my mother realized, these are the foundation on which new learning builds (Bransford & Donovan, 2004). Learning as much as we can about students' existing mental schemes is important if we hope to help them learn. Effective teachers try to activate students' prior knowledge so that, in the course of the lesson, students can build on what they already know, challenge it, rethink it, and refine it.

Because teachers need to pay so much attention to students' preexisting ideas, they often face a situation similar to the one my mother encountered: the student reveals ideas that are plainly "wrong." What should a teacher do when a student has such misconceptions? Many educators believe that if a teacher merely corrects a student's erroneous ideas verbally, those ideas may go underground; they may linger in the student's mind, unrefuted. Instead, the teacher should treat the misconceptions with respect and guide the student in confronting new information that contradicts them. In wrestling with the contradiction, the teacher hopes, the student will modify old mental schemes or create new ones, and in this way genuine learning will occur.

There will be many times when you will be tempted to refute a student's idea or explanation. It is certainly true that you should not allow your student to harbor misconceptions for a long time. But try to find a way to provide convincing evidence for the alternative, more accurate explanation.

Perhaps you can remember a personal theory that you held on to when you were young. How did you eventually learn, through experience and interaction with the material, that you had to adjust your thinking?

Learning and Teaching

A teacher's purpose is not to create students in his [or her] own image, but to develop students who can create their own image.

—Anonymous

This quote refers to the need for teachers to help students build ideas for themselves. They can offer opportunities for students to work iteratively[1] on big concepts; the students

_____
[1] *Iteratively* means repeatedly, on multiple occasions.

can address those concepts over time until they can construct those concepts for themselves. One example is how understanding that the order of the digits in a number tells you the value of the digits. Place value is a huge idea! Students cannot understand place value by having it explained, but when they have the opportunity to exchange bundles of units and bundle the bundles and then represent the bundles in some numerical form, then they can come to make sense of numbers. Representing numbers as numerals is part of the convention we establish. We talk in code to one another, and students need to reinvent that code for themselves. Then the ones, tens, and hundreds columns have meaning, and the number really represents a quantity.

This may seem like a radical idea—that individual students need to reinvent a basic operation we use for arithmetic. But think about what happens if students learn only the mechanical processes of mathematics. When young children are adding numbers, they can learn to "carry a 1" from one column to the next, but if they do not get the *meaning* of this procedure, they will have only a shallow and fragile understanding of what they are doing. Later on in their mathematical education, they will likely get confused because they do not fully grasp what is happening (interview with Dr. Jacqueline Grennon Brooks, 2005).

Education is far broader than just schooling. All the experiences students have at home, on the playground, and in the environments of their lives bear on how they learn. The students' interests, sensibilities, and daily practices all contribute to their mental schemes. That is why the environment is so desperately important to learning. In an inner-city New York school, one teacher takes her low-income students on sidewalk "field trips" to neighborhood places that her students never see (e.g., the subway, the neighborhood market, a municipal parking garage, local parking meters, and an auto repair shop). The teacher situates second-grade math students around the parking meters and generates a list of vocabulary words based on their excursions. Students in this second-grade class get experiential exposure that, coupled with the formal classroom, gives context and meaning to learning (Winerip, 2012).

We base our practices of teaching on learning theories. The emerging relationship between neuroscience and teaching informs our pedagogy and helps us to guide instruction with meaningful context. The more we learn about how the brain works, the more we realize that the way our mind works is dependent on how the neurons in our brain are fired, and that is dependent on the context created for learning. Actively engaged students have more neurons firing, allowing them to use more parts of the brain, connect with prior knowledge, and build on what they already know. John Dewey's progressive era had the right idea when it encouraged the active participation of students in their own learning. This simple story illustrates that type of engagement in the course of a simple lesson:

"My teacher, Ms. Schultz, walked us outside our large brick building in an urban area into the schoolyard and asked us to feel the sun's warmth. It was an autumn day and the air was cool, but the sun felt warm against our faces. Then she asked us to move about and explore our shadows.

"Something Ms. Schultz said in the midst of this experience has stayed with me forever: 'Isn't it amazing, girls and boys, that this sun is 93 million miles away and it still has the power to warm us up?' I remember thinking that the sun must be very, very hot if, after traveling all those miles, it still warmed my skin. I have thought about the sun in that way ever since.

"On the next sunny day, we returned early to the schoolyard and explored our shadows again, noticing how their length changed with the time of day. Experiencing the sunlight in the context of learning about shadows made a big difference to me. I was taken with how different the size of my shadow was at noon, compared with early morning. Experiencing myself in space, responding to the sun's warmth on my body, joining with my classmates in measuring our shadows—all these activities created a mental scheme on which my learning about the sun and shadows occurred. I have always remembered the distance of the sun from the Earth and that when the sun is overhead, around noon, my shadow is the shortest.

"In these simple ways, Ms. Schultz helped create a context that shaped my learning."

Fish Is Fish

One of my favorite children's stories illustrates the role that prior and current knowledge plays in student learning. *Fish Is Fish*, by Leo Lionni (1970), is the story of a young minnow and a tadpole who become friends when they meet underwater in a pond. But the tadpole soon grows legs and explores the world beyond the pond, and then returns to tell his fish friend about the new creatures he sees, such as birds, cows, and people. As the illustrations demonstrate, the fish imagines these creatures as bird-fish, cow-fish, and people-fish, and is eager to join them. The minnow learns the limits of life beyond the safety of the water environment to which he is adapted, but not before we get to see the images of fish with wings as he hears about birds, fish with udders as he hears about cows, and fish walking on their tailfins as he hears about people. You may be wondering what this has to do with learning theories. In fact, it is a wonderful illustration of how learners process new material through their prior and current conceptions. Unless those ideas are acknowledged, learners create mental images that are quite different from those that are intended—in this case, by the minnow's friend, the frog. The implications for teaching are clear: Access students' existing understandings and experiences and draw attention to the kinds of knowledge that help students to learn with understanding (Bransford, Brown, & Cocking, 2000).

Hence, if the frog had provided more details about birds, cows, and people, it would have helped the fish to understand that their body parts have functions that these animals need for survival. Of course, the fish in Lionni's story is endowed with human capacities for thought, but he

Excerpt(s) and illustrations from *Fish Is Fish* by Leo Lionni, copyright ©1970 and renewed 1998 by NORAELEO LLC. Used by permission of Alfred A. Knopf, an imprint of Random House Children's Books, a division of Penguin Random House LLC. All rights reserved.

"Cows," said the frog. "Cows! They have four legs, horns, eat grass, and carry pink bags of milk."

▲ *Fish Is Fish*, by Leo Lionni (1970), is a children's story of a young minnow and a tadpole who become friends when they meet underwater in a pond. It illustrates the role that prior and current knowledge plays in student learning.

does make a good illustration of why it is so important for teachers to understand how people learn.

Understanding by Design

There is rarely one best approach to teaching, based on our understanding of how students learn. Multiple approaches and experiences are very important. Educational researchers have developed a backward design model for planning instruction that takes into account first where we hope the students will be by the end of a unit (Wiggins & McTighe, 1998). This approach, called **Understanding by Design (UbD)**, posits the following questions: What are the goals? What are we hoping the students know and are able to do as a result of experiencing the unit? Where do you want to end up? If you can answer these questions by determining your learning goals for the students, then the next step is to figure out how you will know the students meet these goals. You actually determine what evidence you would need to demonstrate that the students understood it in a way that allows them to make personal meaning for themselves. You may create a project that students would have to complete or some other task that asks them to demonstrate their understanding. The facets of understanding that students should, using this model, be able to demonstrate are: explain, interpret, apply, have perspective, empathize, and have self-knowledge. This looks similar to Bloom's Taxonomy, but

there is no hierarchical order. They are valued outcomes, and not all are met within a particular unit. Now that you have your goals and assessments understood, UbD suggests that you can begin to plan your learning experiences and your mode of instruction through your lesson plans. The lessons, in this way, should contribute to meeting your goals for student learning and the several ways the students can express their understanding. It does indeed seem backward to begin by establishing goals that require you to describe assessing student learning; however, thousands of educators across the country have found this approach to teaching invaluable!

What Is a Curriculum?

In this chapter, you have read about theories of learning and instruction, but what about the actual material you will be required to teach? Educators refer to this required material as the **curriculum**. Who determines the curriculum, and how can teachers express their personal and creative selves when handed a list of topics they must address? Think about these questions as you read the following sections.

Formal, Informal, and Hidden Curricula

The word curriculum derives from the Latin term meaning "running course." It is the overall plan that includes what you will teach and how the material should be arranged and

....

Understanding by Design (UbD) A plan for instruction that starts with the learning goals and assessments and then develops the learning activities and lessons that will lead to those outcomes.

....

curriculum A plan of studies that includes the ways instructional content is organized and presented at each grade level.

presented. A curriculum may be thought of as an organizing tool for the myriad topics that are addressed at each grade level. Curricula are typically organized by content area. There are language arts, mathematics, social studies, foreign language, and science curricula. There is a curriculum associated with any subject matter taught at a given school.

Sometimes, you will hear the official plan of studies referred to as the *formal curriculum*. There is also an **informal curriculum**, which includes all the things you do in the classroom that are not part of the official, prescribed plan. For example, you might use an important local event or news story to create a learning experience closely linked to the students' own lives. In a high school earth science class, the teacher might address an earthquake that was in the news that week and explore the causes for earthquakes, even if this was not the formal topic of study at that moment. Local news events often become the centerpiece of social studies lessons because of their relevance. Although not written into the preplanned curriculum, these informal events bring meaning to the formal curriculum and deepen students' understanding of the concepts they are learning.

In speaking of the informal curriculum, educators often include the concept of the hidden curriculum. The hidden curriculum consists of the social rules and values schools and teachers transmit to students. Hidden curricula are communicated through the rules of conduct, dress codes, social atmosphere, and relationships among teachers, administration, and students in a given school environment. They are hidden in the sense that they are not written down—or at least not presented as part of the subject matter to be learned—but they are very much part of the school experience for both students and teachers. For example, when I was growing up in the middle of the last century, it was customary for the girls in the elementary school I attended to erase and wash the blackboards, also called chalkboards, which are not common in modern classrooms. It was also usual for boys to march in the assemblies carrying the flags in what was called a color guard. I always wanted to carry the flag; however, I knew that I dare not ask. The hidden curriculum dictated what girls and boys would and would not do in this school.

The Role of National Standards and Common Core State Standards

In the United States, the formal curriculum in public schools is established by each state, with individual school districts adjusting it to a greater or lesser degree. Each state, however, relies heavily on the input of national groups that have been actively involved in establishing standards for their discipline. For example, the National Council of Teachers of Mathematics has a great influence on mathematics curricula throughout the country. Today, the Common Core State Standards that you read about in Chapter 3 have great influence over the states in mathematics and English language curricula.

The standards movement has dominated public education since the early 1990s. This movement has prompted subject-area associations to state explicitly what students should know and be able to do at each grade level from kindergarten through 12th grade, resulting in national standards for each subject. Hence, there are national standards for science, language arts, foreign languages, social studies, mathematics, technology, health, and physical education. Local schools' control of their curricula in each area was quite broad until the federal No Child Left Behind (NCLB) Act was passed in 2002. As we explored in Chapter 3, NCLB required that students be held accountable by means of statewide exams that assess their knowledge at various grade levels, often beginning in third grade. That change reduced local schools' control over their curricula. The statewide assessment is often thought of as a one-size-fits-all process because it demands a uniform statewide curriculum if students are to be successful on the tests. With the Every Student Succeeds Act, states will have more control over testing.

Common Core State Standards and Standardized Assessment

Sometimes, local schools' curricula suffer as a result of the inflexibility imposed by standardized assessments. Consider this story of a project in an elementary school where the teachers and administrators had the idea and the funding to build a pond on the school property.

Several years ago, an elementary school in a northeastern suburb began an initiative to build a pond on its school property. The pond would attract birds and insects, the teachers and administrators thought, and they could build an elementary science curriculum around it. They had the pond installed and "seeded" it with a few small koi (similar to goldfish) and water plants.

Grade-level classes took responsibility for monitoring the temperature and turbidity of the pond as well as carefully noticing the life in and around it. The science curriculum in that school grew, with exploration of the properties of the pond being the centerpiece.

Curriculum as Window and Mirror

Ideally, curriculum should be both a window and a mirror. This metaphor, suggested by Emily Style in a 1996 essay (http://www.wcwonline.org/seed/curriculum.html), implies that:

1. Curriculum must provide windows for students into the worlds of others. That is, it should help students learn about other people, other cultures, and other realities.

2. Curriculum must also offer mirrors of students' own reality. It should be connected to their lives in ways that help them see the subject matter as meaningful.

---

informal curriculum Learning experiences that go beyond the formal curriculum, such as activities the teacher introduces to connect academic concepts to the students' daily lives.

I am reminded of how I felt growing up in an inner-city environment and reading *Dick and Jane* basal readers. You are probably familiar with basal readers, which are textbooks used to teach reading. Typically, basal readers are published as a series of books, with each book in the series designed for a particular reading level. Dick and Jane were the main characters in basal readers used to teach reading from the 1930s to the 1970s.

Dick and Jane lived in their own house with a white picket fence and a lawn sprinkler. They had a cute dog and a little red wagon. There is nothing wrong with those things, of course, but I used to ask my mother, "Where do Dick and Jane live?" I did not recognize the surroundings, and I wondered where they could be found. Certainly the private house and lawn sprinkler were not found on my block!

For me, the reading curriculum that relied on *Dick and Jane* may have been a window, but it was not at all a mirror. Many students in other areas of the United States had similar experiences with basal readers. The use of basal readers waned during the 1980s and 1990s because their stories and images did not reflect the diversity of students in classrooms across the country. Basal readers were also thought to be less authentic than other forms of writing, such as regular children's literature. Many states and local districts opted for authentic early-childhood literature as a way to teach reading. Students get a glimpse into many different kinds of worlds, and more types of students see themselves in the reading material.

In many places today, schools use both basal readers and authentic children's literature, offering students a language arts curriculum that includes both formats. Often, local district committees select the required literature for each grade level, and this, in conjunction with a basal reader, forms the backbone of the language arts curriculum. Many of the newer basal readers include some combination of nonfiction, biographies, adaptations of original children's books, condensations of classic children's literature, and original stories. They also feature students of many origins, not only Caucasians.

In this way, the typical language arts curriculum has evolved to function better as both a window and a mirror. Students get a glimpse into many different kinds of worlds, and more types of students see themselves in the reading material.

Adapting the Curriculum to Your Students

One implication of what we have been saying is that you should evaluate the curriculum in light of who your students are. When presented with a curriculum in a subject area, ask yourself, "How can I make this curriculum more relevant to the students in this classroom at this time in their lives?" If we think of learning as a process of reforming mental schemes, then teachers need to begin to understand their students' mental schemes to be successful.

This is a challenging task. One way to accomplish it is to pay careful attention to the experiences of your students. Through discussion and writing assignments, you can invite the students' authentic selves into the classroom and learn much more about them. Know who they are, what their lives are like when they leave your classroom, and what are

From *Dick and Jane* by Scott Foresman by Pearson Education, Inc., or its affiliates. Used by permission. All Rights Reserved.

Come, Dick.
Come and see.
Come, come.
Come and see.
Come and see Spot.

Dick, Jane, and Spot from *We Look and See*.

TABLE 4.2   ●   Questions to Ask About Your Students

Who are my students?

What are their interests, concerns, hobbies, beliefs, and feelings about themselves and others?

Where do they live? Do they have siblings? Do they have both parents at home? Do both parents work outside the home? What do the students do after school?

How can I adapt the formal curriculum to the experiences that the students encounter every day? How can I provide students with a mirror so they will understand that their lives are part of the school curriculum?

WRITING & REFLECTION
FEELING SEEN BUT NOT HEARD

So often, students want to be acknowledged by their teacher in ways that reflect that the teacher "gets" them.

Do you recall an experience in your life as a student where you had a teacher who really understood you as a person and as a learner? Describe that teacher and the relationship you had with him or her. How did knowing you in that way influence you as a learner?

TWO EXAMPLES OF UNDERSTANDING PERFORMANCES

For a social studies unit with the understanding goal "Students will understand that history is always told from a particular perspective and that understanding a historical text means understanding who wrote it":

Students compare two accounts of the beginning of the Revolutionary War, one claiming the British fired the first shot and one claiming the colonists did. They then discuss why the two reports might be different and how they could find out what really happened. They use some of these strategies to figure out which (if either) of these accounts is the more plausible; then they present their explanation to the class.

For a mathematics unit with the understanding goals "Students will understand how percentages can be used to describe real-world happenings" and "Students will understand how to represent numerical information in clear graphs":

In small groups, students collect and compile data about school attendance over the course of two weeks. They calculate the percentage of students who fit various categories (percentage of students absent, percentage present, percentage tardy, and so on). They then create graphs to represent their data visually, collect feedback from the class, and revise their graphs in accordance with the feedback.

Source: From Tina Blythe and Associates, *The Teaching for Understanding Guide*, Copyright ©1998 by Jossey-Bass, San Francisco.

---

their hopes and fears. Then you will be able to make these curricula relevant to your students' lived experiences. Providing the "mirror" helps with preparing them to look out "windows." Table 4.2 lists some questions that can help you explore the world of your students.

Assessment: How Do We Know What They Know?

Closely linked to curriculum and instruction is **assessment**, the process of collecting information to find out what students are learning. As teachers, we are always asking, "What do my students know? How are they able to demonstrate that knowledge?"

Evidence of student learning, like learning itself, is complex and takes many forms. You are probably accustomed to traditional assessments, such as paper-and-pencil tests with multiple-choice, true/false, fill-in-the-blank, and essay questions, used to evaluate students' understanding of the subject matter being taught. Typically, except for the essay questions, these tests are thought of as a measure of what students can recall at the moment, not necessarily what they have incorporated into an existing or new mental scheme.

Many students think of assessments as tests of this traditional type, given at the end of a unit. However, the more we understand about how people learn, the more we realize that an assessment is like a good instructional task and should be part of every lesson, providing feedback to both the teacher and the students about how the students are developing their understanding of the concepts in a unit. Assessments of this type are often called **embedded assessments**.

Many of the questions in the "Writing & Reflection" sections of this text are examples of embedded assessments. These questions are tools for reflection on the current instruction as you are reading the text. Embedded assessments feel like a natural part of the instruction, so you may not be aware you are being assessed!

When we ask students to maintain a journal, write a research report, engage in a debate, design a project, or write an essay explaining a phenomenon, we are using embedded assessments. When these assessments relate directly to tasks or examples in the "real world" outside the classroom, they are also thought of as **authentic assessments**. Activities of this type ask students to perform tasks through which they can express their own ideas. You can see how different these are from tests in which students check true or false, circle a correct choice, or guess at a word for a fill-in question, relying on their recall abilities instead of demonstrating understanding.

Authentic assessment often involves some kind of student performance; hence, this type of assessment is also called *performance assessment*. One type of performance assessment was pioneered by a group of scholars at Harvard University's Graduate School of Education. In an effort called Project Zero, the educators and psychologists were interested in teaching for understanding and in designing assessment tasks called *understanding performances* or *performances of understanding* (Perkins, 1993). Understanding performances are activities that require students to use what they know in new ways or in ways that build their understanding of unit topics. In these performances, students publicly demonstrate their understanding by reshaping, expanding on, extrapolating from, and applying what they already know.

Because of the open-ended nature of authentic assessments and performance-based assessments, guidelines

---

assessment Collecting information to determine the progress of students' learning.

embedded assessments Classroom-based assessments that make use of the actual assignments that students are given as a unit is being taught. These can be used to evaluate developmental stages of student learning.

authentic assessments Assessments that ask students to perform a task relating what they have learned to some real-world problem or example.

TABLE 4.3 ● A Sample Rubric for a High School Class Debate

Category	4	3	2	1
Respect for Other Team	All statements, body language, and responses were respectful and were in appropriate language.	Statements and responses were respectful and used appropriate language, but once or twice body language was not.	Most statements and responses were respectful and in appropriate language, but there was one sarcastic remark.	Statements, responses, and/or body language were consistently not respectful.
Information	All information presented in the debate was clear, accurate, and thorough.	Most information presented in the debate was clear, accurate, and thorough.	Most information presented in the debate was clear and accurate, but was not usually thorough.	Information had several inaccuracies OR was usually not clear.
Rebuttal	All counterarguments were accurate, relevant, and strong.	Most counterarguments were accurate, relevant, and strong.	Most counterarguments were accurate and relevant, but several were weak.	Counterarguments were not accurate and/or relevant.
Use of Facts/ Statistics	Every major point was well supported with several relevant facts, statistics, and/or examples.	Every major point was adequately supported with relevant facts, statistics, and/or examples.	Every major point was supported with facts, statistics, and/or examples, but the relevance of some was questionable.	Every point was not supported.
Presentation Style	Team consistently used gestures, eye contact, tone of voice, and a level of enthusiasm in a way that kept the attention of the audience.	Team usually used gestures, eye contact, tone of voice, and a level of enthusiasm in a way that kept the attention of the audience.	Team sometimes used gestures, eye contact, tone of voice, and a level of enthusiasm in a way that kept the attention of the audience.	One or more members of the team had a presentation style that did not keep the attention of the audience.
Organization	All arguments were clearly tied to an idea (premise) and organized in a tight, logical fashion.	Most arguments were clearly tied to an idea (premise) and organized in a tight, logical fashion.	All arguments were clearly tied to an idea (premise), but the organization was sometimes not clear or logical.	Arguments were not clearly tied to an idea (premise).
Understanding of Topic	The team clearly understood the topic in-depth and presented their information forcefully and convincingly.	The team clearly understood the topic in-depth and presented their information with ease.	The team seemed to understand the main points of the topic and presented those with ease.	The team did not show an adequate understanding of the topic.

Source: 4Teachers.org (2018). Rubistar: Create Rubrics for your Project-Based Learning Activities. Retrieved from http://http://rubistar.4teachers .org/. Copyright 1995-2018 ALTEC at the University of Kansas. Funded, in part, by the U.S. Department of Education Regional Technology in Education Consortium 1995-2005, awards R302A50008 and R302A000015.

for evaluating the final performance are important. These guidelines take the form of a checklist or rubric. A **rubric** defines the expected qualities of student performance and establishes a rating scale. Generally, rubrics specify the level of performance expected for several levels of quality. These levels of quality may be written as ratings (e.g., Excellent, Good, Needs Improvement) or as numerical scores (e.g., 4, 3, 2, 1). Numerical scores can be added up to form a total

score, which is then associated with a grade (A, B, C, and so forth).

Imagine you are assessing student understanding of two sides of a contentious issue, such as the trial of Dr. Jack Kevorkian, who was found guilty of assisting people in committing suicide. (This lesson is described in Chapter 6.) You decide to engage the students in a high school history class in a debate on the issue. Table 4.3 shows a rubric you might use. Notice that there are specific ways to describe student effectiveness and achievement. The highest score a student can achieve on this rubric is 24, indicating that she or he scored a 4 for each category described.

rubric A scoring guide for an authentic assessment or a performance assessment, with descriptions of performance characteristics corresponding to points on a rating scale.

Becoming a Teacher

There is often a disconnect between what we learn about teaching and what we are able to enact in an actual classroom. One reason is that teaching, like many other endeavors, requires practice. Another reason is that we need to examine our beliefs and become comfortable with ourselves as learners as we embark on becoming teachers.

There are no quick and easy ways to make the transition into teaching. But here are some ideas to keep in mind as you consider joining the profession:

- Be comfortable with yourself as a person and feel secure in who you are.

- Wherever possible, give students opportunities to express their own ideas and to be active thinkers.

- Interrogate your students about their thinking. That is, ask them where their ideas come from.

- Make connections between what you are teaching and the students' lived experiences.

- Gain an understanding for yourself of the material you will teach. Using that knowledge, construct activities and opportunities that lead students to engage with the materials for themselves.

- Preparation is a prerequisite for successful teaching. Planning for instruction is very important and one of the rubrics for the edTPA! Always remember, teachers can never be overprepared.

Concluding Thoughts

Is your head spinning from all the theories, philosophies, and movements in U.S. public education you have read about? If so, it is important to remember that your approach to teaching should never be "all or nothing." The boundaries between movements and learning theories can overlap and become blurred.

Understanding more about how people learn helps us know that exploring students' preconceived ideas is essential to planning for instruction. Your plan may borrow principles from learning theories other than constructivism. Naming your personal approach is less important than understanding that it is subject to revision as you grow and learn, and enter classrooms in a more formal role. Your present style of teaching and learning is the result of all that came before you historically and all that you personally have experienced in school. Perhaps you experienced understanding by design or backward planning. Developing consciousness about the role of the teacher and the responsibilities you will have toward your students is important preparation for your future work. Education is broader than schooling experiences. Like you, students learn from formal and informal environments. Their interests are relevant to their abilities to learn. Remember, learning is a complex process, and there is a lot about what goes on in our brains as we learn that we still do not know. We DO know that helping others to learn involves their active engagement.

By discussing how people learn, curriculum, instruction, and assessment, this chapter has provided perspective on part of a big question that all teachers face: Who are my students, and how can I best teach them? In the next chapter, we will explore in detail the nature and diversity of today's students. We will examine demographic trends in the country and consider the ways your pedagogy may be informed by who your students are.

CHAPTER REVIEW

Key Terms

academic language (p. 52)

assessment (p. 62)

authentic assessments (p. 62)

behaviorism (p. 54)

Bloom's Taxonomy (p. 53)

cognitive domain (p. 53)

cognitive learning theories (p. 54)

constructivism (p. 56)

curriculum (p. 59)

educational objectives (p. 53)

embedded assessments (p. 62)

informal curriculum (p. 60)

instruction (p. 52)

Knowledge, Comprehension, Application, Analysis, Synthesis, and Evaluation (p. 53)

learning theory (p. 52)

pedagogical content knowledge (PCK) (p. 52)

pedagogy (p. 52)

personal teaching philosophy (p. 52)

rubric (p. 63)

social cognitive learning theories (p. 55)

Understanding by Design (UbD) (p. 59)

Review the Learning Outcomes

Review each section of the chapter and answer the following:

LO 4-1 Discuss why one needs a special set of skills to become a teacher.

LO 4-2 What makes academic language important for the learner?

LO 4-3 How has neuroscience affected the evolution of learning theories?

LO 4-4 In what ways does backward design for instruction make sense?

LO 4-5 Why are many citizens in favor of the Common Core State Standards?

LO 4-6 How do learning theories explain the statement, "You can teach your students but you cannot learn for them"?

LO 4-7 How does understanding what your students' lives are like help you to be a better teacher?

InTASC Standards

Review the InTASC Standards for the chapter and explain how the chapter addressed each one.

Standard 1: Learner Development

Standard 3: Learning Environments

Standard 7: Planning for Instruction

Journal Prompts

Imagine you are teaching a lesson about a favorite hobby. In what ways would this lesson be a window for your students? In what ways would it be a mirror?

$SAGE edge™

Get the tools you need to sharpen your study skills. SAGE edge offers a robust online environment featuring an impressive array of free tools and resources.

Access practice quizzes, eFlashcards, video, and multimedia at **edge.sagepub.com/koch4e**.

Looking at Today's Schools

iStock/adl21

Who Are Today's Students?

A person's a person no matter how small . . .

—Theodor Geisel (aka Dr. Seuss), *Horton Hears a Who!* (1954)

Learning Outcomes

After reading this chapter, you should be able to:

5-1 Examine the ways in which students may be different from one another.

5-2 Examine factors that might hinder a student's success in school.

5-3 Explain why teachers must have an understanding of their students' lives through the lens of their ethnic, cultural, and daily life experiences.

5-4 Analyze how your students' life histories could explain their performance in your class.

5-5 Assess the importance of knowing who your students are, what their lives are like, and how they learn best.

5-6 Examine the statement that "student diversity is a gift and not a barrier to overcome."

InTASC Standards

- Standard 2: Learning Differences
- Standard 3: Learning Environments
- Standard 7: Planning for Instruction

This chapter looks at the students between the ages 5 and 18 in contemporary U.S. schools. As the quotation from Dr. Seuss suggests, our schoolchildren are important people. Their education is vital not only to their own future but also to the future of our country.

You may be familiar with the Dr. Seuss books—the often silly, rhyming, outrageous stories that delight many children from preschool through graduation from high school. Often, they have deep meaning. In a commentary on Dr. Seuss and his influence, A. O. Scott (2000) of the *New York Times* had the following to say:

> Rather than describe the mental world of children, Seuss labored over his verses and sketches in the hopes of replicating it. His guiding insight was that some version of his words and stories was there to begin with, and that children, in discovering his work, would recognize in it what they already knew.

The significance of these comments is that the students we meet and greet in the classroom come to us with their own stories, backgrounds, and experiences. It is your task to learn about your students—what their lives are like and what hobbies, interests, talents, and challenges they bring to the classroom. Respecting and understanding them as people with their own ideas and experiences is the first step toward becoming an effective educator. Your students will represent the broad diversity of the human condition; they will differ in how they learn, where they come from, their native language, their learning styles, and their prior life experiences.

In this chapter, we address the nature of the learner today. We also acknowledge that teachers make all the difference for all kinds of students from all walks of life.

The Students: A Changing Landscape

Since the mid-1990s, student enrollment in U.S. schools has mushroomed. In fact, when the estimated population of the country surpassed 300 million people in 2006, roughly one quarter were children under the age of eighteen (Annie E. Casey Foundation, 2006).

Total public school enrollment reached a peak in 1971, when the youngest members of the baby boom generation[1] arrived in school (Fry, 2006). Enrollment then dropped off considerably in the 1970s, but it began to climb again in the late 1980s and early 1990s. By the second half of the 1990s, enrollment passed the 1971 mark, and the number of students in school has continued to rise. Between 1985 and 2008, enrollment in public elementary and secondary schools increased by more than one fifth, and by 2015, public school enrollments are estimated to be more than 56 million students in Grades pre-K–12, and more than 6 million students in pre-K–12 private schools, as shown in Table 5.1.

Clearly, the number of students in our schools has been rising rapidly. But who exactly are our students? In the following sections, we will explore the ways in which our students are different from one another and the ways in which they are the same. Diversity, as we will discover, is an opportunity to discover other ways of being in the world. When we embrace difference, we honor the special characteristics of all students.

---

[1] ***Baby boom generation*** refers to those Americans born in the quarter century following World War II, roughly from 1946 to 1964. Some experts use slightly different dates.

TABLE 5.1 ● U.S. Public and Private School Enrollment

Enrollment in Elementary and Secondary Schools, by Control and level of Institution: Selected years, Fall 1970 Through Fall 2020 (Anticipated) (Thousands)

Years	Total	Public			Private		
		Total	Grades PreK-8	Grades 9-12	Total	Grades PreK-8	Grades 9-12
1970	51,257	45,894	32,558	13,336	5,363	4,052	1,311
1980	46,208	40,877	27,647	13,231	5,331	3,992	1,339
1985	44,979	39,422	27,034	12,388	5,557	4,195	1,362
1990	46,864	41,217	29,876	11,341	5,648	4,512	1,136
1995	50,759	44,840	32,338	12,502	5,918	4,756	1,163
2000	50,373	47,204	33,686	13,517	6,169	4,906	1,264
2005	55,187	49,113	34,204	14,909	6,073	4,724	1,349
2006	55,307	49,316	34,235	15,081	5,991	4,631	1,360
2007	55,203	49,293	34,205	15,087	5,910	4,546	1,364
2008	55,235	49,266	34,286	14,980	5,969	4,574	1,395
2009	55,282	49,312	34,505	14,807	5,970	4,580	1,389
2010	55,350	49,386	34,730	14,657	5,964	4,582	1,382
2015	55,546	50,268	35,298	14,970	5,278	3,968	1,311
2020*	55,862	50,774	35,559	15,215	5,088	3,871	1,217

Source: U.S. Department of Education, National Center for Education Statistics. (2016c). *Annual Report of the Commissioner of Education, February 2016,* Table 105.30.

Note: Elementary and secondary enrollment includes students in local public school systems and in most private schools (religiously affiliated and nonsectarian) but generally excludes homeschooled children and students in subcollegiate departments of colleges and in federal schools. Based on the National Household Education Survey, the homeschooled children numbered approximately 1,770,000, and the trend is upward. Excludes preprimary pupils in private schools that do not offer kindergarten or higher. Detail may not sum to totals because of rounding.

*Projected

Ethnic Diversity

Our era of expanding school enrollment has been marked by a significant rise in minority students, driven mainly by an extraordinary influx of Hispanic[2] students, who account for more than 50% of the increase in student enrollment. By 2012, 45% of public school students were considered to be part of a racial or ethnic minority group. In fall 2014, the percentage of students enrolled in public elementary and secondary schools who were White was less than 50% (49.5%) for the first time since these data were reported (see Table 5.2). This represents a decrease from 58% in fall 2004. In contrast, the percentage of students who were Hispanic increased from 19% to 25% (Stepler & Lopez, 2016).

---

[2] *Hispanic* refers to people whose origin is Spain or any of the Spanish-speaking countries of the Americas.

Immigration accounts for a large part of the diversity among today's students. About 25% of youngsters under the age of 18 are part of immigrant families. States with the highest percentage of immigrant families are New Mexico, California, Texas, Arizona, Nevada, Florida, Colorado, New Jersey, New York, and Illinois, states that have attracted the largest number of Hispanic immigrants. Although ethnic diversity is increasing overall, recent decades have seen a new rise in de facto segregation—that is, Whites living in different neighborhoods than minorities. Neighborhoods that are primarily White have a high concentration of White students in their schools, whereas neighborhoods that are predominantly minority have a high concentration of minority students in the schools. In some areas, this segregation has reduced the amount of diversity teachers encounter. Most White students continue to attend schools populated primarily by other Whites; relatively few attend

TABLE 5.2 ● Percentage Distribution of Students Enrolled in Public Elementary and Secondary Schools by Race/Ethnicity: Fall 2004, Fall 2014, and Fall 2026*

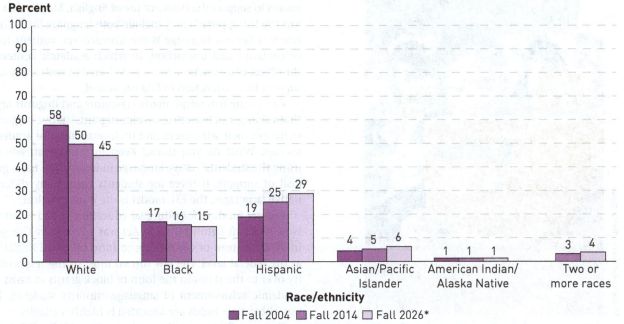

Sources: U.S. Department of Education, National Center for Education Statistics. (2016d). *State Nonfiscal Public Elementary/Secondary Education Survey Data, 2004–05 and 2014–15*, https://nces.ed.gov/ccd/stnfis.asp; and U.S. Department of Education, National Center for Education Statistics. (2016e). *Enrollment and Percentage Distribution of Enrollment in Public Elementary and Secondary Schools, by Race/Ethnicity and Region: Selected years, Fall 1995 Through Fall 2026*, Table 203.50, https://nces.ed.gov/programs/digest/d16/tables/dt16_203.50.asp

Note: Race categories exclude persons of Hispanic ethnicity. Prior to 2008, separate data on students of two or more races were not collected. Although rounded numbers are displayed, the figures are based on unrounded estimates. Detail may not sum to totals because of rounding.

* Data for 2026 are projected.

schools populated primarily by minorities. As a result, many schools are predominantly minority populated.

As enrollment has expanded, so has the number of schools. About half of the students attending the newer schools are White, while White enrollment in older schools has dropped. Most of the newer schools are being built in areas that are predominantly White, while the older school buildings are absorbing most of the Hispanic and other minority students, where neighborhoods are poorer and there is far less available taxpayer money for new schools.

Since the major influx of immigrants has come from countries where English is not the native language, you can imagine that programs designed to help English learners have arisen all over the country, and most especially in the states mentioned previously. English language learners (ELs) are those individuals who are learning English in school and who speak a native language other than English.

Language-Minority Students

Can you imagine going to school in a place where your own native language is not spoken? If your native language is English, that may seem inconceivable. However, for those of you who are reading these pages and who learned English as your second language, the challenge most likely was great and required understanding teachers and schools. By 2017,

22% of school-age children spoke a language other than English at home (Annie E. Casey Foundation, 2017). The number of students who participate in programs for ELs in U.S. public schools was estimated at almost 5 million, or 9.7% of the student population (U.S. Department of Education, 2017c).

Among children who speak a language other than English at home, Spanish is the language most frequently spoken. About three quarters of students who receive special assistance to learn English speak Spanish at home. Yet hundreds of thousands of students come from homes where other languages are spoken. These include Chinese, Vietnamese, Russian, Arabic, and French Creole. Various reports emphasize that, for most of these ELs, success requires targeted and continuing intervention.

Teaching English Learners

The EL programs in which these students participate vary according to the amount of English that is used for instruction. There has been much debate over how best to boost the academic achievement of ELs. **Bilingual education** programs support students with limited English proficiency by teaching them at least part of the time in their native

bilingual education Educating English-language learners by teaching them at least part of the time in their native language.

MediaProduction/E+/Getty Images

▲
Nonnative English-speaking students learn in both languages in bilingual classes.

language. Since the early 1970s, these programs have taken many forms. Some teach academic subjects in the students' native language and also provide English as a Second Language (ESL) classes to help the students learn English. Other models, known as *two-way* or *dual-language programs*, teach fluency in both languages, so that a class of both language-minority and native English-speaking students becomes fluent in both languages. These approaches have several variations and tend to vary from school district to school district. Other programs immerse language-minority students in English-only classes without any native-language communication.

On a recent visit to an elementary school in Queens, New York, I encountered a large sign for parents that read, "We now have a dual-language program in Mandarin." I learned that 87% of the students in this K–5 school were from China and that those students who were native English speakers really wanted to learn Mandarin. Hence, the school began a dual-language immersion program with half of the instruction in Mandarin and the other half in English.

There are many other examples of schools that take pride in their bilingual programs. Yet partly because of the large wave of Hispanic immigration during the past 25 years, the issue of bilingual education has become highly politicized. There are those who believe that only English should be spoken and taught in school. This has prompted some schools to adopt "English-only" programs in which language-minority students have no access to their native language in school. **English as a Second Language (ESL)** programs focus on instruction in English as the primary means to help ELs acquire the language and ultimately meet high academic standards. Students

learn and are taught in English exclusively or primarily—certain instructional materials or instructional techniques may make use of basic native language vocabulary, but only as a means to support the students' use of English. Models that follow the ESL approach may include both language instruction, wherein English language is the instructional content itself, or content-based instruction, in which academic content is the object of instruction, but it is delivered in such a way as to support ELs' acquisition of English as well.

Criticizing this trend, many educators and linguists argue that valuing and honoring new immigrants' native languages enhances their self-esteem and their possibility for academic success. What do you think? Keep in mind that, whereas using the students' native language in instruction has a great deal of support, if there are students with many different native languages, the ESL model is the most practical.

Federal funding for bilingual education ended when the No Child Left Behind (NCLB) Act was adopted by Congress in 2002. Instead of continuing to fund bilingual initiatives at the federal level, the law turned most of the responsibility over to the states in the form of block grants to assist the academic achievement of language-minority students. The way these state funds are allocated is highly variable.

You may find yourself in a classroom with English learners, and it is important to use the most effective strategies to help your students grasp subject matter content while learning English. Many established teachers have taken workshops to learn the best approach for EL instruction—another example of how being a teacher is a commitment to lifelong learning. The best pedagogy helps the EL students gain skills in both the subject material and in using English.

As we explored in Chapter 4, learning something new requires that the learner redesign his or her mental schemes. To do this, the student has to bring his or her existing knowledge into play. Effective pedagogy encourages this process by treating the EL as a "knower," a student with lots of ideas that are temporarily inaccessible to the teacher because of the language barrier. Accessing the student's ideas involves teaching strategies such as

- speaking clearly and at a slower pace;

- using gestures and facial expressions;

- using concrete materials and visuals;

- avoiding idiomatic expressions that are peculiar to English;

- engaging students in group work that is student centered (Kashen, 1994); and

- finding "language buddies" wherever possible—that is, pairing ELs with students who are more advanced in English but also fluent in the learner's native language.

English as a Second Language (ESL) These are "English-only" classroom programs where instruction is solely in English and there is limited access to native language vocabulary.

If you teach a class with both ELs and students who are already fluent in English, your task will be to plan for both populations in ways that enrich the environment. Imagine that two students are using a ruler for a lesson. The native English speaker says to the student who is new to this country, "How do you say 'ruler' in your language?" By sharing in this way, they both become learners. The challenge is to engage all students in helping their classmates overcome barriers to learning.

Religious Diversity

As we saw in Chapter 3, religion has always played a large role in American life and education. The Constitution of the United States guarantees religious freedom to all citizens, and we treasure that right. Yet Americans are divided about how the principle of "separation of church and state" (a phrase coined by Thomas Jefferson) should apply to public schools.

These matters have taken on more urgency in the past few decades as new strains of religious diversity have arisen in the United States. Christians account for 70.6% of the U.S. population, with Protestants accounting for 47% of that total and Catholics accounting for 21% (Pew Research Center, 2015). The total number of Americans who identified their religion as something other than Christian increased dramatically over the last two decades. Religions that barely registered in previous surveys, such as Unitarian Universalists, now have a substantial number of adherents, about 1%. Even the traditional affiliations of Protestant and Catholic contain many subgroups and differences. In addition, over 22% of Americans do not identify with any religion, many of them dropping their affiliations, notably in the 19- to 29-year-old age group. About 6% of Americans are non-Christians, including almost 2% Jewish, and almost 1% each belonging to Hindu, Buddhist, or Muslim denominations.

With such diversity in the nation's religions, teachers have much to learn about the religious beliefs of their students. Religious beliefs bring with them various expectations for an individual's behavior, including observance of customs and traditions. Remember that culture and religion are linked. Understanding who your students are and the role that religion plays in their lives is significant in helping them to learn and in honoring their identities. Understanding the ways in which your own personal religious identity influences your thinking and your relationship with your students will help you to maintain the "consciousness" about yourself that effective teachers require.

Sexual Orientation and Gender Identity

Like religion, language, and ethnicity, **sexual orientation** is an important component of a person's identity. Schools are often the places where teens develop social skills and begin to align with peer groups. For adolescents who do not identify as heterosexual in today's culture, this process of social acceptance and approval is fraught with danger, fear of rejection, and even physical harm.

Typical categories applied to sexual orientation include heterosexual, homosexual (gay and lesbian), bisexual (sexual attraction toward both sexes), and transgender (having characteristics of the opposite sex). The acronym **LGBTQ** is sometimes used to refer to lesbian, gay, bisexual, and transgender people as a group. The "Q" stands for Queer, where "Queer" serves as an umbrella term that encompasses many people as it intersects with sexual orientation and gender identity. It includes anyone who does not associate with heteronormativity; rather, they have nonbinary or gender-expansive identities. Because sexual orientations are often hidden from view, LGBTQ individuals are often thought of as the invisible minority. In schools, fear often prevents these students from revealing their sexual identities; it is therefore important that schools and classrooms provide safe havens for those of our students whose sexual orientation is not aligned with the majority.

Attitudes about sexual orientation are a product of individual family biases and beliefs. Students bring these to school, and LGBTQ youth often have to cope with prejudice and isolation. Lack of family support for these youngsters exacerbates the problem, and there is an enormous fear of stigmatization. These students are at greater risk than others for being harassed and bullied, experiencing depression, and attempting suicide.

For the first time, in 2016, the U.S. Centers for Disease Control and Prevention (CDC) included two new questions in its Youth Risk Behavior Survey. One question asked students about their sexual orientation and the second question asked about the gender of their partners. Twenty-seven states agreed to keep these questions in their survey, and the results indicated to researchers that clearly 8% of high

Honoring diversity requires a respect for the learner and a genuine desire to bridge religious and cultural gaps.

Jeff Greenberg/Universal Images Group/Getty Images

---

sexual orientation An enduring emotional, romantic, sexual, or affectional attraction that a person feels toward people of one or both sexes.

LGBTQ An acronym used to represent lesbian, gay, bisexual, and transgender individuals, and includes Q for Queer, an umbrella connotation that encompasses different ways of experiencing gender and sexuality.

school students, or about 1.4 million teens, report being lesbian, gay, or bisexual. The next group to be counted will be transgender teens. In 2017, for the first time, the CDC sent out its annual survey with a new pilot question on gender identity and expression. The United States will be able to count, for the first time, how many transgender students are in its high schools. A 2017 report stated that about 150,000 high school students, or about 0.7% of 13- to 17-year-olds living in the United States, identify as transgender. These data were released by the Williams Institute at the University of California, Los Angeles, School of Law. The think tank, which researches issues related to sexual orientation and gender identity, based its estimates on statistical modeling rather than direct surveys of children (Blad, 2017). While there is no information available as yet on the number of states that allowed the CDC transgender question to remain on its Youth Risk Behavior Survey, it is hoped that those results will shed more light on the number of transgender students. The reason that these data are so important is to protect the rights of all students, including transgender students. Federal civil rights laws should protect the interests of transgender children, and more complete data could help explain the need for clear, consistent policies related to transgender students to state and local officials.

During the Obama era, schools were put on notice that they could be found in violation of the sex-discrimination protections of Title IX of the Education Amendments of 1972 if they didn't honor students' gender identity. Sadly, the subsequent administration of Donald Trump withdrew this guidance, rescinding the Obama-era ruling. In withdrawing that guidance, the Trump administration left it to state and local decision makers to determine how to handle a range of issues, including what restrooms and locker rooms transgender students should use, whether to call them by their desired pronoun, and how to handle identifying their gender on student records (Blad, 2017).

The experiences of LGBTQ students in schools is captured by the Gay, Lesbian, and Straight Education Network's (GLSEN, 2015) National School Climate Survey. The most recent results indicate that schools nationwide are hostile environments for LGBTQ students, the overwhelming majority of whom routinely hear anti-LGBTQ language and experience victimization and discrimination at school. As a result, many LGBTQ students avoid school activities or miss school entirely. The vast majority of LGBTQ students (85.2%) experienced verbal harassment (e.g., called names or threatened) at school based on a personal characteristic, most commonly sexual orientation (70.8% of LGBTQ students) and gender expression (54.5%). Almost all of LGBTQ students (98.1%) heard "gay" used in a negative way (e.g., "that's so gay") at school; 67.4% heard these remarks frequently or often, and 93.4% reported that they felt distressed because of this language (Kosciw, Greytak, Giga, Villenas, & Danischewski, 2016).

Because all students deserve to work in an environment that is both friendly and supportive, student groups have emerged in high schools all over the country to combat LGBTQ bias and discrimination. These groups or clubs are often called Gay-Straight Alliances; they are student-run

organizations that provide a safe place for students to meet, support each other, talk about issues related to their sexual orientation, and work toward ending homophobia. Teachers can also create safe havens in their classrooms by interrupting statements of bias when they hear or see their occurrence. The GLSEN website offers many suggestions for teachers to enable their LGBTQ students to be full participants in the life of the school.

Socioeconomic Disparities

Another way students differ from each other is in their **socioeconomic status (SES)**, a measure of their standard of living that relates to the family's income. According to recent census figures, 20% of young people under the age of 18 live in families with incomes below the federal poverty level (see Table 5.3). For a family of four with two children under the age of 18, the federal poverty level is $24,339.00 (Center for Poverty Research, UC Davis, 2017). The poverty rate for children is higher than for people in any other age group. Further, almost half of all children living in poverty live in single-parent families. The children of single mothers experience poverty at a rate nearly 4 times higher than children in two-parent families.

Table 5.3 shows the official definition of poverty as related to family size. You may be surprised to see how much a family must earn to avoid being poor in the United States. SES relates to the concept of social capital that we mentioned previously. The point is that the students you encounter will come from various socioeconomic backgrounds. The states with the highest child poverty rates are New Mexico, Mississippi, Louisiana, Kentucky, and Alabama (see Map 5.1).

Higher-income families are directly related to the concept of social capital that we discussed earlier. The more social capital a child's family has, the greater his or her intellectual and cultural advantages. A child with higher SES and more social capital usually performs better than a student with little or no social capital does. We have learned a great deal in recent years about the connection between poverty and intellectual development. Brain imaging has focused attention on the problem of childhood poverty (Balter, 2015). The differences in intellectual development can be staggering for children from poverty when compared to their middle-class peers. Research indicates that students from families living below the poverty line have much smaller and less complex working vocabularies, are less likely to be read to, have less exposure to books in their home, and encounter higher incidences of stress (Coley & Morris, 2002,; Hoff, 2003; Korat & Haglili, 2007; Schwartz & Gorman, 2003). These deficits from the environment in the home and the community result in stark cognitive differences for children of poverty as they enter kindergarten. This is one of many reasons why quality prekindergarten programs are so important.

....

socioeconomic status (SES) A person's or family's status in society, usually based on a combination of income, occupation, and education. Though similar to social class, SES puts more emphasis on the way income affects status.

TABLE 5.3 ● Poverty Thresholds for 2016

Poverty Thresholds for 2016 by Size of Family and Number of Related Children Under 18 Years

Size of family unit	Weighted average thresholds	Related Children Under 18 Years								
		None	One	Two	Three	Four	Five	Six	Seven	Eight or more
One person (unrelated individual)	12,228									
Under age 65	12,486	12,486								
Aged 65 and older	11,511	11,511								
Two people	15,569									
Householder under age 65	16,151	16,072	16,543							
Householder aged 65 and older	14,522	14,507	16,480							
Three people	19,105	18,774	19,318	19,337						
Four people	24,583	24,755	25,160	24,339	24,424					
Five people	29,111	29,854	30,288	29,360	28,643	28,206				
Six people	32,928	34,337	34,473	33,763	33,082	32,070	31,470			
Seven people	37,458	39,509	39,756	38,905	38,313	37,208	35,920	34,507		
Eight people	41,781	44,188	44,578	43,776	43,072	42,075	40,809	39,491	39,156	
Nine people or more	49,721	53,155	53,413	52,702	52,106	51,127	49,779	48,561	48,259	46,400

Source: U.S. Census Bureau.

Map 5.1 ● Child Poverty, 2016

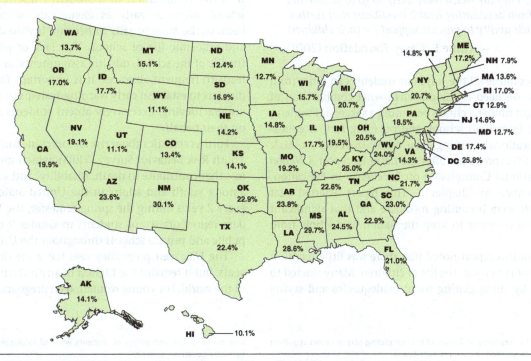

WA 13.7%
OR 17.0%
MT 15.1%
ID 17.7%
WY 11.1%
ND 12.4%
SD 16.9%
MN 12.7%
WI 15.7%
MI 20.7%
NV 19.1%
UT 11.1%
CO 13.4%
NE 14.2%
IA 14.8%
IL 17.7%
IN 19.5%
OH 20.5%
CA 19.9%
AZ 23.6%
NM 30.1%
KS 14.1%
MO 19.2%
KY 25.0%
WV 24.0%
VA 14.3%
TN 22.6%
NC 21.7%
OK 22.9%
AR 23.8%
MS 29.7%
AL 24.5%
GA 22.9%
SC 23.0%
TX 22.4%
LA 28.6%
FL 21.0%
AK 14.1%
HI 10.1%
VT 14.8%
ME 17.2%
NH 7.9%
MA 13.6%
RI 17.0%
CT 12.9%
NY 20.7%
PA 18.5%
NJ 14.6%
MD 12.7%
DE 17.4%
DC 25.8%

Source: Children's Defense Fund (2017). http://www.childrensdefense.org/library/data/child-poverty-in-america-2016-1.pdf

Overlapping Attributes: The Social Context

The aspects of student diversity we have been considering are not isolated and independent. Often they overlap. Consider, for instance, what happens when poverty intersects with the need to learn a new language. The reality of many ELs is that they also represent our poorest children: Many live in crowded housing environments where transportation and employment opportunities are limited and where schools are old and overcrowded. In fact, of all students who live in poverty, more than 28% are Hispanic or Latino, and 36% of all children in poverty are American Indian (Annie E. Casey Foundation, 2016). While these percentages represent a decrease in the number of children from these ethnicities who are living in poverty over the last 5 years, it is still a matter of grave concern. Poverty affects the students' achievement in school, putting many of these students at risk for educational failure. In the next section, we will consider the term at risk and its full implications, but it is important to remember that poverty is not a learning disability and all children have the ability to learn and succeed in school. Differences do not mean deficits; they just mean differences from the norms in public education that were once thought to be White and middle class. The norms are shifting, and it is important that we never think of students who are different in any way as lesser. As future teachers, the guiding question must be: How can I help each child feel successful in school?

Students Who Are at Risk

National research has shown that children living in poor, tough neighborhoods are much more likely to drop out of school, become pregnant as teens, get in trouble with the law as juveniles, and live in poverty as adults, with their own children struggling to succeed. They are much more likely to go to prison and suffer from debilitating health conditions that further limit their ability to provide support for their children.

—Annie E. Casey Foundation (2001)

When we examine all the ways our students can differ from each other, we need to ask ourselves what combination of factors might hinder a child's becoming a successful student, graduating from high school, and pursuing further education or vocational training. The term **students at risk** came into widespread use after the national report *A Nation at Risk* (National Commission on Excellence in Education, 1983) described in Chapter 3. This report asserted that U.S. schools were becoming mediocre and that significant changes had to occur to keep the nation as a whole from declining.

Critics of this report noted that there was little mention of the role of poverty in the life of children. Many reacted to the report by citing glaring social inadequacies and saying that schools could not make up for these deficiencies. There was a "blame the victim" mentality, critics complained, in which students and parents were held to be the culprits. Indeed, schools cannot make up for many of the problems of poverty and degradation, but in turn, educators must not blame their own inadequacies on the students. Both points are at work when we examine who is at risk. The precise definition of the term *students at risk* varies; however, the common attribute is that these students are judged to be seriously in danger of not succeeding in school and hence not completing school.

Failure to complete high school is a key attribute of at-risk students. The **dropout rate** in the United States represents the percentage of 16- through 24-year-olds who are not enrolled in school and have not earned a high school credential (either a diploma or an equivalency credential such as a General Educational Development [GED] certificate). The high school dropout rate has been declining and was down to 5.9% in 2015 (U.S. Department of Education, 2017d). This is encouraging, but we must not forget those young adults who do not complete high school. What puts a student at risk of dropping out or of not getting an adequate education? Social problems in our society make it difficult for even high-ability students to be successful. The greatest social risk factors include substance abuse, child abuse, poverty, homelessness, hunger, depression, and teen pregnancy. For teachers who are from stable homes and environments, it is often difficult to relate to these problems that affect the lives of some students every day. Therefore, it is essential to learn as much as possible about your students' lives.

Single-family households, poverty, and frequent moves that cause students to change schools at nontraditional times contribute to potentially placing students at risk. However, dropping out does not happen spontaneously. It is the culmination of a student's disengagement with school, often as early as elementary school and often because the student fails to become involved in the social and academic life of school. This lack of participation in the life of the school, missing assignments, and failing tests, leads to frequent absences. It is important for schools and districts to establish early warning systems in order to target underachieving, excessively absent students and intervene on their behalf.

Further statistics about risk factors come from the National Youth Risk Behavior Survey (YRBS), which monitors behaviors that contribute to death, disability, and social problems among youth and adults in the United States. Conducted every 2 years during the spring semester, the YRBS provides data representative of students in Grades 9 through 12 in public and private schools throughout the United States.

The U.S. teen pregnancy rate has gone down in recent years, but it remains the highest of any industrialized nation in the world. For young women, teen pregnancy is the major

---

students at risk Students in danger of not completing school or not acquiring the education they need to be successful citizens.

dropout rate The percentage of students who fail to complete high school or earn an equivalency degree.

contributor to high school dropout rates. Substance abuse is a serious problem that crosses all socioeconomic classes. The importance of sex education and drug abuse counseling programs in the schools cannot be overstated. Social media including Facebook, informal social networking sites, and informative websites have given teens better access to information on safe sex and the dangers of substance abuse. This has contributed to lowering the rate of teen pregnancy. Teachers and students can explore useful websites together.

Community and school collaborations including programs to prevent substance abuse targeted to parents of teens, family awareness projects, and parent-teacher associations can prevent students who are at risk from dropping out of school before completing high school. The state of California has "continuation schools" that are designed to meet the needs of young adults who have not been successful in the traditional school environment and have the potential to be dropouts. These schools offer nontraditional classes and enable the students to earn a high school diploma by supporting the students emotionally as they bolster their achievement. A wealth of services including mental health counseling and anger management classes provide possibilities for success for many at-risk teens.

Student Diversity: Challenges and Opportunities

As you might guess, the increasing diversity of U.S. students has led to controversy about educational priorities. In this section, we focus on three areas that have provoked much recent discussion: multicultural education, gender-fair education, and the role of religion in the schools.

Multicultural Education

You may be feeling dizzy from all the data and statistics you have read in this chapter. Why are these details about students important? As we seek to become better teachers, we must understand the origins of our students and the ways their needs can be met in the classroom. If you are not of the same culture, race, ethnicity, or social class as your students, you should make a special effort to understand their needs. You can also turn the diversity of your students into an advantage—an opportunity to share identities and cultures as you create community in your classroom. It is a way to broaden our understanding of the human condition and reminds us that the informal curriculum can be both window and mirror!

If you pursue a career in teaching, you will hear a lot about **multicultural education**, a broad term for many approaches that recognize and celebrate the variety of cultures and ethnic backgrounds found in U.S. schools. Students from groups that have traditionally been underrepresented in the school population—ethnic and racial

multicultural education Education that aims to create equal opportunities for students from diverse racial, ethnic, social class, and cultural groups.

A diverse student body provides the opportunity to learn about other ways of being in the world.

Joe Carini/Perspectives/Getty Images

minorities—have also been understudied. That is, until recently, most educators have not focused on what these students need to succeed in school. We now realize that these students will not be served well and will even become marginalized unless we seek answers to complex questions like the following:

- Whose stories are told in the classroom?

- How do we build community in a diverse setting?

- What is the role of identity formation in our work?

- What can we learn by hearing the stories of those from traditionally marginalized groups? (Nelson & Wilson, 1998, p. xi)

For over 25 years, the **Seeking Educational Equity and Diversity (SEED) Project**, begun by Dr. Peggy McIntosh at the Wellesley Centers for Women, has offered teachers from all over the country the opportunity to

Seeking Educational Equity and Diversity (SEED) Project The national project on inclusive curriculum that promotes multiculturally equitable, gender-fair, and globally aware curriculum and pedagogy through professional development and leadership training for teachers, parents, college faculty, and administrators.

FIGURE 5.1 ● Culturally Relevant Pedagogy

Your teaching should incorporate culturally relevant pedagogy. For a geometry lesson, one teacher had students look for symmetry in the flags of their native countries.

participate in professional development workshops designed to broaden the possibilities for both curriculum and instruction, and teaching in environments rich with students from diverse backgrounds, cultures, and ethnicities (http://www .nationalseedproject.org/). They are able to share strategies for appreciating that diverse learning environments offer a wonderful gift. Emily Style (1996), a director of SEED, offers the metaphor of diverse learning environments being "windows" into the worlds of people other than ourselves and create rich experiences for both students and teachers. As a result of these experiences, teachers are encouraged to develop culturally responsive teaching practices, also referred to as **culturally relevant pedagogy**. These teaching practices have several important attributes:

- They use cultural referents—from all the cultures represented in the classroom—to develop students' knowledge, skills, and attitudes.

- They honor the students' life stories and belief systems, and find ways to incorporate them into the curriculum and learning context.

- They create classroom community by granting voice and legitimacy to the experiences of students from diverse backgrounds.

- They encourage all students to achieve academically by acknowledging the students' personal and cultural identities.

culturally relevant pedagogy Teaching practices that place the culture of the learner at the center of instruction. Cultural referents become aspects of the formal curriculum.

All of these strategies help us to honor the learner and create a classroom community in which each other's stories create the foundation for a caring community.

Culturally relevant pedagogy is one of many instructional strategies that seeks to answer the question: "How can the lived experiences of my students be reflected in the discourse of the classroom?" Consider the planning of a geometry unit in an eighth-grade math classroom in an urban area in the Northeast. Ms. Petersen is in an old, overcrowded school building in an urban area. Ms. Petersen is exploring different types of symmetry that may be found in shapes using several patterns. About one third of her students are Latino, and the rest are of many racial and ethnic origins.

This unit in geometry considers what happens to shapes when they are moved through space. Ms. Petersen has examined the basic concepts in many ways with her class, emphasizing that symmetry may be found in patterns in everyday life and having the students create symmetrical patterns with more than one shape. For instance, she brought in men's ties with many patterns on them and asked students to decide what type of symmetry each pattern represented. She then invited them to explore their native countries' flags. The classroom has three networked computers that students used to print pictures of their flags. The flag designs were examined for geometric shapes and symmetry (see Figure 5.1). It was a lesson that engaged all the students.

After the students had experience with several types of symmetry, Ms. Petersen posed a challenge. In groups of two, the students were to design and create a classroom flag incorporating their room number. The flag had to be in the shape of a rectangle, include two types of symmetry, and appropriately represent the students in the classroom. Students were excited about designing patterns, and they selected the colors from the flags of their various countries of origin to represent themselves. Colors from the flags of Colombia, El Salvador, Mexico, Puerto Rico, Guatemala, South Korea, and the United States adorned the design of Room 303's classroom flag.

What do you think of Ms. Petersen's lesson? Can you imagine how excited the students were that their countries' flags were part of their study of mathematics? The concepts of rotation, reflection, and translation are quite complex in geometry, but by using materials her students could relate to, Ms. Petersen engaged them in a personal way.

We know from research in cognitive science that learning occurs best when students are fully invested in the process—when they can interact with the materials, "play" with them, explore and reexamine the concepts, and then individually make those concepts their own. You can see how culturally relevant pedagogy helps make this possible.

Educating Girls and Boys: Separate or Together?

You may recall from Chapter 3 that Title IX, part of the Education Amendments of 1972, prohibits discrimination on the basis of sex in any federally funded education program or activity. That law might seem to discourage single-sex schooling—the practice of educating girls in separate schools from boys—on the grounds that separate is inherently unequal. In 2006, however, the U.S. Department of Education officially ruled that Title IX does not make single-sex schooling discriminatory as long as it is voluntary and takes place in an environment that also includes comparable coeducational schools and classes. As a result, single-sex schooling has become more prevalent in public schools and public-supported charter schools.

One model for quality single-sex schooling exists in a high-minority area of New York City—the Young Women's Leadership School of East Harlem sent all of its 2013 graduating class to college. Yet there is much debate about single-sex schooling. In the past, all-female schools were typically private schools for the wealthy, and their principles included giving females leadership roles and creating opportunities for them to excel. Many educators feel that if a gender-fair curriculum were commonplace—if it highlighted the lives and accomplishments of women as well as men and used teaching strategies that gave voice to female students as well as to males—the advantages of all-girl environments could be accessible in coeducational environments. That is, females would not need to be separate if indeed they were treated equitably.

Because more single-sex schools and single-sex classes in coeducational settings are now available to children from lower socioeconomic classes, many applaud the Department of Education's ruling. Advocates for single-sex schooling argue that girls in these separate schools will have opportunities for leadership and verbal expression often squelched in coeducational environments. Others worry, however, that single-sex environments may promote stereotyping and discrimination. In fact, many advocates for girls and young women believe that same-sex schools for females will be less authentically rigorous. There are some data that suggest some single-sex environments designed for girls and young women actually cater to misguided stereotypes that girls need to be spoken to quietly, that they need classrooms free from harsh questions and competition, and that they should be analyzing cosmetics to study chemistry (Rivers & Barnett, 2011). Nothing could be further from the truth. A major National Science Foundation (2008) study of mathematics scores revealed that girls, primarily from coeducational settings in 10 states, did as well as boys in mathematics at every grade level. Gender is not a predictor of mathematics ability! Many educators are perpetuating the myth that girls' brains and boys' brains are predictors of achievement in mathematics and science. Be wary of "science" that supports long-held prejudices. Recent studies show that sex differences emerge and are not biological traits fixed at birth (Eliot, 2009). Explore single-sex environments carefully to determine if the students in these classes are being educated in rich and demanding environments and not being taught through the lens of social stereotypes.

The intersection of gender, race, ethnicity, and social class poses challenges for teaching and learning that can be overcome and made into wonderful opportunities for your own and your students' growth. The movement for multicultural education also advocates **gender-fair education**, encouraging teachers to address the needs of females and males in their classrooms in ways that help both genders realize their full potential. With this concept in mind, consider the following story from Ms. Logan's sixth-grade classroom in an urban area in California:

The students are closing their eyes and thinking back to their earliest memories. Ms. Logan says, "To begin, step out of your body and see yourself at your desk with your head down. Now, travel back in time until you are in fourth grade, then third grade. What are you wearing? Who is your teacher? What are you doing? See yourself at home. What does your room look like? Who are your friends? What do you do after school? Now, see yourself as a kindergartner; see how you are playing. What do you love to do? Travel back again until you are a baby. Look around your room. Notice things around you. Now travel back again and here you are—ready to be born! Everyone is so excited, so happy, waiting for your birth. But this time, imagine you are born as the opposite sex.

"Hence, if you are boy, pretend you are born a girl. If you are a girl, pretend you are born a boy. See yourself as a baby, coming home, learning to walk, starting school, attending elementary school. Look at your room and your friends and your activities. Without talking to anybody, create a list of how your life seems different since you were born a person of the opposite sex."

gender-fair education Teaching practices that help both females and males achieve their full potential. Gender-fair teachers address cultural and societal stereotypes and overcome them through classroom interactions.

Ms. Logan really likes this activity because as the students reveal their beliefs about their lives as a member of the opposite sex, they confront stereotypes. Ultimately, they learn that they are really more similar to their classmates of the opposite sex than they are different. As students respond to this exercise, they find they hold various misconceptions: for example, about the paint colors girls or boys would have in their rooms or how they would have to behave if they were of the opposite sex. The discussion gives students a chance to see the ways they are similar, dispelling stereotypes. *(Reprinted by permission of Kodansha America, Inc. Excerpted from* Teaching Stories *by Judy Logan, published by Kodansha America, Inc. [1999].)*

In Ms. Logan's class, boys said that if they were female, they would have to get up extra early to fix their hair. A few of the girls objected to that remark and pointed out that they never get up early to fuss over their hair. Girls felt that if they were male, they would be able to stay out later—only to learn that the boys in their class also had curfews. Some boys insisted that they would do better in writing if they were female, but other boys argued that they were good writers. In the end, these middle school girls and boys agreed that they both loved sports and a lot of different subjects, and that they were probably more the same than different; however, it was clear that the boys had more personal freedom and privileges than the girls.

It's important to remember that treating students *equitably* is not the same as treating them *equally*. **Equity** stands for being fair and just. Because students come from such diverse experiences, identities, and backgrounds, you cannot be fair by treating everyone in exactly the same way. To ensure equality in the learning goals we hope to achieve for each student, we need to notice the differences among our students and use strategies to help each student reach maximum success in the classroom. In a science class, equity may mean asking how to encourage more females' interest. One of the many ways may be to post pictures of female as well as male scientists. In a language arts classroom, equity may mean asking how to engage the boys in more reading experiences. One way may be to integrate action heroes into the literature. In each case, the tacit message is: We are here to support all our students, and we will work to counter any stereotyping and biases in the classroom.

In late 2014, the U.S. Department of Education's Office for Civil Rights released guidance for K–12 schools that offer or want to offer single-sex classes.

To offer single-sex classes or extracurricular activities, schools must

- identify an important objective that they seek to achieve by offering a single-sex class (such as improving academic achievement),

- demonstrate that the single-sex nature of the class is substantially related to achieving that objective,

- ensure that enrollment in the single-sex class is completely voluntary (through an opt-in, rather than an opt-out, process),

- offer a substantially equal coed class in the same subject,

- offer single-sex classes evenhandedly to male and female students,

- conduct periodic evaluations at least every 2 years to ensure that the classes continue to comply with Title IX,

- avoid relying on gender stereotypes,

- provide equitable access to single-sex classes to students with disabilities and ELs, and

- avoid discriminating against faculty members based on gender when assigning educators to single-sex classrooms.

Source: U.S. Department of Education Press Release, December 1, 2014. http://www.ed.gov/news/press-releases/

Religion and Schools

In 1995, President Bill Clinton sent material containing guidelines on student religious expression to every school district in the United States. The letter accompanying these guidelines declared:

Nothing in the First Amendment converts our public schools into religion-free zones, or requires all religious expression to be left behind at the schoolhouse door. While the government may not use schools to coerce the consciences of our students, or to convey official endorsement of religion, the public schools also may not discriminate against private religious expression during the school day.... Religion is too important in our history and our heritage for us to keep it out of our schools.... [I]t shouldn't be demanded, but as long as it is not sponsored by school officials and doesn't interfere with other children's rights, it mustn't be denied. ("President's Memorandum," 1995, para. 5)

That message seems clear enough. Yet issues concerning religion and the schools continue to be controversial. There have been many arguments regarding prayer, Bible readings, religious displays on school property, and similar matters. Many people want schools to promote religious values more openly or at least allow students to do so; others, just as vehemently, demand that schools keep strictly out of religious affairs.

One conflict about religious beliefs and school curriculum involves the teaching of evolution in science classes. A landmark court case (*Tammy Kitzmiller, et al. v. Dover Area School District, et al.*) occurred in the town of Dover, Pennsylvania,

---

equity The act of treating individuals and groups fairly and justly, free from bias or favoritism. Gender equity means the state of being fair and just toward both males and females, to show preference to neither and concern for both.

where the school board insisted that students be required to hear a statement about intelligent design before ninth-grade biology lessons on evolution. (Proponents of intelligent design believe that the diversity of living things can be explained as the work of a designing intelligence; they do not insist on calling that intelligence God.) The statement read to students said that Darwin's theory is "not a fact" and has inexplicable "gaps." Science teachers objected that science class is not the domain to discuss the presence of an all-powerful being, and some parents brought the case to federal court.

In his ruling in December 2005, Judge John E. Jones asserted that the school board's requirement was unconstitutional. The judge said: "We find that the secular purposes claimed by the board amount to a pretext for the board's real purpose, which was to promote religion in the public school classroom." He said that the policy "singles out the theory of evolution for special treatment, misrepresents its status in the scientific community, causes students to doubt its validity without scientific justification," and "presents students with a religious alternative masquerading as a scientific theory." Hence, Judge Jones concluded, it was unconstitutional to teach intelligent design as an alternative to evolution in a public school science classroom.

In another case, in a New Jersey public high school, an 11th-grade history teacher told his students that evolution and the big bang theory of the universe's origin were not scientific, that dinosaurs were aboard Noah's Ark, and that only Christians had a place in heaven. The teacher was audiotaped by a student, and the student's family considered a lawsuit on the grounds that the teacher promoted religious views in a public school history classroom. The incident divided and shocked this New Jersey community (Kelley, 2006), but no formal court case ensued.

In the midst of such controversies, teachers often receive conflicting messages about what they can and cannot teach regarding religion. The best understanding is to recognize that you cannot teach religion in public schools. Similarly, you cannot encourage or participate in student religious activity. However, you can teach about religion and can honor the privacy of religious ritual as long as it does not interfere with the functioning of the school or classroom and is not forced on any other student. The following statement, posted on the website of the First Amendment Center (https://www.freedomforuminstitute.org/first-amendment-center/), was agreed on by a broad range of religious and educational groups:

Public schools may not inculcate nor inhibit religion. They must be places where religion and religious conviction are treated with fairness and respect. Public schools uphold the First Amendment when they protect the religious liberty rights of students of all faiths and none. Schools demonstrate fairness when they ensure that the curriculum includes study about religion, where appropriate, as an important part of a complete education.

Multiple Intelligences: What Does It Mean to Be "Smart"?

This section deals with another type of diversity: the variation in intelligence—or perhaps a better way of expressing it, *intelligences*. Until the 1980s, psychologists believed—and many still believe—that intelligence is a fixed and measurable attribute, calculated by an IQ test. Today, many educators draw on the work of psychologist and neuroscientist Howard Gardner (2006) and accept the **theory of multiple intelligences**. That is, instead of having a fixed, single intelligence, each of us is intelligent in several different ways (see Table 5.4).

From the research of Gardner and others, we now know that babies are born with many capacities. Their intelligences evolve and are expressed in multiple ways. These different ways, or different intelligences, may be more or less dominant in a particular individual. Each individual usually expresses several intelligences, to different degrees. Gardner (1993, 2003) posited a total of eight intelligences. See Table 5.4 for a description.

According to Gardner, each individual has all eight of the intelligences, but no two human beings have the same profiles of intelligence. In other words, we all have these different intelligences in differing strengths and capacities for expression. One way of thinking about this is that each learner's **intelligence profile** consists of a combination of relative strengths and weaknesses among the different intelligences. Moreover, intelligences are not isolated; they interact with one another in an individual to yield many types of outcomes (Moran, Kornhaber, & Gardner, 2006).

Gardner's argument leaves educators with an important mission: finding out how to access all the types of intelligences so that all students can learn to their maximum potential. It is clear that schools traditionally have valued the first two of Gardner's categories—linguistic intelligence and logical-mathematical intelligence—and paid little attention to the others. As teachers, we need to change this emphasis; we need to explore topics in multiple ways to reach more students. When schools stress memorization of key terms without exposing students to other ways to learn about a subject, those students who need tactile or visual representations will often miss the meanings just from words. For example, students who are high in linguistic intelligence will grasp the material, but other students may lag behind and be labeled as underachieving—even though these low-achieving students would do much better if they were given the opportunity to learn and express themselves by other means.

One example of a teacher who organizes assignments that have the potential to express multiple learning styles is

theory of multiple intelligences The theory that intelligence is not a single, fixed attribute but rather a collection of several different types of abilities.

intelligence profile An individual's unique combination of relative strengths and weaknesses among all the different intelligences.

TABLE 5.4 ● Howard Gardner's Eight Intelligences

Intelligence type	This type of learner often. . .
Visual-spatial (picture smart)	• Learns best with visual icons • Is artistic • Is able to read maps, blueprints and graphs, with ease
Verbal-linguistic (word smart)	• Has strong reading skills • Is able to write well • Can process academic lectures effectively
Musical-rhythm (music smart)	• Taps a beat with a pencil or foot or hums softly during silent work time • Processes information by associating it with beats and rhythms that allow them to make sense of data and store it in the brain • Learns and studies best with headphones on
Logical-mathematical (number smart)	• Is good with math and numbers • Is a linear thinker • Needs order and systematic directions or steps in order to process the content
Bodily kinesthetic (body smart)	• Is a good athlete • Has excellent fine motor skills • Benefits from concrete, hands-on learning activities
Interpersonal (people smart)	• Enjoys socializing with others • Needs to interact with others in order to process information • Benefits from group brainstorming
Intrapersonal (self smart)	• Processes information best by working alone in quiet solitude • Finds working with groups to be distracting
Naturalistic (environment smart)	• Gravitates toward natural patterns • Gains brain stimulation when in a natural, outdoor environment • Improves engagement with tasks when exposed to the sights, sounds, and smells of the outdoors

Source: Barger-Anderson, R., Isherwood, R. S., & Merhaut, J. (2013). *Strategic Co-Teaching in Your School: Using the Co-Design Model.* Baltimore, MD: Brookes.

▲ Meeting the needs of students with a wide range of learning styles requires teachers to have more than one way to approach a topic.

Mr. Slomin's sixth-grade science class. He includes a unit on the moon in which students study the moon's phases—how it appears from Earth at different times of the month. Here are Mr. Slomin's instructions for this unit:

The students are required to keep a moon-phase journal over a period of 5 weeks. Each day, they need to record the shape of the moon, the time that they see it, and other information about the moon that can include: how they felt watching the moon, moon poems (original or found), moon facts, or other relevant data about the moon. All these belong in the moon journal. There may be some days, due to weather or other reasons, when the students cannot see the moon. Then, they are asked to develop their own theory about why they cannot see it and keep observing until they see it again. Mr. Slomin's class is accustomed to receiving open-ended assignments. The students trust that he will examine their products as individual creations based on their own interests. At the end of the 5 weeks, the students are asked to present their moon journals and talk about how they felt during the experience of keeping them. To everyone's surprise and delight, Dan, a shy young man who does not participate much in class, created a beautiful painting on each of the nights he could see the moon. Neither his classmates nor his teacher knew how gifted he was. His entries included a relatively small number of words, but his pictures showed close and accurate observations. Dan's artistic talent was a well-kept secret. This assignment allowed him to express his observations through his artistic designs and keen observations.

Perhaps you have had interesting assignments like this one. Think about your own response to this type of experience and how it is meaningful to students.

Multiple Intelligences Are Not Learning Styles

According to Gardner, we all have the multiple intelligences. But we single out, as a strong intelligence, an area where the person has considerable computational power. Your ability to win regularly at a game involving spatial thinking signals strong spatial intelligence. Your ability to speak a foreign language well after just a few months of "going native" signals strong linguistic intelligence (Strauss, 2013).

Gardner's theory of multiple intelligences has had a profound effect on how we think about the ways people perceive the world. A related idea is that people have various **learning styles**. Gardner explains that a learning style is different from multiple intelligences. Learning-styles research developed separately from multiple intelligences and relies heavily on the senses. In Chapter 4, we described learning something as a process of drawing it from the outside and making it your own. *Learning style* refers to the particular way you take in the new idea, event, or concept.

Some people learn best by reading and writing—the traditional approach taken in schools. But researchers (Felder, 2002; Felder & Brent, 2005; Felder & Silverman, 1988) have identified other basic learning styles as well:

- *Auditory learners* learn best through verbal lectures, discussions, talking things through, and listening to what others have to say. For these people, written information may have little meaning until it is heard. Such learners often benefit from reading text aloud and using a tape recorder.

- *Visual learners* need to see the teacher's body language and facial expression to fully understand the content of a lesson. They may think in pictures and learn best from visual displays,

....

learning style The dominant way in which we process the information around us. Different people have different learning styles.

WRITING & REFLECTION
UNDERSTANDING HOW YOU LEARN BEST

Becoming metacognitive about how you learn best provides a window into the experiences of your students. Are you an auditory learner, or do you have to write things down in order to remember them? Do you learn best from video presentations or from a series of visual cues that you can mull over? Do you prefer working alone when you study for a test, or does group work help you more? These questions are prompts for you to write about the conditions under which you learn best.

including diagrams, illustrated textbooks, overhead transparencies, videos, flipcharts, and handouts.

- *Kinesthetic learners* learn best through a hands-on approach, actively exploring the physical world around them. They may find it hard to sit still for long periods and may become distracted by their need for activity and exploration.

When you study for a test, is reading the book enough for you, or do you have to take notes on what you read to remember the ideas? Most people who need to do something physical to make the concepts their own are kinesthetic learners. If you are one, quick—take notes on this chapter! There is so much to know.

Together, the research on learning styles and multiple intelligences has a strong message for teachers: Do not present activities, materials, ideas, and concepts in just one way! Because people learn in different ways and through different personal strengths, it is important to plan your lessons with multiple ways of knowing in mind.

Teaching the Broad Range of Diverse Students

The prevailing question before us is not about what children need to succeed. The research is clear. They need supportive environments that nurture their social, emotional, physical, moral, civic, and cognitive development. Instead, the question becomes, who bears responsibility for creating this environment?

—Gene Carter (2006)

New teachers often draw on their own experiences as learners, and those experiences become the default mode for what is presumed "normal" or "expected" in the regular classroom. As we have seen, however, students today bring to the classroom a wide range of ethnic backgrounds, languages, religions, sexual orientations, learning styles, and intelligences. All of these are embedded in their culture and upbringing. You also have your own identity, embedded in a particular culture with norms and traditions that are dear to you.

To be a successful teacher, you need to become a *student of your students*. Start to view "difference" from the point of view of a learner and ask yourself, "How am I enriched by learning more about my students? How does that contribute to my understanding of the human condition?" In this way, teaching becomes a never-ending story, a new adventure every year, just as Jessica remarked in Chapter 2. Part of your job each year will be to learn about your students and the ways in which they and their backgrounds, languages, learning styles, sexual orientations, and lifestyles prepare them for your classroom.

Concluding Thoughts

The most important theme of this chapter is that differences among students are a gift to welcome in your classroom, not a barrier to overcome. They are a gift both for you and for your students. Unless we meet and interact with people from many walks of life and with different ways of being in the world, we run the risk of closing our minds to all that is possible in the human condition.

This chapter may leave you with more questions than answers, but you can "live into" the questions. Ask yourself: Can I do this? Can I examine my pedagogy and develop teaching strategies that help the young girl from the homeless shelter, the boy from Nicaragua with limited English, the suburban youngster who has more than she will ever need, the musically gifted eighth grader who hates history, the logical-mathematical young woman who wants to be a physicist? Can I learn from them and with them, and help them be all they can be, as others have helped me?

That is the message of this chapter. In Chapter 6, we explore current trends in education. Some of these trends will feel like stumbling blocks, others like welcome boosts. The following anonymous quotation sums it up: "Teachers who inspire realize there will always be rocks in the road ahead of us. They will be stumbling blocks or stepping stones; it all depends on how we use them."

CHAPTER REVIEW

Key Terms

bilingual education (p. 71)
culturally relevant pedagogy
    (p. 78)
dropout rate (p. 76)
English as a Second Language
    (ESL) (p. 72)
equity (p. 80)

gender-fair education (p. 79)
intelligence profile (p. 81)
learning style (p. 83)
LGBTQ (p. 73)
multicultural education (p. 77)
Seeking Educational Equity and
    Diversity (SEED) Project (p. 77)

sexual orientation (p. 73)
socioeconomic status (SES) (p. 74)
students at risk (p. 76)
theory of multiple intelligences
    (p. 81)

Review the Learning Outcomes

Review each section of the chapter and answer the following:

LO 5-1 What are the ways in which students can differ from each other?

LO 5-2 What life circumstances may hinder a student's success in school?

LO 5-3 Why is it so necessary for teachers to understand the nature of their students' daily lives?

LO 5-4 How may your students' life histories affect their performance in class?

LO 5-5 Why is it important to assess how your students learn best?

LO 5-6 How can student diversity be a gift for the teacher and others?

InTASC Standards

Review the InTASC Standards for the chapter and explain how the chapter addressed each one.

Standard 2: Learning Differences   Standard 7: Planning for Instruction

Standard 3: Learning Environments

Journal Prompts

While student diversity is a gift, it may also be a challenge. In what ways do you anticipate that your students will be very different from yourself? How will you learn what their lives are like?

Get the tools you need to sharpen your study skills. SAGE edge offers a robust online environment featuring an impressive array of free tools and resources.

Access practice quizzes, eFlashcards, video, and multimedia at **edge.sagepub.com/koch4e**.

iStock/SolStock

Contemporary Trends in Education

Education is not the piling on of learning, information, data, facts, skills, or abilities . . . but is rather making visible what is hidden as a seed.

—Sir Thomas More, 1478–1535

Learning Outcomes

After reading this chapter, you should be able to:

6-1 Explain why inclusion classrooms look no different from mainstream classrooms.

6-2 Analyze the ways in which students are labeled *gifted* and *talented,* and how inclusion students may also be considered gifted or talented.

6-3 Examine how differentiated instruction meets the needs of all the students.

6-4 Evaluate the role of social and emotional learning for classroom teaching.

6-5 Compare problem- and project-based learning to each other and to the traditional class discussion. Relate this to the STEM and STEAM education movements.

6-6 Examine the effect of the Common Core State Standards on curriculum, instruction, and standardized testing.

6-7 Examine the alternatives to traditional public schooling, including charter schools, homeschooling, and the contemporary trend to privatize many public schools.

6-8 Examine the precautions that schools and teachers take to prevent violence, including gun violence, in the classroom or the school.

6-9 Analyze the legislation ensuring students' rights as part of the U.S. public school system.

6-10 Examine teachers' rights and their legal responsibilities as they perform their professional duties.

InTASC Standards

- Standard 1: Learner Development
- Standard 2: Learning Differences
- Standard 3: Learning Environments

- Standard 5: Application of Content
- Standard 9: Professional Learning and Ethical Practice

Because schools reflect the culture and politics of contemporary society, there are always many trends in education, and we could spend four or five entire books discussing current ones. *Trend* refers to a prevailing tendency that has impacted the lives of students and teachers in schools and that seems likely to remain for the foreseeable future. In this chapter, we will concentrate on several major trends and issues affecting schools across the nation. Some of these trends have been around for over three decades; other trends have emerged in the last decade. Chief among the trends in conventional public schooling has been the inclusion classroom and the attention given to students with special needs.

- Approaches to teaching students with special needs have expanded. Response to Intervention (RTI) is a multilevel teacher response system that identifies students at risk of underachieving and maximizes their chances for success with multiple strategies.

- The emphasis on standards-based testing has had an enormous impact on teaching practice, the construction of the curriculum, and teacher evaluations. The Common Core State Standards (CCSS), adopted by

36 states, modified by an additional 10 states, and adopted for only language arts in one state, are more rigorous than previous curriculum standards and designed to ensure college or career readiness.

- The rising interest in alternative forms of schooling—specifically, public charter schools, homeschooling, small urban high schools, taxpayer-funded alternative schools—has changed the face of the traditional public school.

- The changing ideas about middle schools and the education of young adolescents have yielded school districts with middle grades in many configurations.

- The influence of students' social and emotional learning on their attitudes, behavior, and performance in school has raised awareness of bullying and harassment in the hallways of the schools and at home on the Internet.

- Professional development has become more significant than ever before as teachers work to infuse creativity and imagination in classes where test preparation has become urgent. Helping teachers implement project- and problem-based learning is a major goal of professional development in many schools and districts.

- The STEM education movement, standing for science, technology, engineering, and mathematics education, has dominated school discourse since 2010. Inspired by a desire to foster creative problem solving and examine new approaches to finding solutions, the STEM education movement and its related STEAM education trend (where A stands for the arts) is supported by the Next Generation Science Standards (NGSS, 2013).

- The maker movement, which generally refers to using a wide variety of hands-on activities (such as building, computer programming, and sewing) to support academic learning and the development of a mind-set that values collaboration and experimentation.

- Gun violence has proliferated with attacks by individuals on elementary schools and high schools. Finding ways to prepare school communities for sudden acts of violence has been part of newly designed safety programs for schools.

For you as a prospective teacher, the most significant question behind all these trends is, "How are the needs of so many different types of learners met in one classroom in one school?" As you can imagine, the answer lies in multiple approaches to implementing the curriculum. It is common to find teachers building a large repertoire of activities and experiences for a given topic. It is, therefore, important to remain professionally active and attend conferences, workshops, and professional development programs well after you have left the formal world of teacher education.

The Inclusion Classroom

In Chapter 5, we explored the many ways in which our students can differ from one another—even students in the same grade level at the same school. In this chapter, we examine the extremes on the spectrum of learning—students with disabilities and students who are considered gifted and talented. Both of these groups of students are considered exceptional learners. Teaching exceptional learners requires that teachers stretch themselves and their thinking to consider what works best for these students in their classroom settings.

In Chapter 3, you read about the Individuals with Disabilities Education Act (IDEA) and its various amendments.

The law guarantees that children with disabilities receive a "free appropriate public education." But more than just providing access to education for students with disabilities, the law calls for improved results for these students and the implementation of programs to ensure their continuous progress. The question educators must answer for each student with a disability is, "What does free and appropriate public education look like for this child?" To comply with the law, this education must take place in the least restrictive environment appropriate for each particular student. Hence, to the greatest extent possible, students with disabilities must be educated with children who are not disabled. Originally, this mandate led to the mainstreaming of students with disabilities. Generally, mainstreaming involved having those students with disabilities participate in general education classes for part of the school day and spend the remainder of the day in a separate, self-contained classroom for students with disabilities. Today, the prevailing concept is inclusion, which goes further than mainstreaming. Inclusion involves a commitment to educate students with disabilities in the general education classroom for the entire school day. Any special services the students need are brought to them in the regular classroom. Sometimes this arrangement is called full inclusion to emphasize that the students stay in the regular classroom full time. If students spend only part of the day in the regular classroom, the arrangement is called partial inclusion. Some of you may have been in inclusion classrooms either in the role of the general education student or the student with special needs. In either case, when different student communities socialize and work together in the same classroom, there are positive effects for teaching tolerance and kindness, and for learning.

The field of special education focuses on the services and instructional practices needed by students with disabilities. You may be interested in becoming a special education teacher. Today, because of inclusion, that often means working in tandem with a general education teacher in the same classroom. In addition to having at least two teachers, an inclusion classroom may also have a teacher's aide, who may be specifically assigned to a student in the class with special needs.

Good Schools Are Good Schools for All Students

There was, and in some places remains, controversy about inclusion. Parents of general education students worry that

STEM education A movement that represents science, technology, engineering, and mathematics education. This approach to learning invites students to understand the interconnectedness of science and technology, and the significance of applying mathematical thinking to solving problems.

STEAM education An initiative that adds the arts to the STEM framework. The STEAM movement asserts that art and design must be central to education in science, technology, engineering, and mathematics.

maker movement Refers to using a wide variety of hands-on activities (such as building, computer programming, and sewing) to support academic learning and the development of a mind-set that values collaboration and experimentation.

exceptional learners Students who require special educational services because of physical, behavioral, or academic needs.

least restrictive environment A learning environment that, to the maximum extent possible, matches the environment experienced by nondisabled students.

mainstreaming Having students with disabilities participate in general education classes for part of the school day and spend the remainder of the day in a separate, self-contained classroom for students with disabilities. This leads to full inclusion for many students with disabilities.

special education The branch of education that deals with services for students with disabilities or other special needs that cannot be met through traditional means.

their child's education may be compromised by the presence of students with special needs. They fear, for instance, that the teacher may have to spend so much time with the "special" students that "regular" students get less attention. Other people, however, believe that inclusion helps general education students appreciate people who are different from themselves. The philosophy of inclusion, however, has grown to include all students by eliminating the dual systems of special education and general education students, and creating a merged system that is responsive to the realities of today's student population.

For students with disabilities, there are many critiques of self-contained classrooms. Many educators worry that students in such classrooms are labeled for life. Applied at an early age, the disability label persists over time and limits students' potential. Other critics point out the disproportionate number of minority boys in self-contained special education classes, especially in urban areas. How do these children get placed in such settings? Why is there a larger number of students from one ethnic group and gender than from others? Who is advocating on behalf of students with special needs? These and other questions contribute to raging controversies surrounding special education and its implementation in public schools.

In the past 15 years, the inclusion of students who have been classified as having autism spectrum disorders has engendered a great deal of controversy. There has been an increase in the number of students diagnosed with Asperger's syndrome, an autism spectrum disorder that is characterized by difficulties with social interaction and nonverbal communication coupled with repetitive patterns of behavior and interests. It is a type of pervasive developmental disorder characterized by a delay in the development of social interaction skills. It differs from other autism disorders as it does not affect linguistic or cognitive development. It responds to behavioral therapy, and many children improve with age. It is common for students with Asperger's to require individual aides in the inclusion classroom. The problem is that students with and without disabilities do not fall into neat categories of educational need, so stating that a student has autism, Asperger's syndrome, or other pervasive developmental disorders does not paint an exact picture of the supports or services needed. According to Cathy Pratt (Carr & Pratt, 2007), IDEA clearly states that programming and placement must be individually determined. The mandate from IDEA explains that students with autism spectrum disorders and other disabilities be placed in the least restrictive environment,

Inclusion classes give students with disabilities equitable access to an education.

iStock/FatCamera

demonstrating a clear preference for educating these students in general education settings. The law articulates that students must receive needed supports and services within the context of the regular classroom. When these accommodations are insufficient to ensure educational success, then students can be placed in more restrictive settings.

Wherever you stand on this controversy, it is the consensus of educators and psychologists that segregated settings do not create opportunities for all students to interact and often force teachers into choosing artificial curriculum accommodations, which is in direct opposition to the IDEA. Inclusion classrooms are more common than not, and it is highly likely that you will have an inclusion classroom at some stage in your teaching career.

Types of Disabilities

The number of children and youth ages 3 to 21 who receive special education services represents 13% of total public school enrollment, or about 6.7 million students. Of these, 35% are considered learning disabled (https://nces.ed.gov/programs/coe/indicator_cgg.asp). These are students who have difficulty with reading, listening, speaking, writing, reasoning, or mathematical skills. Students with learning disabilities can be good in one subject area but perform poorly in other areas. For students with learning disabilities, hyperactivity and the inability to follow directions are typical problems.

In some cases, students with learning disabilities have social and behavioral problems. Sometimes, the **learning disability**

learning disability A disorder in the basic psychological processes involved in learning and using language; it may lead to difficulties in listening, speaking, reading, writing, reasoning, or mathematical abilities.

leads to behavioral distress, low self-esteem, and inappropriate behavior in the classroom. Under IDEA, there are 13 categories under which a student is eligible to receive protections and services:

- autism

- deaf-blindness

- deafness

- emotional disturbance

- hearing impairment

- intellectual disability

- multiple disabilities

- orthopedic impairment

- other health impairment

- specific learning disability

- speech or language impairment

- traumatic brain injury

- visual impairment (including blindness)

Source: https://www.specialeducationguide.com/disability-profiles/

Individualized Education Programs

Because there are so many types of disabilities with so many different representations among individual children, the IDEA mandates that, for each student to have a free and appropriate public education, each student with disabilities must be provided with a learning plan. Known as the **individualized education program (IEP)**, this plan outlines long- and short-range goals for the individual student. The elements of a meaningful IEP report include categories describing the student's current performance, statement of goals, special education services, participation with typical students, and participation with state and districtwide assessments (Gargiulo & Bouck, 2018, p. 63). Quality IEP reports depend on having well-written and appropriate goals that address the unique needs of the individual.

This type of form is usually completed by the general education teacher and the inclusion teacher working together. In addition to these teachers, other people typically have input into the child's program, including the school psychologist, school administrators, and the student's parents or guardians. A successful inclusion model depends on the collaboration of all these people.

individualized education program (IEP) A plan, required for every student covered by the Individuals with Disabilities Education Act, specifying instructional goals, services to be provided, and assessment techniques for evaluating progress.

Response to Intervention

Response to Intervention (RTI) is a program that enables schools to identify the specific types of support that struggling students require and to provide this support when it is needed. It is a prevention model that intervenes to identify young students who may be at risk for poor learning outcomes. This organizational framework helps teachers screen all students to determine whether the curriculum and instruction they are implementing are meeting the needs of the majority of students. This screening typically happens for an entire grade and is a means for helping struggling students and preventing them from experiencing academic failure. The RTI program can also identify students with learning difficulties (Brown-Chidsey, 2007).

What makes RTI effective are the ways in which it can prevent academic failure and determine whether a student's underachievement is the result of an actual learning disability or the result of inadequate instruction. RTI is a systematic method for instruction and assessment of students that includes a three-tiered approach to intervening on behalf of students with varying instructional needs.

In Tier 1, all students are assessed to determine if they are meeting grade-level standards for the general curriculum. In Tier 2, students who are performing below grade level receive specific instructional activities to help their academic achievement. These are tailored to the individual and require collaboration between general education teachers and the special education teachers. In Tier 2, students are monitored weekly and, as their skills improve, receive less support until they are fully able to succeed with the general education curriculum as it is implemented in the school. If the students in Tier 2 do not make progress in a specified period of time, instruction is modified and they are further monitored. If they need additional support, the students are moved to Tier 3 services, in which the school conducts a comprehensive evaluation of a student's skills, including the data from Tiers 1 and 2, to determine why the student's performance is significantly different from that of other students in his or her grade and to decide what instructional support the student needs.

If this sounds complicated, that's because it is! However, outcomes from schools that have practiced RTI for years have shown that it raises the educational attainment of students in general and reduces the number of students who need special education services. One of the reasons for this is that the instructional interventions that are recommended have been validated by research and are not loosely constructed. Think about how wonderful it would be to prevent a child's placement in special education simply because he or she needed specific early academic support to achieve success independently. RTI is a framework

Response to Intervention (RTI) A service delivery system in schools aimed at preventing academic and behavioral difficulties as well as identifying the best practices for teaching students with disabilities.

in which we think about organizing curriculum and instruction based on students' responses to screening, tiers of instruction, progress monitoring, and understanding of how the intervention was delivered. The National Center on Response to Intervention provides screening tools, case studies, and descriptions of tiered interventions (http://www.rti4success.org).

Universal Design for Learning

You may be wondering how it is possible to meet the individual needs of the diverse student population that may arrive at your classroom door. The Center for Applied Special Technology (CAST) is a nonprofit educational research and development organization that developed a design of instructional materials and activities, called **Universal Design for Learning (UDL)**, that allows learning goals to be achievable by individuals with wide differences in their abilities to learn. UDL is an effective tool for designing and implementing an inclusive learning environment. It is an instructional resource that helps teachers create curriculum that is sufficiently flexible to meet the needs of individual learners. It provides a range of options for accessing, using, and engaging learning materials—explicitly acknowledging that no one option will work for all students (Gargiulo & Metcalf, 2017).

UDL has three essential components to consider when developing curriculum for diverse learners: multiple means of representation, engagement, and expression. UDL invites teachers to develop many ways to present material, motivate students, and assess their responses. It is a vehicle for diversifying instruction and offers teachers options for how to present materials through learning activities specifically designed to allow for flexibility. Based on scientific research on how people learn, UDL increases opportunities for all students. CAST develops high-quality digital learning materials and engages teachers in online and face-to-face professional development (http://www.cast.org/). The use of technology makes their materials accessible and helps teachers meet the challenges of teaching English language learners as well as students from a wide range of cultures.

The Education of Gifted and Talented Students

A teacher asked a class what color apples are. Most of the children said "Red," a few answered "Green," and one child raised his hand with another answer: "White." The teacher patiently explained that apples were red or green or yellow but they were never white. The student persisted. Finally, he said, "Look inside."

—Adapted from Tara Bennett-Goleman (2001, p. 43)

....

Universal Design for Learning (UDL) Design of instructional materials and activities that allow learning goals to be achievable by individuals with wide differences in their abilities to learn.

This quotation reminds me of how students with "out-of-the-box" thinking often are not rewarded in school because their ideas are not aligned with conventional questioning or expected answers. Sometimes, these thinkers are really gifted or talented students. Most of us typically have less compassion for gifted and talented students than we do for students with disabilities. Conventional wisdom tells us that gifted students always land on their feet, and some of us even feel jealous of their exceptional skills and abilities. Research, however, indicates that gifted and talented learners are in as much need of special educational services as are students with disabilities (Davis & Rimm, 2004). Often, their needs are not met in traditional school settings, and that situation frequently causes depression, lack of interest in school, and underachievement. Many people have an image of gifted students as well behaved, high performing, and compliant. Sometimes, however, they are failing, poorly behaved, and acting out because they are bored and underchallenged. Additionally, fewer gifted and talented students from minority groups or groups of low socioeconomic status are identified than from White, middle- and upper middle-class populations. Part of this discrepancy stems from parent advocacy—parents of higher social status are more likely to push for their children to be included in gifted programs. The discrepancy also relates to the issue of social capital introduced in Chapter 3. Parents with social capital understand how to get their children into special programs. In addition, social capital exposes the learners themselves to a variety of educational and cultural experiences that poorer students often do not gain access to. That early and consistent cultural exposure outside of school contributes to a sense of "giftedness."

As you might guess, the attempt to define giftedness has led to controversy. For much of the 20th century, giftedness was usually measured by IQ tests; people who scored in the upper 2% of the population were considered gifted. Critics pointed out, however, that those tests emphasized a narrow range of skills and tended to discriminate against minority groups. Today, giftedness is defined not so much by test scores as by consistently exceptional performance.

Federal legislation has generally referred to gifted and talented children as those who show high performance capability in specific academic fields or in areas such as creativity and leadership, and who require special services by the school to develop these capabilities. The schools select students for such services using a variety of measures, including recommendations by teachers; test scores; and an understanding of certain identifying features of gifted and talented students, such as the pace at which they learn and the depth of their understanding (Maker & Nielson, 1996).

Services for the gifted and talented learner can provide enrichment (broadening the curriculum) or acceleration (speeding up the student's progress through the curriculum). Enrichment activities for the gifted are usually classroom

iStock/Zinkevych

Providing resources and experiences for gifted and talented learners.

based, whereas accelerated programs may allow students to skip grades or graduate early from high school. Accelerated programs range from segregated grade-level classes to high school programs such as the International Baccalaureate (IB) program and advanced placement (AP) courses. The IB program is a rigorous course of study concentrating on mathematics, science, and foreign language, and is internationally recognized. AP courses offer college-level classes while students are still in high school, and students may receive college credit for them if they score high enough on the culminating AP exam.

There is no universally agreed-upon answer to the question of who is gifted. Many people believe that all children are gifted in different ways. The National Association for Gifted Children (NAGC) defines a gifted person as:

> Students, children, or youth who give evidence of high achievement capability in areas such as intellectual, creative, artistic, or leadership capacity, or in specific academic fields, and who need services and activities not ordinarily provided by the school in order to fully develop those capabilities. (NAGC, n.d.)

Some gifted people have general abilities such as leadership skills and the ability to think creatively. Other gifted people have more specific abilities such as special aptitudes in mathematics, science, or music. By these standards, the U.S. Department of Education estimates that approximately 6% of the student population in the United States is considered gifted (NAGC, n.d.). In many cases, gifted students learn differently from their classmates in several important ways:

- They learn new material in much less time.

- They tend to remember what they have learned, making reviews of previously mastered concepts a painful experience.

- They do not need to watch the teacher to process what is being said, and they can process more than one task at a time.

- They become passionately interested in specific topics and have difficulty moving on to other learning tasks.

- They are able to operate on higher levels of thinking than their age peers, are comfortable with abstract and complex thinking tasks, and need a minimum of concrete experiences for complete understanding (Winebrenner & Brulles, 2012, p. 12).

Finally, many people now recommend "gifted inclusion." That would prompt us to design regular classroom activities that offer gifted and talented students opportunities to expand on the unit of study. This is a common occurrence in classrooms of students with many different abilities. Clearly, teachers need to offer varying instructional strategies and adjust their pedagogy to recognize the many types of learners with whom they may work.

Differentiated Instruction

Although there is great diversity among students, all learners want to be valued and need support, encouragement, kindness, and compassion. Examining student diversity provides teachers with the challenge of meeting the differing needs of students who may have exceptional learning needs, special learning profiles, language and ethnic differences, and cultural and socioeconomic differences. Sometimes, strategies for meeting the needs of these learners are developed through collaboration with a specialist, someone who has been trained in a field such as special education, gifted education, or bilingual education. The RTI model and the UDL process are two good examples of how instruction is specifically designed for students with special learning needs. This is a research-based model of differentiation. The various programs for gifted and talented students represent another model of differentiated instruction.

Whether in collaboration with a fellow teacher or not, you will be responsible for developing teaching strategies that can accommodate the learning experience to a wide range of student abilities. Teaching to diversity has a name. **Differentiated instruction** or **differentiation** has become an important educational philosophy recognizing students' varying background knowledge, learning profiles, abilities, interests, and language. It is the basis for developing instructional practices that engage all learners through multiple approaches, tasks, and activities.

Differentiated instruction is another example that refutes the concept that all children should be taught in the same manner. The movement for gender-fair education, for

---

differentiated instruction/differentiation The practice of using a variety of instructional strategies to address the different learning needs of students.

Students may be engaged with different activities in the same classroom with the same teacher.

example, identified the different needs of girls and boys in the classroom resulting from the different ways they are socialized (Sadker & Zittleman, 2009). The movement first focused on the needs of girls but then went on to consider new ways to help boys succeed. Overall, the important message for teachers is that equality of treatment does not guarantee equity. Equity is what we should strive for because it provides equal opportunities for all students to succeed.

What teachers ask students to do on behalf of their own learning must be geared to their individual needs and strengths, and designed to help them achieve to their fullest potential. In other words, one size does not fit all. One type of activity or lesson will probably not reach all of the students. When you approach teaching a topic, ask yourself questions such as:

- In how many different ways can I engage my students in this unit of study?

- How many different types of representations can I use for a concept?

- How can I support students with learning disabilities and challenge the gifted learner, while at the same time exciting all learners to find their inner confidence?

- What are the strengths of my students with disabilities? How can I teach to their strengths and not focus on what they cannot do?

Differentiated instruction is based on the following set of beliefs:

- Students who are the same age differ in their readiness to learn, their interests, their styles of learning, their experiences, and their life circumstances.

- The differences among students are significant enough to make a major impact on what students need to learn, the pace at which they need to learn it, and the support they need from teachers and others to learn it well.

- Students learn best when they can make a connection between the curriculum and their interests and life experiences.

- Students learn best when learning opportunities are natural.

- Students are more effective learners when classrooms and schools create a sense of community in which students feel significant and respected.

- The central job of schools is to maximize the capacity of each student (Tomlinson, 2014).

Social and Emotional Learning

Social and emotional learning (SEL) refers to individuals' abilities to manage their emotions, develop caring and concern for others, make responsible decisions, establish positive relationships, and handle challenging situations effectively. School programs that help students to develop these skills have been shown to be effective in preventing violence, substance abuse, and related problems, and in helping students succeed academically (Zins, Bloodworth, Weissberg, & Walberg, 2007). The Collaborative for Academic, Social, and Emotional Learning (CASEL) is a nonprofit organization that was founded by Daniel Goleman, author of Emotional Intelligence (2006). It works to advance the evidence-based practices for incorporating SEL into the curriculum in as many schools as possible nationwide.

It comes as no surprise that students' learning is influenced by social and emotional factors and that an anxious, afraid, or alienated student has a diminished capacity for learning. Helping students to communicate, make decisions, and solve problems increases the likelihood that they can develop a positive attachment to school and experience greater academic success (http://www.casel.org/).

SEL skills are explicitly taught through planned, systematic, and evidence-based classroom instruction, and many of the activities that compose an SEL curriculum could be integrated with academic learning areas. These carefully structured learning programs engage students from pre-K through high school in experiences that build their self-awareness, self-management, social awareness, relationship skills, and responsible decision making. A related component to the SEL approach is the development and maintenance of caring classroom communities. This text explores those types of caring classroom communities further in Chapter 9. Well-managed learning environments are places where students feel safe, respected, and challenged, and where teachers are able to model and provide opportunities for students to practice their social and emotional skills. Teachers need to be in control of their own emotions and be confident that they will be able to interact with youngsters in a way that helps them to improve, feel good about themselves, and contribute to the classroom community.

Researchers examined 213 school-based universal SEL programs involving 270,034 kindergarten through high school students. What they found through this meta-analysis was that students who participated in these programs demonstrated significantly improved social and emotional skills, attitudes, and behavior. Their academic performance reflected an 11-percentile-point gain in achievement over similar students who did not participate in universal SEL programs (Durlak, Weissberg, Dymnicki, & Taylor, 2011). These data are significant and speak to the importance of helping children and young adults develop skills that help them solve personal, social, and emotional conflicts.

To develop creative classroom experiences, certain trends have traction—they hold the attention of students and of the educational community at large because they offer learners opportunities to think for themselves, create new designs, and solve compelling problems.

The Power of Projects and Problems for Student Learning

Looking for a history teacher, a suburban high school ran the following advertisement in the local newspaper:

"Responsible for implementing curriculum specializing in the time period of 1500–1700 by designing lessons reflecting the theory of multiple intelligences, integrating with other domains using project-based learning and technology."

The phrase toward the end of the ad, "project-based learning," is one you will hear frequently. Both project- and problem-based learning are contemporary trends aimed at ensuring that students address content areas with depth and skill. Students with diverse needs and learning profiles have been shown to benefit from the use of these strategies.

One major characteristic of both these approaches is that students work in groups, with three to five students organized around a central learning task. This technique had its beginnings in the **cooperative learning** movement, which became popular in the 1990s. Every member of each group is assigned a task, and each task is important for the goal to be reached. The students in the group are responsible for their individual learning as well as the group's learning. They work toward the common goal of promoting each other's and the group's success.

cooperative learning An instructional approach in which students work together in groups to accomplish shared learning goals.

Project-Based Learning

To see what project-based learning looks like, consider a challenging project for a sixth-grade math class in the following story:

In Mr. Roberts's sixth-grade math class in an urban middle school, a visitor is immediately struck by what the students are doing. Students are working in groups of four to construct a model classroom, using cardboard boxes, glue guns, poster board, markers, and construction paper. Centimeter sticks and measuring tapes are scattered around each work station. When asked about their work, students eagerly show their sketches, which indicate the scale of their model and use principles of ratio and proportion. Clearly, this class is learning about mathematical concepts through a design project.

Mr. Roberts is convinced that the students will develop a deeper understanding of the concepts of ratio and proportion as a result of designing and constructing the model classroom. He is preparing a written assessment on this topic to more fully understand what the students know.

The design challenge, a term from engineering design, began with certain specifications. The ratio was stated in advance, using proportional units of 2 cm equal to 1 foot. The challenge also specified that the classroom contain (1) seating for 18 students, (2) a teacher's desk, (3) a discussion area with a couch, arm chairs, and an area rug, and (4) ample board space. Certain constraints were imposed as well: The students may not use materials other than those supplied by the teacher, and the final model should be no larger than 40 cm long × 40 cm wide × 18 cm high. The materials provided include foam board, cardboard, construction paper, markers, glue guns, cutting tools (handled by the teacher and other adults), and assorted recyclable materials, such as wooden spools from sewing thread, cardboard paper-towel tubes, cereal boxes, and other assorted containers.

Working in groups of four, the students present their designs to the entire class after completing their model.

▲ In project-based learning, students work together to meet shared learning goals.

iStock/lisegagne

They demonstrate how they have met the specifications and constraints of their design challenge and explain why their model classroom contains objects that are in appropriate proportion to the rest of the room. They provide a rationale for the arrangement of the students' and teacher's desks. Throughout this performance, each member of the working group has the opportunity to present his or her understanding of the project and of ratio and proportion. All the students get feedback from their classmates. Engineering practices implemented through the use of design challenges are an important component of the NGSS (2013).

This story demonstrates how **project-based learning** adds creativity and depth to a curriculum, promoting more meaningful learning than rote memorization or worksheet activities. Projects can be designed for any subject area, and they often embrace concepts from several disciplines. They also accommodate students with different learning profiles and abilities, helping students work from their own strengths. Everybody becomes engaged in completing the task or constructing the final product. As the newspaper advertisement indicated, projects typically reflect the theory of multiple intelligences and help students integrate knowledge from different domains.

Projects are challenging for teachers because they require more time and more materials than talking and doing worksheets, which is often the instructional device used when teachers are teaching to the test. A project is a carefully planned and organized experience involving thoughtfully selected groups. Although classrooms engaged in projects can be noisy at times, the students are usually self-directed and invested in their work.

Problem-Based Learning

Closely related to project-based learning is **problem-based learning**. Both strategies emphasize connections to real life, but project-based learning usually results in the construction of something, whereas problem-based learning focuses on a problem, the solutions to which may take many different forms. Problem-based learning is often more open-ended. The following story shows problem-based learning in action:

In Ms. Rhodes's fourth-grade Vermont classroom, a unit on recycling and conservation prompted the class to consider the amount of milk wasted in the school cafeteria during lunchtime. Ms. Rhodes introduced the problem by explaining to the class that the custodian had mentioned how many half-full milk cartons were tossed into the trash during lunch. "So many children—wasting so much milk," he said. Ms. Rhodes asked the class to consider the challenge of finding out just how much milk is wasted in a typical day in the cafeteria.

The students' problem was twofold: (1) how to calculate the volume of milk wasted and (2) how to enlist the help of all the students in the school to curb this waste.

The class secured the help of the custodian, who brought discarded, but not empty, milk containers to the classroom each day for a week. Working in groups of four and using graduated cylinders, the students measured the amount of milk wasted each day. They constructed a huge bar graph titled "Milk Waste" outside their classroom, labeling the axes with "day of the week" and "liters of milk wasted." Under the graph, they posed the question, "What can YOU do about the amount of milk we waste in our school?" The students also visited classrooms, talked about the problem, and gathered suggestions. By the end of the school term, there was a 70% decrease in the amount of milk wasted!

As this story demonstrates, problem-based learning can help students make connections between school subjects and the world outside of school. Conservation takes on new meaning when students relate it to their own lunchtime habits.

Notice, too, that the problem the students faced was not a simple one. They were not told how to measure the amount of milk wasted. Instead, they faced an **ill-structured problem**, one for which they had to figure out their own approach to the question. With ill-structured problems, the solutions and the steps for reaching them are not clearly defined. In this way, they resemble real-life problems, which are usually complex and messy, and require creative and critical thinking skills. To solve ill-structured problems, students need to make decisions based on the facts they gather and their beliefs about the best way to proceed. Solutions emerge from the process, and there may be more than one solution to a single problem.

Karen Rasmussen (1997) describes how a 12th-grade geology teacher designed his entire course around six ill-structured problems. Each unit lasted 6 weeks. His goal was to teach students that scientific findings have a lot of relevance outside the school building. In one unit, for example, students received a letter stating that a volcano in Yellowstone Park was showing signs of activity. If it erupted, the middle third of the United States could be wiped out. The students were asked what should be done. In response, they worked in groups to study volcanoes, determine the probability

---

project-based learning A teaching method that engages students in extended inquiry into complex, realistic questions as they work in teams and create presentations to share what they have learned. These presentations may take various forms: an oral or written report, a computer technology-based presentation, a video, the design of a product, and so on.

problem-based learning Focused, experiential learning (minds-on, hands-on) organized around the investigation and resolution of messy, real-world problems.

ill-structured problem A problem that lacks clear procedures for finding the solution.

that such an event would occur, and describe the effect a major natural disaster would have on jobs and politics in the region. The teacher encouraged the students to locate information on the Internet. Students prepared a final paper for this unit and also presented oral reports. Their suggestions included

- drilling into the volcano to relieve the pressure,

- developing evacuation plans, and

- not informing the public at all. Some students reasoned that because the volcano was unlikely to erupt, there was no way to predict or prevent an eruption, and widespread panic would lower property values and scare industry away from the area.

None of these suggestions were right or wrong, but each had to be supported by the students' research (Rasmussen, 1997).

I want to emphasize that project- and problem-based learning can be applied in any subject area. The next story focuses on a high school course in government in which students consider a controversial social and political issue:

In a senior-level high school government course, students are shown a video of the trial of Jack Kevorkian, a doctor who was given a 10- to 25-year prison sentence in Michigan for assisting in the suicide of a terminally ill patient. As is made clear in the video case, Dr. Kevorkian (now deceased) dismissed counsel and represented himself. He had been acquitted of similar charges several times previously, but in this case, he was found guilty of second-degree murder.

At the point when students are studying the case, Kevorkian is ill. After serving less than 10 years in jail, he has appealed for parole to the governor of Michigan. The students are asked to make the case for or against granting Kevorkian parole, using data they collect from news reports, the video case, and their own research.

Students must present an argument with no fewer than five pieces of information to support their claim. Their teacher encourages them to learn as much background information about this case as possible, including the ways this case differs from previous cases in which Kevorkian was brought to trial. Students are also required to understand the parameters of second-degree murder and to decide why or why not they believe the verdict to be just and fair.

In this class of 24 high school seniors, opinions are almost evenly split. Three groups favor granting parole, and three favor refusing parole. Students' arguments cover a wide range of topics, from the techniques for assisted suicide to the actual poisonings Kevorkian helped perform. Although no one is clearly right or wrong in the conventional sense, the quality of the problem solving influences some students to reconsider their original decisions when they have heard all the arguments.

In a conversation with the teacher, Alex Winter, I was struck by the following remark: "When students are engaged in determining solutions to problems that exist in their real world, they use all of their mental resources to contribute to the solution. I find that I have to say very little. My role is that of a mediator—organizing presentations and moderating the conversations."

Have you ever thought of teaching in the way that Winter suggests? His technique reminds us, as discussed in detail in Chapter 4, that teachers may tell students many things in the classrooms, but teaching is not telling.

To sum up the discussion of project- and problem-based learning, note that these two approaches have several characteristics in common (Torp & Sage, 2002, pp. 15–16):

- Students are engaged problem solvers.

- Students work in groups and collaborate to find the best solution to a problem.

- Teachers are coaches and guides, modeling interest and enthusiasm for learning.

- Projects or problems deal with real-life issues that students care about.

- Students use interdisciplinary resources.

- Students acquire new skills as they work on different tasks.

- Students struggle with ambiguity, complexity, and unpredictability.

Whether project- or problem-based, however, students are given the opportunity to develop a set of concepts about the topic through their own explorations and collaboration with their peers. Each project- or problem-based experience has a set of big ideas or core concepts that will result from the experience. Those ideas become internalized in a much deeper and meaningful way through the journey the students take to reach those understandings.

The STEM and STEAM Education Movements

The descriptions of project- and problem-based learning model the attributes of the STEM education movement, representing science, technology, engineering, and

▲
Students collaborate on solving a problem.

mathematics education. This multidisciplinary approach to learning invites students to understand the interconnectedness of science and technology, and the significance of applying mathematical thinking to solving problems. The NGSS (2013) emphasize the interconnectedness between science and technology content, and the ways in which scientific and engineering practices engage students in a deeper understanding of content in the life, physical, and earth and space sciences. Science and engineering practices have many parallels, and using engineering practices to support scientific ideas is just one way that project- and problem-based learning align with the STEM education agenda. For example, teachers are asked to use the processes of scientific investigation and the engineering design process to extend a typical bridge-building lesson to include many topics in science and lots of experimentation. Preparing students for the interdisciplinary challenges of the real world is the underlying goal behind the STEM education movement.

STEAM is an educational initiative that adds the arts to the STEM framework. Developed by the Rhode Island School of Design, the STEAM movement asserts that art and design must be central to education in science, technology, engineering, and mathematics. "The goal is to foster the true innovation that comes with combining the mind of a scientist or technologist with that of an artist or designer" (http://stemtosteam.org/). The STEAM movement emphasizes creativity and design, countering the system of standardized, rote learning that teaches to a test. STEAM projects invite students to solve real-world problems using the arts and STEM fields as tools. For example, a math teacher in Andover, Massachusetts, takes her students to an art museum for a class in geometry. The students learn that scale in geometry is the same thing as perspective in art (Krigman, 2014). In the real world, both scientists and engineers use models. They use sketches, diagrams, simulations, and physical models to make predictions about how a physical system may behave. Being able to sketch,

for example, helps engineers to communicate their ideas quickly. The world is rapidly becoming an environment where interdisciplinary skills and knowledge are required and valued.

Variation Among States: The Emergence of the Common Core State Standards

States develop their own standards and tests for subject areas, and there is enormous variability from one state to the next. In fact, when federal mandates required standardized testing under the No Child Left Behind (NCLB) Act, students in some states performed better on the state standardized tests than they did on national math and reading tests. Some educators believed that these states were setting the achievement bar too low. Because schools, administrators, and teachers—and the states responsible for them—faced financial consequences if students failed to show adequate progress, there was some incentive to make the standards easy to meet.

In 2009, a movement to establish common curriculum standards was begun with funding by the Gates Foundation and other philanthropic organizations. Participants included the National Governors Association and the Council of Chief State School officers. The result is the Common Core State Standards, adopted by 36 states, modified by 10 states, and only adopted for English language arts (ELA) for one state. The CCSS for language arts and mathematics is intended to help level the playing field for all the states, and its widespread use would be matched with the same standardized tests in all the states, eliminating the variability of the assessments from state to state.

It is significant to note that the CCSS set the bar for content area achievement much higher than many states have become accustomed to. The emphasis is on critical thinking and analytical skills rather than on rote memorization. The standards are not a curriculum but a guide to curriculum development, describing what students should know and be able to do in the content areas by the end of each grade level. The goals set by the standards are designed to ensure students' college and career readiness. To that end, there are large instructional shifts required of teachers as they examine the grade-level learning goals for ELA and for mathematics. Some defining features of the CCSS include:

English Language Arts

- Reading content rich nonfiction—as opposed to only reading stories

- Making claims from evidence found in texts—analyzing what we read

- Regular reading of complex texts and academic language—practice with syntax and vocabulary through more intense reading of complex texts

Mathematics

- Greater focus on fewer topics

- Linking topics across grades

- Pursuit of conceptual understanding and procedural skill and application

For both mathematics and ELA, the CCSS require students to approach topics deeply, thoughtfully, and critically, understanding the "why" behind what we say and do in each content area. There is a good deal of controversy surrounding the implementation of these standards, with teachers and administrators understanding the depth of professional development required. Many states and districts are opting out of standardized testing based on these standards until programs authentically representing their goals are in place.

The Achievement Gap

> *What might happen if we paid less attention to outcomes, as measured by test scores, and more attention to how children learn, which is one of the most important processes of education? . . . Studying the ways in which children learn could help us focus on cultural differences between and among the children who sit in the same classroom, and on how those cultural differences might be used to empower learning rather than to stand in its way.*
>
> —Ellen Condliffe Lagemann (2007)

Perhaps the most discouraging effect of the NCLB legislation has been its effect on low-achieving schools and districts, precisely the constituents it had hoped to serve. After the first 6 years under the NCLB legislation, the gap between high- and low-achieving students had actually widened (Planty et al., 2008). Although accountability is terribly important, the implementation of one high-stakes test per grade level has forced many teachers to ignore the types of creative, problem-based teaching strategies that have been discussed in this chapter—strategies that engage students in their own learning. Consequently, the very students we are hoping to hook become discouraged by a lifeless curriculum.

Moreover, many teachers themselves are discouraged by the effects of high-stakes testing on their teaching.

In a study of 376 elementary and secondary teachers in New Jersey, teachers indicated that they tended to teach to the test, often neglected individual students' needs, had little time to teach creatively, and bored themselves and their students with practice problems as they prepared for standardized testing. (quoted in Cawelti, 2006, p. 65)

A basic assumption of the U.S. Department of Education is that maintaining high expectations is necessary for improving achievement. This is, however, only one part of a potential solution. Achievement gaps between ethnic groups and groups of differing socioeconomic status are not caused entirely by schools. They are caused by powerful social and family characteristics that affect children long before they start school and continue to operate as they enter school (Brooks-Gunn, Duncan, & Aber, 2000; Hart & Risley, 1995; Lareau, 2003). This does not mean that social and economic disadvantages—the absence of social capital—cannot be overcome in schools. But substantial learning goals cannot be achieved by enforcing a standardized testing program that few low-income students can become invested in. As we noted in Chapter 5, children of poverty enter kindergarten with significant cognitive deficiencies when compared with middle-class peers. Poverty, however, is not a learning disability, and the deficits that present themselves from low-income areas can be remedied through pre-K programs and high expectations for all our students as they enter kindergarten.

Many people speak of an "opportunity gap," defined as the pervasive lack of high expectations, lower per-pupil spending, and lack of access to educational resources for many of the nation's least advantaged children. The ways in which opportunity gaps can lead to achievement gaps takes the focus off the individual students and onto the circumstances to which they were born. Despite the discouraging effects of the mandatory testing due to NCLB, the results highlighted a pervasive and serious achievement gap along the lines of race and socioeconomic status.

Alternatives to Traditional Schools: School Choice in the 21st Century

In today's national school culture, schools that do not meet state standards for 2 consecutive years are subject to penalties by individual states. Depending on where you live, parents may move their children into other, higher-performing schools. Essentially, federal law obligates school districts to replace low-performing schools. Under the new legislation, schools that miss certain targets are required to provide students with tutoring or the option to transfer. This requirement has given a boost to charter schools, which are an alternative kind of public school. Since the first charter school opened in Minnesota in 1991, the charter school movement has grown to more than 6,900 charter schools with an estimated 3 million students.

Another alternative to traditional schools is **homeschooling**. More and more parents dissatisfied with public schools have begun to investigate the options for teaching their children at home. What do you think is behind this movement?

As a teacher, you may end up working in a charter school, or you may teach children who have been homeschooled in the past.

The Rise of Charter Schools

In 1999, charter schools represented 1% of public schools; today, they are more than 6% of public schools. A **charter school** is a public school that has a specific written charter

---

homeschooling Educating children at home rather than in a school; parents typically serve as teachers.

charter schools Publicly funded elementary or secondary schools that are granted a special charter by the state or local education agency.

from the school district, the state, or another governing agency. The charter typically exempts the school from selected rules and regulations that apply to other schools. In exchange for these exemptions, the school agrees to be accountable for producing certain results set forth in the charter in a specified period of time. Every 3 to 5 years, a school's status is reviewed; the school's right to exist can be revoked if the school has not met the standards promised in the charter.

By 2017, 44 states, the District of Columbia, and Puerto Rico had established charter school laws. This means that concerned citizens, educators, or government officials can bring a plan for a charter school to the local or state education agency, and if the plan meets the established requirements, there is a strong possibility that the school can be established. In 2017, there were 17 states that had at least 100 charter schools and nine states that had over 50 charter schools. There are currently six states without charter school laws: Kentucky, Montana, Nebraska, North and South Dakota, and West Virginia.

The belief is that charter schools have the potential to develop new and creative teaching methods and that these innovations can thrive in a system that is not constrained by the usual rules and regulations. Many educators also hope that charter schools will foster a positive spirit of competition, encouraging traditional public schools to reform their practices.

While the charter school sector is rapidly growing, there is no clear evidence that charter schools are significantly more successful than traditional public schools. In 2003, The National Assessment of Educational Progress (NAEP), for example, found no significant advantages for charter schools in reading or math performance (NAEP, 2005), and low-performing charter schools have since closed. More recent assessments indicate that students in charter schools are performing, on average, as well as their public school peers. There is a great deal of variability in charter school performance. Charter schools are producing positive effects for some subgroups of students—particularly poor and Black students—and in the elementary and middle school grade levels. Urban charter schools appear to be producing much more impressive results, compared to district schools, than the total national population of charter schools, which is particularly good news given the high concentration of charter schools in our nation's largest cities (Mead, 2015).

One of the serious problems associated with charter schools in low-income areas is that they tend to enroll the highest-achieving students, leaving the traditional public schools with a less heterogeneous group of students. Consequently, the public schools from which the charter schools' students came usually experience a loss of academic standing. In some cities, those now low-performing schools are being closed.

Because many different groups of concerned citizens can start charter schools, often without any prior training in education, professionals who do research in the area of learning and teaching are concerned about the charter

school movement. Analyzing the success or failure of charter schools is complicated, however, because there are so many different types serving so many kinds of students. As one team of researchers explains:

> One of the most important difficulties in studying charter schools is that many of them are targeted specifically at particular student populations and thus serve dramatically different kinds of students than regular public schools do. Although most states require charter schools to have open enrollment policies, charter schools can still target specific populations by describing themselves as schools for a particular kind of student or by otherwise encouraging a certain kind of student to apply for admission. (Greene, Forster, & Winters, 2003)

Remember that charter schools are publicly funded but independently run, and hence it is necessary to keep asking the independently run charters, "How are you doing?" This is a reminder that teaching and learning are highly complex activities and that schools are complicated organizations functioning on behalf of diverse students with a broad range of differences.

Who Teaches in Charter Schools?

Approximately half of the charter school states stipulate that their teachers must be certified by meeting the certification requirements of their state. For the remainder, the requirements vary. In some states, individuals may apply for a waiver to the certification requirement. In the District of Columbia, teachers do not have to be certified at all. In Illinois, charter schools may be able to employ noncertified teachers if they have a bachelor's degree, 5 years' experience in the area of degree, a passing score on state teacher tests, and evidence of professional growth; for all such noncertified teachers, mentoring must be provided.

Most professional educators, like the author of this book, believe that a formal program in learning to become a teacher is vital for anyone who wants to teach. For this reason, I hope that all charter schools will eventually require certification. This will ease some of the doubts about the value of charter schools for U.S. education.

Types of Charter Schools

There is no typical charter school in the same way there is no typical public school. Be assured that charter schools vary in composition, curriculum, teacher preparation, administration, and philosophy. Some charter schools are based on a particular focus or concentration. Charter schools are designed to be innovative and sometimes emphasize a main theme, such as STEM charters or arts and music charters. Some charter school programs focus on the basics—reading, writing, and the traditional school subjects with which some students struggle. Some charters look just like traditional public schools, and some serve a particular community. Some are dropout prevention programs, adult education programs, online programs, charters that serve day care needs, and charters that work with children who want to go to college (Center for Education Reform, 2017). Despite being free public schools, charter schools are not accountable to state or local education authorities in the ways that traditional public schools are. This frees them from red tape, but it also holds them accountable only to their own charter school boards. Since they are using public funds, many taxpayers worry about the charter schools' systems of accountability.

Small Urban High Schools

One unintended result of the 2002 NCLB Act was a movement to reimagine existing schools. Many large urban school districts began to deconstruct their massive over-populated high schools and create smaller schools, sometimes focused on an area of study or a theme and often coexisting on the same large campus. The pressing problem in education remains closing the achievement gap between low-income students in urban schools—predominantly people of color—and their more advantaged, middle-class peers in predominantly White suburban schools. To that end, the Bill and Melinda Gates Foundation and other benefactors contributed funding to create high-performing high schools in urban areas. Often, this meant the closing of large urban high schools where the student population was more than 4,000 and creating smaller high schools of no more than 100 students per grade. Small schools were formed to create and sustain a culture of achievement in inner-city schools.

Recent studies have shown that students who attend the new smaller urban high schools have a better chance of graduating than those in larger urban high schools (Bloom & Unterman, 2012). Creating this change for urban youth is not without its troublesome baggage. For example, schools that are in the process of closing by losing a grade each year have abysmal graduation rates. Disadvantaged urban teens often get "lost" in the anonymity of many large urban high schools, and studies find that smaller is better because it increases opportunities for achievement and graduation. Still, the debate is not over, and many who support large urban high schools suggest that there are more course offerings and that certified personnel lead academic departments and promote professional development. Still, the small urban schools movement's success is about more than just size. New, smaller schools create specialized and rigorous curriculum and recruit teachers to their themes or dominant areas of study. In New York City, graduation rates from smaller high schools in the first decade of the 21st century were significantly higher than were the rates from their large urban counterparts. Clearly, more research is needed before definitive answers are obtained. With all the experimentation in public

school structure and design, there are more students than at any other time in the country's history who are being educated at home and not attending any school.

Homeschooling: Another Nontraditional Option

A few decades ago, homeschooling represented a fringe element of the educational landscape, but currently it is a fast-growing trend. In 1999, an estimated 850,000 U.S. students between the ages of 5 and 17 were being homeschooled (U.S. Department of Education, 2001). By 2014, the number of homeschooled children had more than doubled as more families questioned the efficacy of traditional schools in preparing their children academically and socially for a global economy and a highly competitive marketplace. (In these statistics, students are considered to be homeschooled if their parents report them as being schooled at home for at least part of their education and if their part-time enrollment in public or private schools does not exceed 25 hours a week.) At the current time, more than 2.3 million students are being homeschooled, with a vast number of websites supporting curriculum construction and resources for home-schooled children.

Homeschooling is considered one of the fastest-growing forms of education in the United States. Once thought of as the purview of White, middle- or upper middle-class families, homeschooling is gaining popularity among minorities. Families decide on homeschooling for a variety of reasons. Previously, the main thrust for homeschooling was to impart a worldview, a set of moral and/or religious beliefs to children. More recently, common reasons include individualizing the curriculum and accomplishing more academically for each child. Other reasons include safety factors, providing an environment free from physical violence, drug and alcohol abuse, bullying and teasing, and unhealthy sexuality (Ray, 2014). Clearly, some elements of homeschooling, including the lack of pressure to perform and a freedom of choice concerning the curriculum, are appealing alternatives to mandated curriculum that is based on standardized testing. Schooling children at home also allows religious training that by law their children would not receive in public school.

Some critics of homeschooling worry that most parents cannot provide the academic support their children need to learn a wide range of subjects. After all, certified teachers are trained in educational methods and in curriculum content areas, and most parents are not. However, a growing number of companies cater to parents who homeschool by providing curriculum materials. In addition, the Internet now offers an abundance of educational resources that were not available a decade ago. Many previously reluctant parents now choose to homeschool their children because of the wealth of materials available online. The significant rise of online precollege courses has been an aid and motivation for families considering homeschooling.

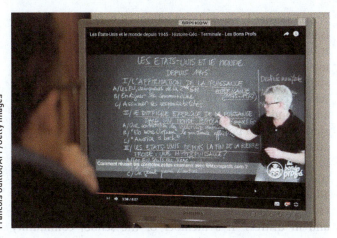

Francois Guillot/AFP/Getty Images

Middle School: A Movement in Transition

In the early 1900s, the dominant school configuration was 8 years of primary school followed by 4 years of secondary school. This "8–4" model was called into question as more and more students attended public school. In 1899, the National Education Association (NEA) issued a report calling for secondary school to begin in the seventh grade, citing that time—the beginning of adolescence—as a "natural turning point in a pupil's life" NEA, 1899). Nevertheless, it was another 15 to 20 years before the junior high school model of Grades 7 through 9 emerged and began to proliferate.

Originally, junior high schools were thought of as preparatory grounds for the academic rigor of high school. By the late 1960s and early 1970s, however, various models for reorganization of school district grades were being considered to meet desegregation requirements. Further, many junior high schools were seen as focusing on content mastery rather than on the psychological and emotional needs of early adolescents.

Some people express concern that students miss the socialization that occurs in schools. The entire experience of "going to school" is composed of much more than lessons, athletics, and theatrical and musical performances. It is a daily and annual ritual event that defines the growth and development of children. As we saw in previous chapters, many cultural beliefs and social values are transmitted through the "hidden curriculum" of schools. Students meet peers who represent a cross-section of their community—students with different learning styles, abilities, opinions, strengths, weaknesses, and ways of being in the world. So one must ask, are homeschooled children denied all these opportunities?

Proponents of homeschooling point out that parents have formed networks to engage their children in social, musical, and athletic events outside the home. Homeschooling does not mean isolation. Some studies indicate that few homeschooled children are socially deprived and that homeschooled children in general have a good self-concept. Most state governments regulate homeschooling to at least some degree. In some of these states, parents merely have to notify the educational authorities that they are schooling their children at home. In other states, parents must submit their children's test scores or other professional evaluations of academic progress. The strictest states have further conditions, such as requiring that parents file a plan or program of study before they can gain permission to homeschool their children. Since every household that home schools their children does not contribute to the tax base for public schooling, it is just one reason to keep track of this trend.

By the 1980s, many school reformers endorsed a new "middle school" concept intended to create an educational experience more appropriate for young adolescents. The goal was to make the old junior high school more developmentally responsive by changing the grade configuration from Grades 7–8 or Grades 7–8–9 to Grades 6–7–8 and designing new organizational structures such as interdisciplinary teams (Juvonen, Le, Kaganoff, Augustine, & Constant, 2004). The teams would ensure that a group or cluster of students would be taught by the same four- or five-subject area teachers, thus creating a sense of community and closeness.

In the following decades, many school districts converted their junior highs to middle schools, but the process was far from uniform. There are several ways of organizing the middle grades, and despite well-intentioned and committed educators, middle schools do not yet fully serve the needs of young teens. The history of the middle school movement suggests that the middle school became the norm because of societal and demographic pressures and not because of hard evidence to support the need for a separate school for young teens.

For these reasons, organization of the middle grades is still in flux. Recent research produced evidence that transitions to the Grade 6–7–8 middle schools were often harmful to students, citing a drop in achievement scores compared to same-age peers in K–8 schools (Rockoff & Lockwood, 2010;

WRITING & REFLECTION
HOMESCHOOLING

Imagine you are the parent of a fifth grader and you are preparing to homeschool your child. Which of the contemporary trends in education would pose the greatest challenge for you as your child's primary teacher? Explain how you would overcome the obstacles to implementing this trend.

Schwerdt & West, 2013). The middle school transition is difficult for many youngsters as they leave the self-contained supportive atmosphere of one teacher in Grade 5 and move to often seven different teachers in the school day. There are issues of adolescent aggression that confront many middle school students as well. Whereas middle schools were seen as a nurturing bridge to high school, there is now a movement in some areas back to more K–8 schools (Tamer, 2012). It may be that sixth graders are too young to make this type of transition, although there is no hard and firm evidence for that assertion. Because the U.S. educational system has been struggling with meeting the needs of early adolescents, there is concern in some parts of the country that middle schools may not be the answer. A large Florida study was able to compare students' achievement in several different grade-level school models, including K–8 and K–6, then 7–8, and then Grades 9–12 configurations. The 6–7–8 transition was found to be the place where urban youth suffered an onslaught of educational failure (Tamer, 2012). While the Florida study is concerning, there has been no broad national study to determine the optimal age and stage of development to send students into a major transition.

Creating a Safe School Climate: The Concern About Violence in Schools

Although the vast majority of the country's students will never be touched by peer violence in their K–12 school careers, serious incidents of school violence have rocked the headlines and shaken confidence in school safety. In 1999, the Littleton, Colorado, high school, Columbine, was the scene of a violent school attack by two students that claimed the lives of 14 students and a teacher. This was the most violent school attack in U.S. history until it was eclipsed by the 2007 rampage at Virginia Tech University in Blacksburg, Virginia, which claimed 32 lives, including 27 students. In February of 2012, a teenager at Chardon High School in Ohio opened fire on classmates in the cafeteria, killing three students and injuring two others. In December of 2012, a 20-year-old fatally shot 20 children and six adult staff members in a mass murder at the Sandy Hook Elementary School in Newtown, Connecticut. More recently, on February 14, 2018, a former student gunman killed 17 students at Marjory Stoneman Douglas High School in Parkland, Florida. Incensed by this challenge to their lives, Stoneman student survivors sparked a protest movement that is shaking up the establishment and putting pressure on lawmakers to eliminate the availability of guns, especially assault rifles. Other high school students have joined their Florida counterparts and staged protests locally and in Washington, DC. The state of Florida has increased the age at which an individual can legally purchase a gun to 21. Because these incidents of targeted violence have become more frequent, school shootings have prompted educators to examine how, if at all, these incidents, and other less serious ones, could have been prevented.

In Chapter 1, we explored school climate and the ways it is evident when you enter a school as a student or teacher. It may even be evident to a regular visitor. The school climate is a result of the relationships that exist among the students, teachers, parents, and administrators within the school community. In a school with a climate of safety, adults and students respect each other and, importantly, students have a positive connection to at least one adult in authority. When a climate of safety is created, it is sensed in a school; there is a feeling of emotional wellness. In this type of school climate, problems can be raised and addressed in peer groups and with counselors before they escalate. It becomes noticeable when a student is disturbed and in distress. If a member of the school community shows enormous personal pain that could lead to harm—to the student himself or herself or to others—it becomes a cry for help that is answered. The small-schools movement in large urban areas helps to ameliorate the potential for student violence simply because the smaller number of students helps to ensure that one does not get lost in a crowded school environment. Despite these attempts at school safety, schools are implementing additional specific lockdown procedures to guard against lone gunmen attacks. Teachers are being asked to participate in workshops to learn the best responses to these gun violence emergencies. Research into the causes, patterns, and perpetrators of gun violence in schools has been spotty; however, in the wake of recent school tragedies, there is a movement for further studies (Ollove, 2018).

The box titled "Creating a School Climate That Promotes Safety and Connectedness" lists some important factors that help establish a safe school climate. In Chapter 9, I discuss the classroom community and the ways to think about teaching as forging relationships with students. On a school-wide basis, all the participants in the school community—the administrators, parents, school secretaries, custodians, groundskeepers, as well as the teachers and students—must contribute to the establishment of a climate of safety.

▲ High school students on the streets of Washington, DC protesting the proliferation of gun violence in schools.

SOPA Images/LightRocket/Getty Images

CREATING A SCHOOL CLIMATE THAT PROMOTES SAFETY AND CONNECTEDNESS

Working together, the U.S. Department of Education and the Secret Service have produced a guide to help schools create a climate of school safety. According to this document, the major components and tasks for creating a safe school climate include:

Assessing the School's Emotional Climate

- How do the students and teachers experience the daily life of the school?
- Is there a culture of respect?
- Are students' emotional needs being met?
- Is everyday teasing and bullying dealt with immediately?

Creating Connections Between Adults and Students

- Do students have a positive relationship with at least one adult?
- Does each student feel there is an adult he or she can talk to about problems and concerns?

Breaking the Code of Silence

- In many schools, students believe that revealing another student's pain or problems breaks a special peer code. This belief often forces troubled students to go it alone.
- In a safe school climate, students are willing to break the code of silence to get help for a peer.

Involving Everyone

- Are all members of the school community involved in creating policy and practices that help each member respond to stressful and potentially harmful events?

Source: Fein, R. A., Vossekuil, B., Pollack, W. S., Borum, R., Modzeleski, W., & Reddy, M. (2004). *Threat Assessment in Schools: A Guide to Managing Threatening Situations and to Creating Safe School Climates*. Washington, DC: U.S. Secret Service and U.S. Department of Education.

Protecting the Rights of Students

Clearly, students have a right to be safe in school. That is one basic right that cannot be denied. What other rights do students have?

In most states, education of children has been compulsory for more than a century. Children must go to school or, as we discussed previously in this chapter, to a reasonable home-based alternative to school. Obviously, though, schools cannot do whatever they like with this captive audience. Along with schools' obligation to educate students, students deserve to have certain rights, but exactly what those rights should be is not always evident. A number of recent laws and court cases have raised serious questions about the subject. Some of the issues that have come to the fore will be explored.

Before reading further, stop a moment and think: What kinds of student rights do you suppose are covered by law? And how do you suppose the recent concern about school safety has affected students' rights?

The Right to Privacy

Do you know where all of the information about your educational history is kept? Are your health records in the same place? Does the file contain records of your student loans and other information you might not like to share with everyone? What if you have a learning disability—is that documented in your file? Who has access to this file? What are your rights?

The **Family Educational Rights and Privacy Act (FERPA)** of 1974, also known as the **Buckley Amendment**, is a federal law that requires educational agencies and institutions to protect the confidentiality of students' educational records. It applies to all school systems and individual schools, including colleges and universities, receiving federal financial assistance or funding.

FERPA allows students and their parents to have access to the student's records kept by educational institutions. The law also states that no one outside the institution may have access to a student's educational records, nor can the institution disclose any information from the records without the written consent of the student or, for students under the age of 18, their parents. Congress passed this act in response to instances of parents or students being denied access to their records or information about students being improperly used.

FERPA clearly states that parents of students in attendance at a school have the right to inspect and review the education records of their children. Further, if the parents (or students older than 18) challenge the contents of the records, they must be given a hearing. At this hearing, the parents and student have the opportunity to insert their own written explanation into the record. The intent is to make sure the records are not inaccurate, misleading, or otherwise in violation of the student's privacy or other rights.

Family Educational Rights and Privacy Act (FERPA)/Buckley Amendment
A federal law requiring educational agencies to protect the confidentiality of students' educational records.

As a college or university undergraduate or graduate student, you should know what is in your personal records at your institution. Once you are 18 years old, your parents have no inherent right to inspect your educational record; that right becomes yours alone. Parents may, however, gain access to so-called directory information, which includes simple facts that would not compromise a student's privacy, such as enrollment status, major field of study, degrees received, and so on.

Recent Challenges to FERPA

Until 2001, no cases involving violations to FERPA were brought to the U.S. Supreme Court. In 2001, however, the court heard a case concerning the oral reporting by peers of student grades. In Oklahoma, in the Owassa Independent School District, a mother was disturbed when her son's teacher asked the class to grade each other's quizzes and then had students call out the grades so she could record them. This mother felt that the calling out of grades by her son's peers was a violation of his right to privacy. She lost the case; the Supreme Court ruled that peer grading did not violate FERPA.

A second case was brought to the Supreme Court by a college student at Gonzaga University in Washington State. The teacher certification officer at that university overheard a student discussing a teacher candidate's alleged sexual harassment of another student and proceeded to conduct an investigation, place remarks about it in the student's record, and deny teacher certification to that student. The supposed victim of the sexual harassment denied that it occurred and never pressed charges. The alleged offender sued the university for violating FERPA. This case made its way through various levels of the state court system and finally reached the U.S. Supreme Court in 2002. The justices ruled that FERPA did not give "enforceable rights" to individuals. Rather, it was up to the Department of Education to enforce FERPA by denying funding to educational institutions that violated the law.

Although this Supreme Court ruling may prevent individual students from collecting damages for violation of their privacy, FERPA still offers protection through the power of the purse. Because educational institutions do not want to lose their federal funding, they will be careful about allowing practices that infringe on rights established by FERPA.

Compromises on Privacy

In this age of readily accessible data, it often feels as though anyone can gain access to another person's information just by having Internet access and finding that person on Facebook. It is not quite that easy to get educational records. Unfortunately, however, since the Columbine High School shooting in 1999, educators and police agencies have felt an increased need to identify, collect, and share information in a coordinated effort to prevent a recurrence of this type of student violence. Events such as the terrorist attacks at the World Trade Center towers and the Pentagon on 9/11 have also made the sharing of information seem more imperative.

The scope of student data collected has expanded greatly since FERPA was passed in 1974. For example, student records now include data relating to the student's needs for specific educational services. Moreover, requests for student information now come from a growing number of sources inside school systems (including counselors, principals, school social workers, special education personnel, classroom teachers) and outside school systems (military recruiters, university researchers, law enforcement officers, the courts, college admissions personnel, the media, social services agencies, and others).

Some additional laws do help protect the new wealth of information. IEPs are protected under IDEA, and parents must have ready access to their child's IEPs. However, the information in an IEP is considered confidential, and schools are restricted from releasing it to people who do not have a legitimate educational interest in the child. Similarly, federal law ensures the right to privacy of individual students' scores. Nevertheless, the USA PATRIOT Act of 2001 created the possibility that, with a subpoena, authorities could gain access to a student's confidential information without the knowledge of the student or the parents (Vacca, 2004).

Clearly, educational institutions need to exercise careful monitoring of when and to whom student data are released. As a teacher, you, too, should be sensitive to your students' rights to privacy.

STUDENTS' AND PARENTS' RIGHTS UNDER FERPA

- The right to inspect and review educational records.
- The right to request amendment of educational records.
- The right to exercise some control over the disclosure of information from educational records.

- The right to file a complaint with the U.S. Department of Education if a school or other educational agency fails to comply with the act.

First Amendment Rights of Students

Congress shall make no law respecting an establishment of religion, or prohibiting the free exercise thereof; or abridging the freedom of speech, or of the press; or the right of the people peaceably to assemble, and to petition the Government for a redress of grievances.

—The First Amendment to the U.S. Constitution

Bettmann/Getty Images

It is commonly accepted that, in schools and classrooms, the need for legitimate teaching and learning requires rules of behavior that, at times, restrict the speech of students. Yet the Supreme Court ruled in *Tinker v. Des Moines* that "students do not shed their constitutional rights when they enter the schoolhouse door." In this 1969 ruling, the Supreme Court upheld the First Amendment right of high school students to wear black armbands in a public high school as a form of protest against the Vietnam War. Wearing the armband was considered symbolic speech. According to the court, school administrators could prohibit the armbands only if the administrators showed that the protest would cause a substantial disruption of the school's educational mission. (Do you think the case would have come out differently if school administrators had demonstrated that the armbands caused loud debates to break out in class?) Similarly, in the 1973 case of *Papish v. the Board of Curators of the University of Missouri*, the Supreme Court ruled in favor of the First Amendment rights of Barbara Papish, a graduate student, after the university expelled her for distributing a controversial leaflet containing profanity and a cartoon of policemen raping the Statue of Liberty.

Other court decisions, however, have supported schools in their attempts to restrict students' speech. In 1986, the court ruled in favor of the right of Washington State high school administrators when they disciplined a student for delivering a campaign speech that was full of sexual innuendo at a school assembly. In this case, *Bethel School District No. 403 v. Fraser*, the court expressed the view that school administrators had the right to punish student speech that violated school rules and that interfered with legitimate educational objectives. As another example, in the 1988 case of the *Hazelwood School District v. Kuhlmeier*, the court upheld the right of school administrators to censor materials in a student-edited newspaper that concerned sensitive issues, such as student pregnancy, that could be considered an invasion of privacy. Also accepted is the school district's right to impose dress-code restrictions on students—and teachers. Schools may require students to wear uniforms, and they may also impose reasonable grooming and dress codes for their teachers.

Overall, it seems that the Supreme Court has tried to strike a balance between the right to free expression and schools' need to maintain a productive learning atmosphere. In day-to-day terms, teachers and administrators make their own decisions on the basis of established school policies as well as common sense. Think back to the speech and dress policies of the schools you have attended. Do you think a reasonable balance was struck between individual rights and an orderly learning environment?

The First Amendment also addresses freedom of religion, and here the issues become even thornier and more confusing, as noted in Chapter 5. There are many legal questions surrounding the separation of church and state and the First Amendment's clause about free exercise of religion. In general terms, public schools must remain neutral about religious beliefs, but does this mean, for instance, that a student-led religious group cannot meet on school grounds? Does it mean that teachers cannot lead their students in reciting the Pledge of Allegiance, which includes the phrase "under God"?

The courts have been actively tackling these issues, and decisions made over the next few years may affect your classroom. Right now, to sum up the impact of various laws, court cases, and federal guidelines, it is fair to say that the following rules apply:

1. Prayer cannot be a regular part of the public school day.

2. Worship services, including Bible readings, may not be practiced in public school.

3. Public schools may not intrude on a family's religious beliefs.

4. Teachers and administrators in public schools may not advocate religious beliefs.

5. Extracurricular religious groups may meet on public school grounds as long as they are not led by a teacher or school official.

6. Many states require that schools include the Pledge of Allegiance in their daily schedules, but the practice remains the subject of court challenges. Individual students may not be forced to salute the flag if this conflicts with their religious beliefs.

The Rights and Responsibilities of Teachers

Like students' rights, teachers' rights are protected by the Constitution. As agents of the government, public school teachers are protected by state constitutional provisions, statutes, and regulations as well. They are also held accountable to these regulations and may be dismissed if they are not meeting their obligations. This section gives a brief overview of the legal rights and responsibilities attached to the teaching profession.

Teachers' Rights

Although private school teachers do not enjoy as much protection as public school teachers, both are protected by the Civil Rights Act of 1964, which prohibits racial, sexual, or religious discrimination in employment. Teachers' employment rights are further protected by the due process clause of the 14th Amendment to the Constitution, which provides that no state may "deprive any person of life, liberty, or property, without due process of law." This **due process** requirement means that school boards and state agencies must follow established rules when deciding to dismiss or discipline a teacher.

In most states, teachers are also protected by **tenure** statutes. These statutes define a probationary period during which a teacher's performance is evaluated. If the performance is deemed acceptable, a teacher may receive tenure, and then his or her contract is automatically renewed each year unless there is a specified cause for dismissal. Legitimate causes for dismissal vary from state to state. In Illinois, for example, a teacher's certificate may be revoked or suspended for immorality, a health condition detrimental to students, incompetence, unprofessional conduct, neglect of duty, willful failure to report child abuse, or "other just cause" (Illinois School Code, section 21–23a). Many public policy officials protest that teachers' tenure status is too difficult to revoke once a teacher has earned tenure. This is the subject of much controversy today as teachers' unions are being challenged by state and federal policies mandating rigorous evaluation of teachers and, in some cases, the abolition of tenure.

Teachers have a number of other rights, such as freedom of expression and the right to personal privacy. The Civil Rights Act of 1964 prohibits racial, sexual, or religious discrimination in employment. By tradition, a teacher is reasonably free to teach according to his or her best understanding of subject matter and instructional methods. But the content taught by the teacher must be relevant to and consistent with the teacher's responsibilities; a teacher cannot promote personal or political agendas in the classroom.

Community members gather in support of school improvement.

Bloomberg/Getty Images

Protected by the First Amendment, teachers can express their personal opinions; however, they must not use this freedom to undermine authority and adversely affect the working relationships in a school. Teachers enjoy limited rights to personal privacy. A teacher's personal life may lead to disciplinary action only if it affects the integrity of the school or district and hampers the teacher's effectiveness.

Teachers' Legal Responsibilities

Teachers have many ethical and professional responsibilities to their students, the parents, the school, and the district. They also have certain legal responsibilities, established by state law or by court cases.

For example, teachers must take reasonable precautions to keep their students safe. If such precautions are neglected, the teacher or the school may be held legally responsible. Teachers and schools have been sued when students were injured in the classroom, on the playground, or on field trips.

One important legal requirement is that teachers must report child abuse and negligence when they believe they have noticed it in one of their students. Child abuse is a state crime, and each state has specific reporting guidelines. Consider North Carolina's statute:

> Any person or institution who has cause to suspect that any juvenile is abused, neglected, . . . or has died as a result of maltreatment, shall report the case of that juvenile to the director of the department of social services in the county where the juvenile resides or is found. The report may be made orally, by telephone, or in writing. The report shall include . . . the name and address of the juvenile . . . the nature and extent of any injury or condition resulting from abuse [or] neglect . . . and any other information which the reporter believes might be helpful in establishing the need for protective services or court intervention. (quoted in Smith & Lambie, 2005)

due process A formal process, such as a legal or administrative proceeding, that follows established rules designed to protect the rights of the people involved.

tenure A status granted to a teacher, usually after a probationary period, that protects him or her from dismissal except for reasons of incompetence, gross misconduct, or other conditions stipulated by the state.

In some states, teacher candidates must complete child abuse seminars before they are allowed to have their own classrooms. In these seminars, they learn the symptoms of child abuse, sexual abuse, emotional abuse, and neglect. In many school systems across the country, there are support services to help teachers by providing in-service classes on child, sexual, and emotional abuse and neglect.

Many districts also have specific procedures for reporting bullying and sexual harassment among students. Teachers cannot sweep these incidents "under the rug"; they must report them in a timely fashion. In Chapter 9, this subject is discussed again because it is a crucial part of building classroom community.

Concluding Thoughts

From inclusion to gifted education, and from problem-based learning to test preparation, public schools in the United States struggle to find the best way to educate all of their students. *Complex, diverse,* and *challenging* are good adjectives to describe students and the world in which they are educated. Pursuing a career in education requires that you consider all these factors, but it also holds the promise of making a difference for the most vulnerable of our citizens—our children.

There is a strong possibility that the school or district in which you teach will have inclusion classrooms because nearly 10% of all students in public schools have a disability. You will be exposed to approaches such as project- and problem-based learning that can make your students' school experience truly challenging and rewarding. At the same time, you will need to deal with the Common Core State Standards and the testing associated with them in the content areas of English language arts and mathematics. You will also be asked to protect the rights of your students as you seek to contribute to a climate of safety and equity. You may be asked to participate in school safety professional development including the responses to gun violence in the schools.

You may be drawn to the charter school movement, which seeks alternative ways to educate students who are often ignored by traditional schools. You may be part of an antibullying task force in your school. You may be asked to teach to the test in your school or district and explore how you can do that and implement project-based learning at the same time. Wherever contemporary trends and pressing issues lead, there will be new ones to catch up to, especially as digital communication continues to challenge the way we think about teaching and learning.

There are contradictions here—forces pulling you in different directions. Being a teacher means finding your own way of reconciling these various demands. In the next chapter, information technology, no longer a trend but an integral way of life that is finding a home in the world of teaching and learning, will be explored. It, too, brings both demands and significant benefits for you and your students.

CHAPTER REVIEW

Key Terms

charter schools (p. 98)

cooperative learning (p. 94)

differentiated instruction/ differentiation (p. 92)

due process (p. 106)

exceptional learners (p. 88)

Family Educational Rights and Privacy Act (FERPA)/Buckley Amendment (p. 103)

homeschooling (p. 98)

ill-structured problem (p. 95)

individualized education program (IEP) (p. 90)

learning disability (p. 89)

least restrictive environment (p. 88)

mainstreaming (p. 88)

maker movement (p. 88)

problem-based learning (p. 95)

project-based learning (p. 95)

Response to Intervention (RTI) (p. 90)

special education (p. 88)

STEAM education (p. 88)

STEM education (p. 88)

tenure (p. 106)

Universal Design for Learning (UDL) (p. 91)

Review the Learning Outcomes

Review each section of the chapter and answer the following:

LO 6-1 Discuss the advantages of inclusion for special needs and general education students.

LO 6-2 *Exceptionality* refers to populations of students who have special needs and who are gifted and talented. In what ways are meeting their needs the same?

LO 6-3 Why is differentiated instruction one way to satisfy the diverse learning needs of students?

LO 6-4 How does the social and emotional learning movement meet the needs of all students?

LO 6-5 How are project- and problem-based learning related to the STEM and STEAM movements?

LO 6-6 How do the Common Core State Standards affect curriculum?

LO 6-7 How can charter schools and homeschooling meet the needs of some students?

LO 6-8 What are the elements of a strong safety protocol for schools?

LO 6-9 What are the dominant features of students' rights?

LO 6-10 Discuss how teachers' rights are protected.

InTASC Standards

Review the InTASC Standards for the chapter and explain how the chapter addressed each one.

Standard 1: Learner Development

Standard 2: Learning Differences

Standard 3: Learning Environments

Standard 5: Application of Content

Standard 9: Professional Learning and Ethical Practice

Journal Prompt

Discuss a current trend in teaching that poses a challenge to you as a future teacher.

Get the tools you need to sharpen your study skills. SAGE edge offers a robust online environment featuring an impressive array of free tools and resources.

Access practice quizzes, eFlashcards, video, and multimedia at **edge.sagepub.com/koch4e**.

7

Classroom Teaching
in a Digital World

On any given day, the average American teenager consumes just under nine hours of entertainment media, excluding time spent in school or for homework.

—Common Sense Media, 2015 Census

iStock/MachineHeadz

Classroom Teaching in a Digital World

On any given day, the average American teenager consumes just under nine hours of entertainment media, excluding time spent in school or for homework.

—Common Sense Media, 2015 Census

Learning Outcomes

After reading this chapter, you should be able to:

7-1 Discuss how student immersion in social media and their use of smartphones impacts teaching and learning in the classroom.

7-2 Describe the debate about using smartphones in the classroom: pros and cons.

7-3 Describe how teachers can help students manage information overload.

7-4 Explain how Internet technology can support learning.

7-5 Discuss the importance of teaching about Internet safety.

7-6 Analyze why having Internet access only at school is not enough in today's educational landscape.

7-7 Examine how assistive technology in the classroom can benefit students with disabilities.

InTASC Standards

- Standard 3: Learning Environments
- Standard 5: Application of Content

- Standard 8: Instructional Strategies

Communication and access to information has been radically transformed in the 21st century. While the technology revolution began decades ago, access to sources of information through the Internet and the use of social media have inundated our culture and our world, creating an environment vastly different from the one that existed only 10 years ago. Far-reaching changes in digital technologies have produced large shifts in our ways of thinking and behaving, leading us to reconsider the act of teaching and learning in light of how we use digital technology. Mobile devices allow for accessing the Internet wirelessly and constantly. How often do you text? Shop online? Check Facebook? Use Instagram? Use Snapchat? The smartphone has also given way to an explosion in teens' media consumption, and the rise of media multitasking habits has followed. Mobile devices account for nearly half of the screen time used by tweens (ages 8–12) and teens (ages 13–18). A 2017 survey of more than 5,000 American teens found that three out of four owned an iPhone (Twenge, 2017). With access to the Internet and social media apps in the palm of their hands, today's tweens and teens live very different daily lives than their predecessors. The students born between 1995 and 2012 in every corner of the nation and in every type of household, rich or poor, of every ethnic background, are living their lives on their smartphones. Where there are cell towers, there are teens on smartphones (Twenge, 2017).

Teenagers send, on average, about 4,000 text messages a month, with girls texting over 1,000 more messages per month than their male peers. Teens connect through social media sites, often experiencing the need to be connected as a form of "addiction." Understanding how our students are spending their time with digital technologies requires us to reconsider how we teach and how students learn, perhaps integrating their devices in meaningful ways. In this chapter, we explore the possibilities, pitfalls, and advantages of engaging students in digital technologies in school and at home.

One question for you as a future teacher—for all of us in education—is this: Although all aspects of daily life have changed so dramatically, why have the design and conditions of classroom learning and teaching remained somewhat unchanged? I say somewhat because iPads and other tablets can be found in many public and private school classrooms alongside wireless laptops, and some teachers do seize the opportunity to engage their students in new learning experiences. A large number of schools have classrooms that use electronic whiteboards, and many teachers use portable wireless devices as part of their daily teaching routines. By and large, however, instruction lags behind the advances in technology. That is most pronounced in poorer school districts where the digital divide is most apparent. This refers to the "haves" and the "have-nots" in education, as some schools are more likely to be able to afford the latest technologies.

This chapter addresses the ways information, knowledge, communication, and understanding can be redefined in this period of unparalleled digital access. It also underscores the fact that the same inequities that have dogged U.S. education since its earliest days persist in the digital age.

It is important to keep in mind that even though the Internet holds the promise of infinite knowledge, what gets delivered more often than not is infinite *information* (Orenstein, 2009). Sometimes, when we are inundated with data, it is difficult to make sense of it and connect to that which is most important. It falls to the classroom teacher, in any grade level and in any subject, to ask himself or herself, "What is the best way to make use of iPads, netbooks, smartphones, streaming videos, and other communication tools that are available to my students?" For some teachers, it is overwhelming to answer this question, but to ignore what is available for teaching and learning in any area of the digital universe is to deny the way your students and you spend time outside of school. Using technological devices to enhance teaching and learning is one way of connecting to many students' lived experiences. The technology connection, however, must make sense by providing the class with an experience, a challenge, or data it could otherwise not have access to. It must also be challenged as teachers interrogate their students' use of smartphones and social media apps and help them to use their devices responsibly. Hence, in addition to teaching *with* technology, teachers are being urged to teach *about* technology.

Students and Social Media

As early as 8 years old, in second grade, students are bringing smartphones to school. Most likely, your future students will spend a good deal of time on their smartphones, and as they get older, they will be connected to social media sites that they use, in addition to texting to connect with their peers (See Figure 7.1).

Marc Prensky (2001) has referred to people who have lived all their lives with online access and digital communications as **digital natives**. It is now apparent that classroom teaching needs to acknowledge and support the ways in which you and your students are digital natives, having grown up with easy access to wireless Internet and a variety of apps that foster communication and ask users to create content and post it online. Digital technology, especially smartphone technology, is an integral part of our lives, and more and more, it is part of the work teachers do as educators in the 21st century. Do not confuse digital natives, however, with digital learners. Technology does not necessarily teach material, but it makes information and the possibilities for learning more accessible and potentially more effective.

It is also important to acknowledge that today's teens and tweens are in many ways less social than their predecessors because their social life is lived on their phones. This has important implications for encouraging healthy social dialogue in school and fostering teamwork experiences that help students gain skills in face-to-face communication.

Classrooms and Smartphones

Although smartphones have been around in the pockets and backpacks of the nation's students for several years, there remains no simple answer about what to do about them. This a critical juncture at which schools and districts need to establish policies concerning student smartphone use by assessing the degree to which wireless mobile technology should influence the school day. Since fewer elementary and middle school students carry smartphones, the issue began to dominate the discourse of high schools. There is no national database on smartphone policies; however, there are a variety of approaches, from abstinence to one day a week, or only at lunchtime and after the end-of-day bell. There are schools that allow students to carry their smartphones each day and follow the policies set down by their teachers in each subject.

Recently, elementary and middle schools have set policies limiting smartphone use and requiring a student to obtain special permission to carry one to school. Despite this, some middle school principals allow students to use their devices during lunch periods or in the hallways. There does not appear to be a consensus, because there is a lack of research exploring the effect of smartphone use on academic achievement.

Clinical psychologist Richard Freed (2015) asserts that high levels of smartphone use by teens often have a detrimental effect on achievement because teen phone use is dominated by entertainment, as opposed to educational applications, or apps. Others argue that smartphone use for learning could be a great equalizer in terms of giving children from all sorts of socioeconomic backgrounds the same device with the same potential. At least some teachers have experienced smartphone use in the classroom as less effective for students with low literacy skills who find it challenging to use smartphones (Barnwell, 2016). While a Stanford study (Darling-Hammond, Goldman, & Zielezinski, 2014) of at-risk students' learning with technology concluded that providing one-to-one access to devices in school provides the most benefit, the study did not mention smartphones as a choice tool for greater academic success.

Still, having an Internet-enabled device in the hands of every student can be a powerful tool for learning. The National Education Association has a link for using smartphones in the classroom, and teachers have found many apps that enhance student learning and performance (Graham, n.d.). For example, one app for keeping students on top of their work is Remind (www.remind.com), where students sign up to receive text messages when assignments are due. Teachers can use the app to communicate with the class and their parents. Teachers report that this app helps students get better organized. A number of apps are useful for teaching social science courses, such as iAmerica, an app for understanding U.S. history and the U.S. Constitution. Many other apps provide access to information, while video capabilities on cell phones enable students to videotape their

digital natives People who have grown up using the digital "language" of computers, video games, and the Internet.

FIGURE 7.1 ● Most Popular Teen Social Media Sites

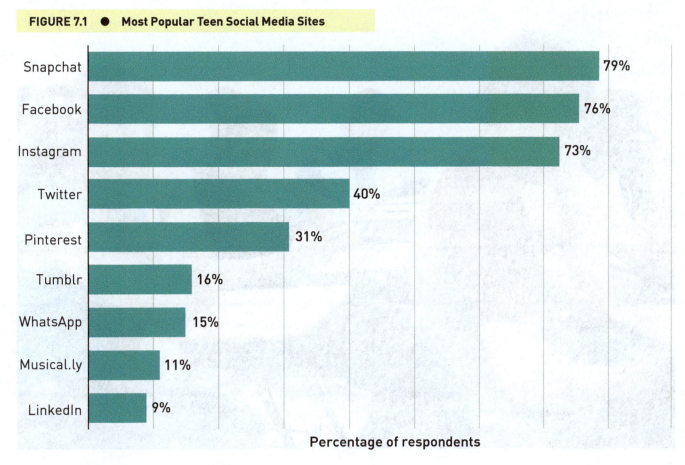

Percentage of respondents

This graph details the leading social media and networking sites used by teenagers and young adults in the United States as of February 2017.

Source: Statista. (n.d.). Reach of Leading Social Media and Networking Sites Used by Teenagers and Young Adults in the United States as of February 2017. Reproduced with permission. https://www.statista.com/statistics/199242/social-media-and-networking-sites-used-by-us-teenagers/

results in a science lab, for example, and post it to a class website. Smartphones' array of reading and writing apps are also handy for doing research, sharing blogs, e-reading, and keeping mobile diaries (Lynch, 2016). Teachers who have success using smartphones in the classroom argue that intentional use of these devices for productive work has much to teach young people.

Imagine you are in a classroom with Wi-Fi access, and your class is doing research on the causes of the Civil War. Or perhaps students are exploring a science problem related to global warming. They may be checking real-time data relevant to a topic they are studying while in the classroom. With Internet access and ubiquitous smart-phones, iPads, or tablets, the ease with which students can access a wide variety of information—and the seamlessness with which this information gathering can be integrated into the rest of their work—makes it possible for you to be truly creative as a teacher. Because there is easy access to content, today's students often do not have much patience for step-by-step instructions or carefully writing things down. Because perseverance is important in learning, integrating smartphone technology in the classroom has to be gradual and purposeful so that

students acquire new skills, not lose qualities necessary for learning. Remember, a teacher's skill, student motivation, and the context for using technology are what helps students learn, not the technology itself.

The Problem of Information Overload

Once I was a scuba diver in the sea of words. Now I zip along the surface like a guy on a Jet Ski.

—Nicholas Carr (2010)

There is a wealth of information on the Internet. Sometimes it can be overwhelming. Is there simply too much of it out there?

Information used to be scarce, and having more of it was considered a good thing. Now, it feels as though we are at a saturation point, with more information than we will ever need. One of the disadvantages of this overload is that it is easy for some students to get overwhelmed. Many teachers who use the Internet for project- and problem-based learning caution that students need to be taught how to use inquiry-based methods powered by technology. Technology has to be suited to the content and based on a true understanding

Smartphones are ubiquitous in many American high school classrooms.

of how learning occurs. How do students make sense of what they find online? Researchers have found that there is a lot of clicking from one site to another to find what they are seeking. According to Nicholas Carr (2010), "When we go online, we enter an environment that promotes cursory reading, hurried and distracted thinking, and superficial learning" (p. 116). Carr worries that people are losing their capacity for the kind of sustained, deep contemplation and reflection required to read serious works of fiction or nonfiction. With that in mind, teachers cannot automatically assume that when their students read something online they "get it." Learning is about making the material your own, mulling it over, and being able to express it and apply it in a new context. Using Carr's metaphor, the Jet Ski approach to reading text may not yield as much comprehension as the scuba diver may find.

The following story gives a simple example of the benefits of a connected elementary school classroom; you can also see how the teacher avoids the problem of overloading her students with irrelevant information:

Ms. Frank's inner-city third-grade class is studying China—a fact evident from the Chinese lanterns hanging along clotheslines overhead. In the current portion of the unit, the students are being challenged to design and construct a model of a Chinese hanging scroll. They must meet certain specifications; for instance, each scroll must provide three pieces of information about the inventions and customs of China. Today, the students are beginning the research process for completing this design challenge, and Ms. Frank is discussing how to do research on the Internet.

The students sit at rapt attention and are visibly excited about beginning the project. They listen carefully to the directions for accessing three specific websites they will need to do their research. Ms. Frank has chosen these sites in advance because they provide easy access to the information the students need, they are at the right reading level for her class, and they do not include anything inappropriate or overly distracting.

Ms. Frank announces that students will work in groups of four, and she assigns group names based on the work students have already done on this unit. The groups are called Great Wall, Yeh-Shen, Chinese New Year, Red Envelope, Chinese Lantern, and Dragon. The students nod and smile in recognition of the group names.

The students have access to tablets that use the school's wireless network to access the Internet. Students log on to the wireless network using the password Ms. Frank provides. The groups work well together, carefully accessing the three specific websites Ms. Frank has instructed them to go to. It is clear that they have done this kind of work before; using wireless tablets for research on the Internet is second nature to them. As they gather data, you can hear comments like, "The Chinese invented the compass!" and "Scroll down." Students read aloud statements about the invention of paper money and kites. In each group, the students jointly decide on the information to select from the websites, and they record their data in design portfolios. Within a few minutes, they have collected plenty of information, and they move on to the next step in designing a hanging scroll.

When a class is researching a topic on the web, it is useful to filter the websites in advance, as Ms. Frank did, so that students do not waste their time on unproductive sources. In that way, teachers help students manage the information available and avoid problems of information overload. As you prepare units for your students, look for websites with useful links for many different topics or themes. That will make it easier for you to identify good resources for particular units. In this example, the websites are a source of data that are used to complete an investigation—a design challenge. It makes it possible to have ready access to information.

Internet Technology and Learning

In Chapter 4, we saw that learning requires the learner to be actively engaged with the material to be learned. Many educators believe that technology encourages this process. Others, like Mr. Carr, worry that students lose focus online.

How exactly does technology help get students involved in learning? Entire books have been written on this subject, but here is one important point: Because new technologies are interactive, it is easier to create environments in which students can learn by doing, receive feedback, and continually refine their understanding. Through this process, students

Computer-based projects can include artifacts downloaded from the web. The potential to expand upon students' learning is part of technology integration.

Ariel Skelley/DigitalVision/Getty Images

take charge of their own learning. By integrating technology into the classroom, you promote students' passionate involvement in their own learning, allowing them to be adaptable and flexible and to go beyond "education as usual" (Fisch, 2006). Most students are also familiar with the technologies being employed for classroom learning, and they can bring the skills of their real worlds into their classroom. Interactive websites allow for content to be read, heard, observed, and experienced. The convergence of media elements such as text, audio, video, and animation into a seamless flow of content holds new promise for teaching and learning. Your role is to find the ones that have the most potential to be tools for student learning and focus the students' attention on how they will use the material and apply it to a new context.

Supporting Student Learning

The interactivity of digital technologies takes many forms, but most educators agree there are several major ways that it supports learning by (1) allowing students to deal with

GUIDELINES FOR INTERNET RESEARCH

- Research is not simply a list of questions for which students find answers. Students' research should focus on finding the information they need to solve a problem or complete a project.
- As they use technology, students need to stay focused on the problem they are trying to solve or the area they are exploring.
- Guide students in interpreting and using the data they find.
- Guide students in finding creative and innovative ways to present their information.

- Encourage students to use the information they gather on the Internet to further other students' understanding of the topic.
- Invite students to collaborate with other students in designing a final product.

Source: Adapted from B. Stoker, 6 Internet Safety Tips for Teachers https://www.studiesweekly.com/6-internet-safety-tips-for-teachers/)

real-world problems as part of the curriculum, (2) expanding the possibilities for simulations and modeling, (3) creating local and global communities of learners, (4) creating and uploading meaningful content, and (5) taking an online course or tutorial.

Real-World Problems

Technology fosters the use of real-world, exciting problems in the classroom curriculum. Imagine you are working with middle school students on a unit about weather and global warming. Using the Internet, students can find real-time weather data about present conditions as well as archival data showing trends over time. They can focus on a given part of the world or compare different areas. The learning occurs as the teacher helps the students to make sense of the data and their implications for global climate change.

Now, imagine that a high school social studies class is exploring world population, comparing the number of births per day in China, India, and the United States. From the Internet, students gather the most current information related to population growth in these countries—data that have far-reaching implications for consumption of natural resources. This kind of real-world context makes the unit come alive for students. Yet the data retrieval requires only about as much time as it takes to read this paragraph! The learning occurs as teachers help students analyze the data and draw conclusions.

Simulations, Modeling, and Augmented Reality

Students can learn a great deal through **simulations**. Often, these real-world activities would be impossible to bring into the classroom. Suppose you want your students to understand the movements of planets in the solar system. Obviously, you cannot bring Mars and Venus to class, but you can use simulation software that shows the planets in motion and allows students to view the system from different positions. The story that follows is from the author's own experience using the WorldWide Telescope (WWT), available at www.worldwidetelescope.org:

I have just returned from visiting the planets Mars, Jupiter, and Saturn. It was an exciting trip that revealed so many details of these planets—my, how huge Jupiter is! It took much longer to reach Jupiter from Earth than to reach Mars.

Okay, this was a virtual trip, but the views were breathtaking, and knowing I could "travel" anywhere in our solar system or the entire universe with my computer mouse was quite exciting. I was using the WWT available on the Internet. Replete with real images from the finest space and ground telescopes, this computer portal allows the viewer to visit real images in the solar system, the Milky Way galaxy, and beyond to other galaxies. I started on planet Earth, traveled to Mars, then Jupiter, and then on to Saturn and back to Earth. It was a quick trip in real time, but I began to get a feeling for celestial relationships: the planets that are closer to us and those that are farther, those that are much bigger than ours and those that are smaller.

WWT has been used by researchers, educators and the public to explore the universe since its release in 2008. In 2015, WWT became an open-source project supported by the broad community of users and developers. WWT blends images, information, and stories from multiple sources into a seamless, immersive, rich media experience. It allows students and adults to use its images and tell their own stories, make presentations, and share them with others. The software creates a realistic simulation with actual images taken from space. It is an extraordinary teaching tool.

Similarly, students often learn by creating **models**. For years, science students have created models of atoms and molecules, usually static ones made of plastic or Styrofoam pieces. With a computer, students can create atomic models in which the electrons move in cloudlike orbitals, and the software provides feedback about the correct number of protons and neutrons.

Do you suppose that simulations and models are useful mainly in the physical sciences? That is far from true. In social science, for example, simulations can model social dilemmas and engage students in finding their own creative solutions (see Figure 7.2).

Extending one's perceptions of the environment belongs to a class of images called **augmented reality (AR)**. AR is a live, direct or indirect, view of a physical, real-world environment whose elements are augmented by computer-generated sensory input such as sound, video, graphics, or global positioning system (GPS) data. The view of reality is modified by a computer or a smartphone application. As a result, the technology functions by enhancing one's current perception of reality. By contrast, virtual reality replaces the real world with a simulated one. AR uses the technology found in the gaming world and applies it to the real world by creating a way to infuse virtual images and events into real settings. For example, the yellow first-down line on your television screen during football games is an example of AR at work. These kinds of virtual visualizations implanted onto real settings can create historical images for real buildings, demonstrate hidden sides of protected

simulation A computer program or other procedure that imitates a real-world experience.

model A representation of a system or an object, such as a small physical structure that imitates a larger structure or a computer program that parallels the workings of a larger system.

augmented reality (AR) AR is a live, direct or indirect, view of a physical, real-world environment whose elements are augmented by computer-generated sensory input such as sound, video, graphics, or GPS data.

FIGURE 7.2 ● A Scene From American History Prior to the Revolutionary War

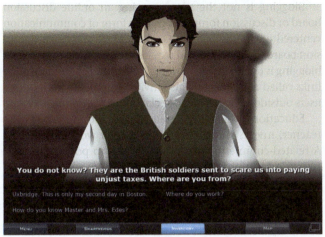

Mission US: For Crown or Colony? Produced by Thirteen Productions, LLC and WNET. Used with permission.

▲

An example of a computer generated simulation depicting events leading up to the American Revolution.

museum artifacts, or allow the user to write messages virtually on a real site. Many believe it is the future of interactivity for technology in education. Besides giving immediate feedback to users, many simulation, modeling, and AR technologies also provide opportunities for later reflection and discussion—and this point leads to a third key benefit of technology.

Communities of Learners

Many classes have their own web pages, a site where teachers communicate with students and create an online extension of the classroom. The shared class web space has many uses; the teacher can post announcements and schedules, and it can facilitate informal communication among the students and teacher.

On any given topic, teachers can promote focused discussions online through the use of discussion boards or forums. You may already have participated in such reflective discussions using Blackboard courseware or a similar course management system in your college classes. Technology-supported conversations can help students refine their thinking, and they help build a sense that everyone is working together in a learning community.

Technology easily extends the learning community beyond the immediate classroom. In Chapter 8, we examine the rise of global networks in which students from around the world collaborate to solve problems and share their cultures. Using technology, students from different places can work on the same projects with multiple solutions and collaborate via shared classroom websites, tweets, blogs, and e-mail. A deep sense of community is created as the groups work toward shared goals and communicate with one another about the strategies needed to solve a mutual problem.

The Flipped Classroom

Regardless of the subject area, many teachers, especially at the secondary level, use PowerPoint or other presentation software to present ideas to their classes. Presentation software enables teachers to record a slide show, including voiceover and annotations. The presentation can then be converted into a file that is easily distributed online and accessible to anyone with a smartphone or other device. Simply described, the flipped classroom gets its name from the distribution of classroom presentations as "homework"—what students need to examine before coming to class. Class time is then spent solving homework-type problems or responding to in-depth questions as students wrestle with the content from the presentations they examined on their own.

Often, class time is spent interacting with peers in small groups as teachers exchange ideas with students about their pressing questions and difficulties with the content. Hence, the name, the flipped classroom: homework problem solving and question answering become class time, and presentations by teachers using cutting-edge technology become homework. The technology employed is referred to as *screencasting*, and classes that employ this technology for instruction are often part of the flipped model. Screencasting is a digital recording of computer screen output, also known as *video screen capture*, containing audio narration.

As we explore what can happen when students take more ownership of their learning by examining teacher presentations prior to coming to class, we begin to see the classroom as the hub of interaction with peers and teachers that represents teaching and learning as cognitive psychologists would describe it—a dialectic, a give and take, an interaction between peers and teachers that helps students make meaning of content.

There are many versions of the flipped classroom, and there are educators who think of it more as an ideology than a methodology. That is, whatever it takes to interact with students and engage them in asking their own questions about the content and have them working in small groups to tease out meaning is an important ideology about helping students to learn. Other uses of screencasting include asking students to create a video explaining an assignment or solving a problem. You can then keep this assessment to show growth later in the year. You can enable students to become digital teachers by allowing them to create tutorials, which also demonstrates their understanding. You can share the tutorials with the class to build a classroom video library (Lynch, 2018). As you enter the teaching profession, look for its occurrence in the classrooms you observe and in which you participate. There may be several versions of the flipped classroom, but what is common to most is that interaction with students and students' interactions with each other are integral to the learning process, and presentation time through screencasting is integral to the teaching time.

QR Codes in Education

 A **QR Code** consists of black square dots that are arranged in a square grid on a white background.

"QR" Code is short for a "quick response" code. When you scan a QR code, you are transported to an online digital world. Employing the use of QR codes to direct students to online resources offers a high level of interaction. It has the potential to be very motivating for students as they use a scanning app on their smartphones or tablets and get transported to a relevant website or websites. According to Hopkins (2013), scanning a QR code can bring the digital world to the printed paper world. The digital resource to which a QR code sends you could be a website, a YouTube video, or a preformatted text message. Often, there are QR codes in commercial use—a QR code next to the advertisement for a movie will direct you to its trailer.

In the classroom, QR codes can link to sites that showcase students' work for parents and other community members. QR codes can be linked to images of historical figures, and after scanning the code, you are directed to a video of the person. A periodic table of the elements with a QR code next to each element's symbol might link to a YouTube video showing the properties of that element (Hopkins, 2013). Imagine a science fair poster board with a QR code linked to a video of the process of the experiment or sustained inquiry unfolding! QR codes can also link to students' stories about themselves as they display art work at an art expo at school. Websites are available to help you create your QR codes, and many scanning apps are free.

Creating Digital Content

A surge of new technologies and social media innovations are altering the digital landscape. Wikipedia, for example, was launched in 2001 and now features more than 40 million articles in more than 290 languages. A **wiki** is a website or other online resource that fosters collective authoring by allowing many users to add content or edit the existing content. Social media platforms such as Facebook, Twitter, and Snapchat are also avenues for changing and adding content.

Blogs

Most likely you're aware of the rapid proliferation of **blogs,** online journals on which a writer posts frequent observations and others respond with their own comments. It seems that everyone, from music fans to politicians, now has a blog. Blogs are becoming increasingly popular with teachers, too, because they offer a forum for expression for students as young as the second grade.

Blogging is not the same as using an online discussion board or discussion forum. Blogs are a form of communication centered on the individual (Ganley, 2009). Although discussion boards are directed and require specific, focused postings, blogging is open-ended, allowing users to add content through links called *tags*. Blogging also invites comments from online users outside of the immediate classroom community.

Educational blogging, guided and monitored by the teacher, invites students to publish their work on the site. A related-comments link allows readers to post comments. Hence, educational blogging gives students an opportunity not only to publish their writing but also to receive and respond to comments from their classmates and the rest of the world!

Twitter

Twitter is an online social networking service that enables its users to send and read text-based posts between 140 and 280 characters, known as "tweets." A simple form of social media, Twitter makes communication among communities quick and easy because Twitter messages have a finite number of possible characters. The service rapidly gained worldwide popularity, with more than 330 million users as of 2017. Using Twitter is a handy way to connect to other people with similar interests with whom you share ideas, ask questions, and gather data. For educators, Twitter has professional communities that link users to resources and to other teachers who share your ideas and questions. For classroom use, teachers and students can share tweets and even write a story as a collaborative community. Students can create a story taking turns to contribute one line each.

The Twitter app is used most frequently on smartphones, and it has become ubiquitous, including its use by government agencies, school districts, and high-ranking officials in many walks of life. In a classroom setting, Twitter can be used to contribute to a discussion and also gives students and teachers a way to keep the conversation going long after the class is over.

Facebook

Facebook is a social networking service and website that by 2018 had over 2 billion users worldwide. Many of you, I suspect, have your own Facebook page, as do I.

QR code A type of two-dimensional barcode that consists of black modules arranged in a square pattern on a white background. When scanned, the QR code links to a website or a video or some printed material that is available digitally.

wiki A website or other online resource that fosters collective authoring by allowing many users to add content or edit the existing content.

blog (short for weblog) An online journal using software that makes it easy for the user to create frequent entries; typically, visitors can add their own comments and responses.

Twitter An online social networking service that enables its users to send and read text-based posts of up to 280 characters, known as "tweets."

Facebook A social networking service and website that by 2018 had over 2 billion users worldwide. Users must register before using the site, after which they may create personal profiles, add other users as friends, and exchange messages, including automatic notifications when they update their profiles.

Many tweens and teens also have their own Facebook pages. As you know, users must register before using the site, after which they may create a personal profile, add other users as friends, and exchange messages, including automatic notifications when they update their profile. Additionally, users may join common-interest user groups, organized by workplace, school or college, or other characteristics.

As a teacher, you can use Facebook as a communications hub. Create a public page or smaller closed group for your classes to keep parents informed, distribute homework or permission slips, and share photos or videos from classroom activities or field trips. Anyone can "like" a page on Facebook, and students who do will see updates in their newsfeed. Groups, on the other hand, allow you to limit membership. You can also message-mail all the members of a group. Maintaining a page or group is also a useful way to establish a presence as a teacher without blurring the line between your personal and professional lives. You can interact with parents, students, and colleagues via your page or group, calling it, for example, "Ms. Smith's Ninth-Grade English Class." Of course, it is important to understand and comply with your school's social media policies.

Engaging with students online through Facebook is one way to model appropriate communication online as well as offline. Facebook publishes tips for teachers as they use this platform with their students.

Picting

Using images instead of text to convey ideas is a phenomenon known as **picting**. Facilitated by mobile apps like Snapchat and Instagram, picting is exceptionally popular with today's tweens and teens. Outside of the classroom, researchers assert that today's youth spend 90% of their time with image-based materials (Norris &

Soloway, 2017). Hence, students are coming to school with an established digital footprint on Facebook, Twitter, Snapchat, or Instagram before they even walk through the classroom door.

Snapchat, a picting site, is a social media service that allows users to send pictures and videos to their friends, and these images disappear within 24 hours. They are considered "picture conversations," and just as verbal conversations disappear, so do "snaps." Using mobile technology on their smartphones, students send and receive snaps among their group of permitted friend users. **Instagram** is another picting app; however, it is a permanent record of favorite photos or videos. Users have a profile and newsfeed similar to Facebook, and a user can adjust privacy settings on an Instagram account.

Some teachers are putting these apps to work in the classroom. One example is using Instagram to chronicle the events in the life of the classroom. A class photographer can showcase the story of your classroom and post this image story to the class website. Younger students can capture images of objects that correspond to letters on an ABC scavenger hunt.

Teachers can use Snapchat to create 10-second videos that students can record, for example, to give book reviews or to share a recommendation on the latest book they have read. Some teachers experience Snapchat as an easy way for kids to practice speaking, especially a new language (Romano-Arrabito, 2017).

Picting is another way that teachers can use the tools that students rely on outside of the classroom so that students can see school as relevant to their lives. There are critics who feel that school should be the place to escape social media apps, and they shy away from embracing new types of digital literacy.

Implications of Digital Communication

Think about the implications of Facebook, Twitter, Snapchat, Instagram, blogs, and texting. In the current wave of wireless communication, handheld devices have implications for teaching and learning and for assessment. The end user of the content or information is also an author of content along with everyone else who is interested in a given topic. This situation challenges our thinking about information and its reliability and veracity. Not only experts have access to cutting-edge information; there is increasing reliance on communities of experts that are redefined to include us all. Again, we are reminded that the most meaningful

---

FACEBOOK TIPS FOR TEACHERS

- Know your school's policy on using social media in the classroom and comply.
- Use public pages for your classes to post homework assignments and other updates.
- Use groups to control membership and facilitate discussion.
- Be a role model of a good online citizen.
- Report inappropriate content to Facebook.

Source: http://www.facebook.com/safety/groups/teachers/

---

picting Using images instead of text to convey ideas.

Snapchat A social media app that allows users to send pictures and videos to their friends, and these images disappear within 24 hours.

Instagram A social media app that allows users to maintain a permanent record of favorite photos or videos. Users have a profile and newsfeed similar to Facebook.

learning involves inquiry processes, reflection, and active, committed participation by the learner.

Parents, Teachers, and Students Online

There are new tools through which parents can track their child's progress at school. Several companies have developed software that allows parents to view a password-protected, web-based grade book that tracks student attendance, homework completion, and grades on tests and projects. The site may also be like a class webpage or Facebook page and indicate what the homework assignment is for each class, the due dates, and the criteria for the assignment. Many parents and teachers have embraced the use of these tools because it fosters consistent communication between parents and teachers. Although teachers have used e-mail as a form of communication to parents, these secure websites allow parents to intervene early if students need guidance because they can be updated daily on their child's performance. It allows teachers to communicate with parents on a timely basis.

Many software companies have specialized in services for schools, teachers, students, and parents. Often, a school, district, or county hires a software company to meet the needs of their locale by providing electronic services to teachers, parents, and students. As recently as 5 to 10 years ago, parents had to wait for written progress reports or a parent–teacher conference to learn how their children were doing in school. Now, those data may be readily available on their smartphones. Students and their parents can readily check their grades or missing assignments, often on a daily basis. Paper grade books are a thing of the past for most teachers in most schools and districts across the country. Opinion is mixed on whether the web-based record keeping is more or less work for the classroom teacher. What do *you* think?

Internet Safety

Teaching your students about safe Internet use is extremely important, whether you are using the Internet in your classroom or not. As a teacher, you need to be a trusted source for your students. As you use the apps and communication tools of everyday life, you should make your students aware of the significant dangers they might encounter with their online presence. The following suggestions are guidelines for safe Internet use with your students.

- **Read and reference your school or district's Acceptable Use Policy.** Be sure you are familiar with your school or district's guidelines for proper Internet use.

- **Teach students about legal issues surrounding Internet use.** Teach your students not just how to use the Internet but also about plagiarism and copyright issues, and how to effectively use the Internet to perform research.

- **Have lessons on Internet safety.** Be sure your students are aware of how to avoid websites with inappropriate messaging, including those that are violent, objectionable, or pornographic. Good resources may be found at NetSmartz.org.

- **Know what they're up to when you're not around.** Keep informed of what students are doing online when you are not around. Ask them about the apps they use most and how much time they are spending on screens. Show them you are interested in their well-being and debate the pros and cons of screen time.

- **Protect your online identity.** The interactive, two-way nature of the web gives marketers the ability to collect data about individual computer users. Companies collect personal information about children and teens as their websites encourage youngsters to share their hobbies, interests, and other personal preferences. This invasion of privacy is commonplace on the Internet.

- **Have an open-door policy about cyberbullying and Internet safety.** Cyberbullying can have devastating consequences for individual students, for which some school districts are held liable. Cyberbullying refers to willful and repeated harm inflicted through the use of electronic devices. It occurs when a child, preteen, or teen is tormented, threatened, harassed, humiliated, embarrassed, or otherwise targeted by another child, preteen, or teen using the Internet, interactive and digital technologies, or smartphones. Cyberbullying has become more prevalent as teens' use of texting, Facebook, Instagram, Snapchat, and Twitter on their smartphones has skyrocketed in the last 5 years. Chapter 9 addresses this issue in depth.

Source: Adapted from B. Stoker, "6 Internet Safety Tips for Teachers," https://www.studiesweekly.com/6-internet-safety-tips-for-teachers/

All of these are important issues, and school districts have taken steps to address them. Most school districts and libraries have installed blocking and filtering technologies to safeguard against offensive websites. Schools and districts are also implementing Internet safety workshops and discussions. As a teacher, you need to be aware of the potential problems in students' Internet and wireless electronics use and make sure sufficient safeguards are in place. Chapter 9 addresses how to create community in the classroom and provides more information on cyberbullying.

WRITING & REFLECTION
FACEBOOK AND YOU

Think about how you use Facebook. Consider how you would use a Facebook page with a seventh-grade social studies class. What might be the title of the page? What images would you post? How could it help students learn about a topic? What is the nature of the discourse on this Facebook page? Discuss how using Facebook could be both a boon to student understanding and a burden for classroom teachers.

The Digital Divide

Although all students are expected to develop **digital literacy,** some struggle if they come from schools and home backgrounds in which technology is not widely accessible. In a world that is so information rich, we have to remember that technology access is not equal. The American Library Association's (2018) Digital Literacy Task Force states that digital literacy is "the ability to use information and communication technologies to find, evaluate, create, and communicate information, requiring both cognitive and technical skills."

The **digital divide,** a term coined by David Bolt (2000) in a book of the same name, is "the gap between those with regular, effective access to digital technologies and those without" (p. 17). On one side of the divide, people have easy access to technological resources and know how to use them. On the other side, people have substantially less access, less experience, and correspondingly less knowledge about how to use the technology. The distinction is not only between those who have computer access at home and those who do not. The digital divide also refers to the quality of hardware, software, and connectivity that is available to users across social classes. Who are those with less technological access and experience? Families living below the poverty line rarely have computers and broadband connections in their homes (see Figure 7.3). Students living in poverty are twice as likely as other students to access the Internet at school only. Although instructional computers, tablets, and laptops with wireless access have become commonplace in high-needs, high-poverty schools, these tools do not fully make up for the lack of mobile technology access outside of school. America's digital divide is also a matter of geography, with about 25% of rural communities having no access to broadband Internet service. Students in poor rural areas rarely have access to Internet-enabled public libraries or coffee shops. Access to the Internet at home has been found to be an important factor in students' ability to use digital resources for word processing, information processing and presenting, and connecting through social media platforms.

The Pew Research Internet Project reported that 89% of Americans use the Internet (Anderson, Perrin, & Jiang, 2018). Of those who lack a high-speed connection at home, 11% have smartphones that can access the Internet. They found that age, education, and household income were the strongest predictors of broadband adoption. The number of people who use a dial-up connection for Internet access has held steady at 3% of American households. Researchers have determined that the quality of work that can be done through Internet access is hindered by connections such as dial-up due to the speed of connectivity. Even smartphones offer limitations not shared by broadband connections. To help underserved populations develop digital literacy, a means of closing this technology gap caused by lack of access at home and in informal learning environments where young people are increasingly using small mobile devices to access the Internet must be found.

Assistive Technology

The term **assistive technology (AT)** refers to devices that promote greater independence for people with disabilities by enabling them to perform tasks that would otherwise be difficult or impossible. AT can take many forms, from simple to complex. For students with visual impairments, for example, a simple type of AT is a keyboard with large symbols that makes it easier for the students to type. A more complex form is speech recognition software that converts the student's spoken words into text on the screen. Similarly, screen reader software can read aloud the information displayed on a computer screen.

In the past, for blind students who read by means of braille (a writing system that uses raised dots identifiable by touch), curriculum materials were usually converted through a lengthy process that required 2 to 4 weeks' lead time. Now, with computer technology, relevant materials can be converted at the time they are needed. With a computer program, text that the teacher types into a word-processing document is transformed into braille

digital literacy The ability to use information and communication technologies to find, evaluate, create, and communicate information, requiring both cognitive and technical skills.

digital divide The gap between those with regular, effective access to digital technologies and those without.

assistive technology (AT) A device or service that increases the capabilities of people with disabilities.

FIGURE 7.3 ● Lower-Income Americans and Technology

Lower-income Americans continue to lag behind in technology adoption

% of U.S. adults who have the following . . .

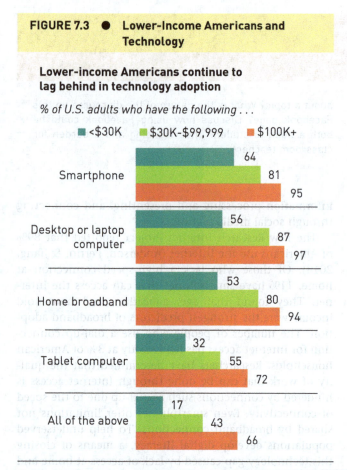

■ <$30K   ■ $30K-$99,999   ■ $100K+

Smartphone
64
81
95

Desktop or laptop computer
56
87
97

Home broadband
53
80
94

Tablet computer
32
55
72

All of the above
17
43
66

Source: Pew Research Center. (2017, March 21). *Lower-Income Americans Continue to Lag Behind in Technology Adoption.* http://www.pewresearch .org/fact-tank/2017/03/22/digital-divide-persists-even-as-lower-income-americans-make-gains-in-tech-adoption/ft_17-03-21_low-incometech_adoption

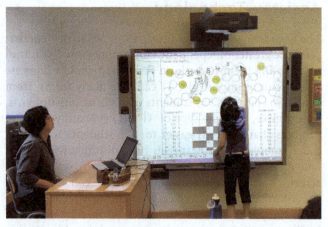

ullstein bild/ullstein bild Premium/Getty Images

▲ A SMART Board assists a student with disabilities by providing interactive technology controlled by the student and displayed for the class.

and printed on a braille printer within seconds. This technology makes it possible for the teacher to include blind students in the same activity as the rest of the class at the same moment.

For disabled students whose fine-motor skills do not allow them to write easily and without pain, note taking is

an arduous task. Teachers with interactive whiteboards in their classrooms can save the notes written on the board and print them for these students. An **interactive whiteboard,** typically the size of a regular chalkboard, is linked to a computer. Teachers can project images from the computer onto the board. When a student or the teacher writes on the board with a special marker, the notes can be saved as text in the computer.

In the following story, students with a wide range of learning disabilities experience a lesson on maps using a SMART Board, a brand of interactive whiteboard:

On the day that I visit their classroom, the 10 students in Ms. Mandel's self-contained special education second-grade class are learning about maps. Seated on a carpeted area in front of a SMART Board, they tell me that a map is a bird's-eye view of the earth from above.

Ms. Mandel chats with the children about maps that are found on the subway, on trains, in the mall, and at a major sports complex. She uses the SMART Board to display different types of maps. One map has roads, street names, stores, gas stations, and houses. There is a produce map with images relating to fruits and vegetables grown in New York, where the school is located. Still other maps show weather changes, vacation spots, and geographic features.

The children can manipulate a pointer and direct it to different images on the map. By manipulating the image of a car or a plane, they can take a ride from one destination to another. Taking turns with the pointer, the students respond to questions on cards located in a wall "pocket" next to the SMART Board. Each card has a number corresponding to the map type and a question like, "How would you get from Amy's house to The Home Depot?" or "What is the name of the town closest to the dairy farm?"

Deeply engaged in this activity, the students do well manipulating objects and moving them to destinations on the SMART Board. They are using the technology creatively. One student tells me, "We are having a great time." The questions on the cards involve the class in interpreting symbols, locations, and directions, and I am struck by the way these students with various learning disabilities are making sense of the maps and are developing higher-order thinking skills.

This story highlights ways technology can reduce or eliminate the barriers to learning experienced by students with disabilities. But do not suppose that only special technology is suitable for these students. The technology you use with all your other students—the same technology that enhances meaningful learning, reflection, and discussion—also provides benefits for those who are

. . . .

interactive whiteboard A whiteboard that works together with a computer to display and save information.

disabled. For instance, a student who struggles to write with pen or pencil may find it much easier to write on a computer. A wide range of software programs are available that help students with writing, reading, mathematics, and general organizational skills. This is another reason why easy access to Internet technology is essential for all Americans.

Concluding Thoughts

Although teachers look forward to new ways of teaching students, they face many challenges imagining how the traditional classroom is becoming transformed to reflect the high-tech world around us. Remember that as exciting as the new technologies are, they are tools for learning and teaching, not the end in itself.

In today's classrooms, the traditional hierarchy is deconstructed. Many students can find information as quickly as teachers can, and that means our role as teachers must change accordingly. Teachers should take full advantage of the ways technology can promote independent learning through real-world projects, simulations, and collaborative investigations. At the same time, teachers have to guide students in negotiating the overload of information so that they use their time wisely and focus on greater depth than may be possible from casual surfing of websites.

Teachers should make sure that students gain the digital literacy they will need in later life. To do so, teachers need to meet their own high standards for understanding technology and its uses in education. Further, teachers need to seek ways to use technology to "level the learning field" so that all of the students are served equitably by our schools.

We now know that the average young American spends nearly every waking minute, except for the time in school, using a smartphone or another electronic device. Consider how empowering it would be for educators and students to use these devices for the very purpose of teaching and learning. In the next chapter, we consider online learning and the role that popular course and tutorial sites play in teaching and learning, and perhaps in your future classroom.

CHAPTER REVIEW

Key Terms

assistive technology (AT) (p. 121)
augmented reality (AR) (p. 116)
blog (short for weblog) (p. 118)
digital divide (p. 121)
digital literacy (p. 121)
digital natives (p. 112)

Facebook (p. 118)
Instagram (p. 119)
interactive whiteboard (p. 122)
model (p. 116)
picting (p. 119)
QR code (p. 118)

simulation (p. 116)
Snapchat (p. 119)
Twitter (p. 118)
wiki (p. 118)

Review the Learning Outcomes

Review each section of the chapter and answer the following:

LO 7-1 How do you think today's students' attachment to their smartphones affects their school lives?

LO 7-2 What is your opinion of using smartphones in the classroom?

LO 7-3 How can teachers help facilitate information access on the Internet?

LO 7-4 How can learning be made more accessible using the Internet?

LO 7-5 What are the important aspects of Internet safety for students?

LO 7-6 How is the digital divide an example of inequality in the United States?

LO 7-7 When would you use assistive technology with your students?

InTASC Standards

Review the InTASC Standards for the chapter and explain how the chapter addressed each one.

Standard 3: Learning Environments

Standard 8: Instructional Strategies

Standard 5: Application of Content

Journal Prompt

What digital tools can you imagine using with your future students?

Get the tools you need to sharpen your study skills. SAGE edge offers a robust online environment featuring an impressive array of free tools and resources.

Access practice quizzes, eFlashcards, video, and multimedia at **edge.sagepub.com/koch4e**.

Tanya Constantine/Blend Images/Getty Images

The Global Classroom

More people collaborate and connect on more stuff than
in any other time in the history of the world.

—Thomas Friedman, *The World Is Flat* (2006)

Learning Outcomes

After reading this chapter, you should be able to:

8-1 Explain how online high schools can foster critical thinking and collaboration in the global marketplace of ideas.

8-2 Explain why globalization can enhance the learning experiences and the lives of today's students.

8-3 Describe how the language of the digital age and serious learning games help students take control of their own learning.

InTASC Standards

- Standard 3: Learning Environments
- Standard 6: Assessment

- Standard 8: Instructional Strategies

This chapter explores how digital communication has made connecting with ideas and people from around the world a part of the everyday classroom experience. As a result of seamless and portable access to the Internet, students and teachers from all over the world can communicate electronically, sharing their cultures, their school lives, and their larger world. Students can work side by side even if they live thousands of miles apart. They can take courses online from anywhere in the world, and online high schools are emerging as the line between virtual and classroom-based learning continues to blur. It is unclear how many K–12 students take online classes, because states have not been tracking courses taken online. However, researchers have estimated that in 2017, there were over 3 million students taking more than 4.5 million courses online (Herold, 2017). Online course enrollment continues to grow. In addition to individual courses, there are students enrolled in online schools. In each state, there is a rise of cyber charter schools, publicly funded but privately run. In many states, thousands of students are enrolled full time in online schools commonly known as *virtual schools*; however, there has been little research exploring how these schools are doing. Online schools may be state run, privately managed, or cyber charter schools. Several elite online high schools are privately managed by universities. Online teaching and learning have important implications for how students learn on smartphones, tablets, and computers.

Online Education in the Knowledge Economy

Teachers are educating students to become part of an information society in which the creation, distribution, and manipulation of information is a significant economic and cultural activity. As part of what is known as the **knowledge economy**, businesses operate through the collaboration and shared problem solving of people across the globe, transforming information into creative innovations for an ever-changing technological world.

In June 2017, 74 students graduated from Stanford Online High School (SOHS), begun by the elite university of the same name. The University of Nebraska, Brown University, Yale University, National University, George Washington University, Cornell University, Indiana University, and the University of Missouri are among many other colleges and universities that are awarding high school diplomas while charging private school tuition and offering financial aid. In addition, thousands of other students enrolled in concrete schools take one or more online courses per year from the many offerings available through new online high schools sponsored both by universities and rapidly proliferating for-profit online schools. Over 3 million precollege students and more than 8 million college students take at least one online course per academic year. Perhaps you are taking the course for which this book was written online!

The term **online learning** is used to refer to a wide range of programs that use the Internet to provide instructional materials and facilitate interactions between teachers and students, and in some cases among students as well. Online learning can be fully online, with all instruction taking place through the Internet, or online elements can be combined with face-to-face interactions in what is known as *blended learning* or *hybrid courses* (Staker, 2011). Although there is little research to date examining the

---

knowledge economy An economic system in which the use and exchange of knowledge plays a dominant role. In this kind of economy, knowledge is both an economic asset and a key product.

online learning The use of the Internet to provide programs of study or individual courses that offer instructional materials and interactions between teachers and students.

Glenn Koenig/Los Angeles Times/Getty Images

impact of online learning on educational productivity for secondary school students, the International Association for Online Learning, a nonprofit advocacy group, has several reports related to effective online teaching and learning that you will find useful should you be asked to teach an online course.

What do you think it would be like to be a student in an online high school? As of the 2015–2016 school year, 528 full-time virtual schools enrolled 278,511 students, and 140 blended schools enrolled 36,605 students (Molnar, 2017). Thirty-four states and Washington, DC, had full-time statewide online schools operating in 2016, and 21 states had blended schools. Often, the full-time online high school student lives in a remote area, was previously homeschooled, or is deeply involved in an extracurricular activity that is incompatible with a traditional school. When SOHS began in 2017, it was designed to meet the needs of a diverse group of students who did not have access to excellent traditional education. That year, there were 750 students enrolled in SOHS, 48% of them full time. They came from 46 states and 32 countries.

A standard online course blends synchronous seminars with asynchronous lectures and interactive online components in a flipped classroom model (Scarborough & Ravaglia, 2014). The students in a typical class session at SOHS simultaneously watch a streamed lecture with video clips, diagrams, and animations. When they have comments or questions, students click into a queue and teachers call on them by choosing their audio stream, which can be heard by all. If any of you have participated in an interactive webinar, it is similar and includes a window where students can instant message each other. In many cases, you are seeing the students' faces in the online class and responding to them as you would in person. The students who are taking a full five-course load at SOHS must be present for ten 60- to 90-minute seminars a week and for an additional 15 to 20 minutes that are recorded by the teachers and viewable asynchronously. Part-time students take two or three courses and are usually enrolled in a brick-and-mortar school in addition to being enrolled with SOHS; they use the courses at SOHS for advanced study. For assessment, students at SOHS must find a Stanford-approved proctor to oversee their exams. Fridays are devoted to clubs, colloquia, presentations, and assemblies, all online. All students can meet each other face-to-face in a 2-week residential summer session at Stanford or informal parent-organized meetups (Scarborough & Ravaglia, 2014).

The academic program of SOHS is rigorous, and students are required to meet high standards. Because of the blended, flipped classroom approach, students and teachers interact often and there is a definite sense of community. Elite online high schools, like SOHS, boast high graduation and college admissions rates. This is in contrast to virtual high schools nationwide, which had far lower graduation rates than the national average of 83% (Molnar, 2017). Although overall school performance ratings were only available for 18 of the 34 states with virtual schools, the data reveal a pattern of underperformance compared to their traditional counterparts. These data speak to the need for clear and specific oversight of the virtual and blended schools that are not functioning as elite private schools.

Because the world is a global marketplace, five states require some form of online learning for high school graduation. Michigan was the first to do so in 2006, followed by Florida, Virginia, Arkansas, and Alabama. Educators and policy makers want to ensure that high school graduates are proficient with information communication technologies. The main reasons why school districts make online learning opportunities available to their students are to provide courses not otherwise available at their schools and to provide opportunities for students to recover course credits from classes missed or failed (Watson, Murin, Vashaw, Gemin, & Rapp, 2013). In addition, students gravitate to online educational sites to fuel their interests. Community, state, national, and global collaborations are part of everyday functioning in today's world. This challenges teachers to think about how to create learning opportunities online because many schools offer blended courses, and most students engaged in online courses work on those courses while at school.

Globalization and Learning

As the world has shrunk through electronic communication, the ways in which we teach and learn have expanded. Now that teachers and students can reach people and investigate ideas with the tap of a finger or the click of a mouse, how can these connections contribute to the intellectual discourse of the classroom? We need to examine the teacher's role in light of our unlimited access to information and people.

The Flat World

In his best-selling book *The World Is Flat*, Thomas Friedman (2006) uses the metaphor of a flat world to describe

Ariel Skelley/DigitalVision/Getty Images

▲ Working together to accomplish a task can be face-to-face or virtual.

the leveling of the playing field on which industrialized and emerging-market countries compete. Friedman recounts many examples of **globalization** in which companies in India and China are becoming part of global supply chains that extend across oceans, providing everything from service representatives and X-ray interpretation to component manufacturing. He also describes how these changes are made possible through intersecting technologies, particularly the Internet.

In a flat world, Friedman explains, the work done by corporations is no longer conducted vertically—that is, in a structure of workers and supervisors, with each person at each level having different specific tasks. Rather, much of the work has gone horizontal: Corporate analysts examine each step in a process and ask whether the firm is a leader in that step. If not, they determine who in the world can best do that work at the appropriate level of quality and the lowest possible cost. The firm then contracts with providers for each service. The firm itself performs only those functions it does best. This arrangement is known as *outsourcing*, and many functions formerly performed by U.S. workers are now being outsourced to workers in other countries who can do these jobs better, more cheaply, and faster. Remember, one does not have to be in the same geographical location to be a coworker in a company.

The flat world creates significant challenges for teaching and learning. For our students to fully participate in the global community, they require **global competence**—the attitudes, knowledge, and skills to live and work successfully in our interconnected world (Tichnor-Wagner, 2016). Global competence also involves the development of affective

---

globalization The increase of global connectivity, integration, and interdependence in economic, cultural, social, and technological spheres.

global competence The attitudes, knowledge, and skills to live and work successfully in our interconnected world (Tichnor-Wagner, 2016). Also involves the development of affective skills such as empathy and respect for others in order to be engaged and effective citizens of the world.

---

skills such as empathy and respect for others in order to be engaged and effective citizens of the world. While there are still school classrooms that resemble the ones our grandparents attended—with the teacher front and center and the students listening and writing at their desks—there are many more beginning to resemble the global classroom of the future, both in technology access and in access to the global marketplace of ideas.

The Global Student: Having Information Versus Constructing Meaning

One of the first steps in preparing ourselves and our students to function in a data-rich global knowledge economy is to explore the ways in which having a lot of information is different from gaining a lot of knowledge.

In today's digital age, learning *how* to learn becomes more important than *what* we learn. Thus, it is the individual with curiosity, imagination, and a passion for learning who will be most successful in the global knowledge economy. Curious students work hard at learning and eagerly find new opportunities to learn. Hence, when we gather information, we reflect on it, apply it to different contexts, examine its meaning, and try to communicate it to others—and then we are starting to be knowledgeable. Finally, we can create something new and innovative out of what we have learned, and we then reach the apex of Bloom's Taxonomy, discussed in Chapter 4.

Learning How to Learn

The kind of information teachers used to ask students to memorize is now available on the Internet, usually just a few keystrokes or taps on the touch screen away. Consider this memorable anecdote:

> "Learn the names of the rivers in South America." That was the assignment given to Deborah Stipek's daughter Meredith in school, and her mom, who was Dean of the Stanford University Graduate School of Education, was not impressed. "That's silly," Stipek told her daughter. "Tell your teacher that if you need to know anything besides the Amazon, you can look it up on Google." (Wallis & Steptoe, 2006, p. 4)

Because simple facts are easy to locate, today's students require what educators refer to as more depth of understanding and less breadth. In other words, key ideas and topics should dominate the curriculum, not lists of facts that can be found easily enough on the web.

Educators also talk about the importance of **metacognition**, the understanding of one's own learning processes. Students with metacognitive skills know how to

---

metacognition The understanding of your own thinking and learning processes.

approach a learning task. They have good learning strategies. In other words, they have learned how to learn.

The projects and problems described in Chapters 6 and 7 illustrate some ways of developing metacognitive skills and depth of understanding. As students work in teams, both in their classrooms and online, they risk making mistakes on their journey to finding solutions and consensus. They develop critical thinking—making connections between ideas and events—and they learn how to keep on learning.

Worldwide Collaboration

Knowing how to work with others to solve a problem is an essential skill, and knowing how to collaborate across a digital learning environment adds another dimension. Around the world, teachers are using online education tools to bring a global perspective to their students by developing cross-cultural education projects that bring the diverse cultures of the world into their classrooms.

A growing number of schools are using Skype videoconferencing to collaborate nationally and globally. Skype is free communication software that allows you to make calls, instant message, and videoconference online. Imagine your class is reading a book by a favorite author, and the author is your Skype guest where the students communicate through the class SMART Board in real time! Mike Artnell, an author and artist, virtually visits elementary school classrooms thousands of miles from where he lives. The students engage with him about his stories and his illustrations, and he demonstrates his drawing techniques and engages students in the wonders of his creativity (http://www.teachhub.com/using-skype-classroom).

Teachers and students can Skype with partner classrooms across the country or across the world. Imagine taking your class on a virtual around-the-world field trip. Collaborative project-based learning is easily accomplished through the Skype for educators' website (https://education.microsoft.com/skype-in-the-classroom/overview). There are projects listed that invite collaborating classes from all over the world. In one project, students from Iran, Taiwan, and Delaware planned the autumn week in which they would plant daffodil bulbs. They then looked for their emergence in the spring, carefully observing when they started to bloom and taking the air temperature each day. Each class kept a record of the weather indicators and their latitude and longitude; the photos of the daffodils and their weather data were shared on a project website (https://sites.google.com/site/daffodilandtulip/). Students got to experience what latitude and longitude really meant when they located their partner schools on a world map. Climate patterns and global climate change became topics of conversation.

The International Education and Resource Network (iEARN) is another collaborative project site that has been around for more than 20 years. iEARN is a nonprofit organization made up of more than 30,000 schools and youth organizations in more than 140 countries.

iEARN-USA, a branch of iEARN, empowers teachers and young people to work together online using the Internet and other communications technologies. More than 2 million students each day are engaged in collaborative project work worldwide through iEARN-USA (http://www.us.iearn.org/). There are more than 100 projects in iEARN-USA, all designed and facilitated by teachers and students to fit their curriculum, classroom needs, and schedules. Projects take place in the iEARN-USA Collaboration Centre. To join, participants select an online project and look at how they can integrate it into their classroom. With the project selected, teachers and students enter online forum spaces to meet one another and get involved in ongoing projects with classrooms around the world who are working on the same project.

An iEARN project is a collaborative academic endeavor between two or more groups of students and educators in different parts of the world. Collaborative projects not only help teach content but also help students to develop skills such as communication, time management, teamwork, and facilitation. These skills enable students to function globally and cooperatively, sharing information and ideas, and learning how to "to think outside the box"—a necessary skill for promoting innovation.

Skills for the 21st Century

Jean Pennycook is a science educator from California who studies Adélie penguins for three months on Cape Royds in Antarctica. Each year, she travels there to observe the penguins and the shrinking polar ice and communicate, through her webcam, with classrooms all over the world. Her work is one example of the ways that our global reach has shrunk the size and scope of our world, making accessible to students a vast array of experiences that would otherwise remain hidden from them. What types of skills do our students need to navigate these virtual terrains?

Knowing More About the World. Students are global citizens now. They need to understand the world economy, be able to identify the nations in the developed and developing world, become sensitive to foreign cultures, and learn foreign languages.

Thinking Outside the Box. Students need to think creatively to solve problems, seeing patterns where others may see chaos. Interdisciplinary combinations—design and technology, mathematics and art, music and science—spawn innovative ideas and products for the global economy. Interdisciplinary study aligns with the contemporary STEM and STEAM movements discussed in Chapter 6. Creativity expert Ken Robinson (2006) felt that "we get educated out of creativity" in school. It is essential, therefore, to foster creative problem solving by providing students with challenging problems and guiding them to find solutions.

Managing New Sources of Information. Students need to develop skills that help them manage the vast amount of information to which they are exposed. For one thing, they must learn to distinguish between reliable and unreliable information.

Developing Good People Skills. With so much being accomplished online, we can get the mistaken notion that good people-to-people communication is unnecessary in today's marketplace. However, most recent innovations involve collaboration among teams of people. The ability to work and communicate with others—often people from different cultures—is essential.

Teaching in the Global Classroom

After all that has been said so far about the flat world, the global student, and the needs of a technology-driven world, you must be wondering, "What does this mean for teaching?"

First of all, it means that your job as a teacher is to demonstrate a love and a passion for learning. In the words of Thomas Friedman (2006), "You can't light the fire of passion in someone else if it does not burn in you to begin with" (p. 305). You cannot expect your students to become curious and inventive if you do not display those qualities yourself. It also means that you should help students develop ways of thinking and knowing the world by helping them refine their abilities to collaborate; their metacognitive skills; the skills of managing, interpreting, validating, and acting on information; and their willingness to think outside the box to come up with new solutions. It is an exciting time to be a teacher, and you can imagine what is possible for your future global students, like using Skype to connect to students who are native speakers of the foreign language you may be teaching. Students learning English in other parts of the world can connect with your students for help as students around the world do peer teaching and forge solid friendships with each other locally and internationally. Classroom learning is shedding its walls and expanding through the digital universe.

Teaching With Digital Media

Skype

In the project space of the Skype for Education website (https://education.microsoft.com/GetTrained/skype) a teacher from Japan posted the following suggestion for a collaborative project:

> My high school and jr. high is in Hiroshima prefecture in Japan. We are interested in using Skype to help our students practice their English, learn about foreign cultures, and basically have a "window to the world."

High school or junior high school classes that want to participate in some form of cultural exchange, comparing and contrasting different foods, clothing, music, pop culture, customs—you know, nothing too heavy—using simple English come together once in a while with prepared questions and something that they want to present—and hopefully gain understanding and respect for others while practicing English.

A teacher from Oklahoma, not far from Tulsa, responded to this teacher's request, and a conversation between the classes occurred. Exploring the projects can offer a sense of the scope and magnitude of teaching in a digital world. There are so many possibilities!

Serious Learning Games

Gaming has the potential to change education as computer and video games permeate our culture and students use them for learning on tablets, smartphones, and other portable electronic devices. When developed correctly, games can engage players in learning that is specifically applicable to school curriculum (Klopfer, Osterweil, & Salen, 2009). The Public Broadcasting System (PBS) offers educational games for young learners in content areas including math, reading, science, social studies, music, and art. Trends in serious gaming for education suggest that video games can enhance classroom learning by having a positive effect on a broad range of learning outcomes including engagement, motivation, content mastery, and sustained interest in the subject area (Young et al., 2012).

So what can we say about the benefits of gaming for learning? First, the type of games being explored should be defined. **Serious learning games**, also called **digital learning games**, are those that are designed for a primary purpose other than our entertainment. They target the acquisition of knowledge as its own end and foster habits of mind and understanding that are used within an academic context (Klopfer et al., 2009, p. 21). Learning games are associated with formal or informal learning environments or with self-learners interested in acquiring new knowledge or understanding. For example, conceived for out-of-school use, several middle school English language arts (ELA) learning games are tablet-based game ecosystems consisting of embedded, skill-based literacy games and a virtual library with many different texts. Users engage with the games by browsing and reading books, meeting characters from literature, and creating their own stories.

This game world aims for students to read more and practice syntax, vocabulary, morphology, and spelling skills. It seeks to engage and encourage students to persist in these literacy activities. The design principles on which these games are based rely on years of study by psychologists and literacy specialists, and align with the Common Core State Standards that emphasize more reading and writing, greater rigor in those experiences, and more time on task with ELA skills.

The research on how to engage and encourage persistence is essential to the design of games that students actually want to play. In self-determination theory, psychologists Deci and

gaming Used in this context, *gaming* refers to playing computer and video games. Video game culture is a form of new media that has enormous potential for teaching and learning.

serious learning games/digital learning games These games target the acquisition of knowledge as its own end and foster habits of mind and understanding that are generally useful or used within an academic context.

iStock/FatCamera

Ryan (1985) identified activities that satisfy individual needs for autonomy, competence, and connectedness. By meeting these needs, these activities promote persistent engagement. When engaged in a favorite activity, students may enter a state of flow, the unselfconscious involvement in an activity during which nothing else seems to matter and a sense of time is lost (Csikszentmihalyi, 1997). Research shows that teenagers experience flow 44% of the time they are involved in sports or games, and that people experience more flow when they are reading books than when they are watching television (Csikszentmihalyi, 1997). Games contribute to a state of flow by encouraging the use of a set of skills to overcome a challenge. Players then move on to learning new skills and facing new challenges. Combining conditions that contribute to flow and self-determination promotes persistence, a critical skill for learning.

Game designers create environments where users can play games that enhance vocabulary and spelling skills, literacy comprehension, math skills, and science understandings while deriving pleasure from the game experience. Well-designed games create a nonthreatening environment and allow students to persist at their own pace. Several game designers create platforms for students to connect with one another and share game strategies. Gaming researchers believe that the use of games and game technologies for learning content will become pervasive. Successful serious learning game designers capitalize on the enjoyment human beings derive from solving problems and take advantage of their tenacity; they keep trying until they succeed (Gee, 2008).

Although there is little conclusive research to correlate computer and video gaming with student achievement, there are promising findings (Young et al., 2012). Serious learning games for language learning show evidence of enhancing student learning not only by the users but by those watching the games being played. In addition, deep understanding of content takes time, reflection, and active engagement—all strengths of video games.

Effective serious learning games encourage the kind of persistence that promotes a growth mind-set toward learning (Dweck, 2006). Psychologist Carol Dweck's research on growth mindsets is rooted in repeated studies that show that people with a growth mind-set believe that intelligence is an attribute that develops over time with hard work and persistence.

Other research suggests that in addition to being motivating, playing computer and video games affects brain function and plasticity (Bavelier & Green, 2009). Some research indicates that playing action video games on a regular basis can alter a player's attention skills. These include low-level vision, monitoring several objects at once, or searching through a cluttered scene; multitasking; task switching; and a general speeding up of perceptual processing. Exploring video games from PBS (PBSkids.org/games) for primary-grade learners reveals a host of choices where the learners are problem solvers. They acquire understanding through the multistep processes of solving the problems as they play the games. An art education game downloaded from one site contains paintings from great masters belonging to various periods of artistic creation, from the early Renaissance to Surrealism and beyond. As the game unfolds, the paintings are reorganized and some are missing; students need to find the missing works of art and place them in their proper period. All this happens quickly, with fifth graders manipulating the mouse and discovering how to make the best display. Players today use tablets to engage with the games, eliminating the need for a mouse.

"Business Education" is a set of online high school games that tests students' knowledge of business strategies. Users create their own company and product, and participate in simulations including the Business Game, the Entrepreneurship Game, and the Finance Game. In this high school program, simulations approach reality as students need to apply the principles they have learned in their business education classes. The Business Game gives students the chance to experience a business scenario in which they develop and market a new product. This provides training in pricing issues, product positioning, sales and marketing budgets, stock levels, and production versus demand. Students build relationships with simulated mentors and coworkers through daily interaction using e-mail and video phone calls (Schaffhauser, 2010). Serious learning games can be found at the Center for Online Education (http://www.onlinecolleges.net/50-great-sites-for-serious-educational-games/).

Today's high school students take simulations seriously and do not see them as second best to the real thing. Although different from learning games, simulations offer a somewhat risk-free environment, one where learners are free to experiment, make mistakes, and rethink and redesign without fear of destroying something that cannot be easily replenished in a traditional setting. A report from MIT suggests that, although gaming and simulations cannot single-handedly change the way a subject matter is taught, they can promote deeper understanding through active engagement. Serious learning games allow students to apply what they have learned and refine their understanding of content in a safe, risk-free environment.

Digitally Inclined Students

Teachers report that their students prefer digital media over other types of instruction and that digital media increases student motivation and stimulates discussions. Digital media supports teacher and student creativity. What is really significant here is acknowledging the many types of digital media to which students and teachers are exposed and then asking: "How can these media serve teaching and learning and extend our understanding of the world?" Ever-increasing numbers of teachers are joining virtual professional communities and using social networking tools in their personal and professional lives. These technologies hold the promise of exciting changes in K–12 education, including using digital media to foster more creative and collaborative learning environments, engaging students in using new tools to produce content and take charge of their learning, and creating more possibilities for real-time cross-cultural conversations with students from all over the world.

Precollege students who take online courses to supplement traditional courses offered at their brick-and-mortar schools are changing the face of U.S. public education. These virtual classes are becoming more and more popular. In *synchronous* distance learning, students are virtually present through the Internet at the same point in time. More commonly, though, the learning environment is *asynchronous*—that is, students from different geographical areas work at different times.

One of the significant advantages of **virtual schools** is that they can provide courses otherwise unavailable to a local student. This is especially important in rural areas, where one school often serves all students from pre-K to 12th grade and the financial resources for extensive enrichment courses are unavailable. Some school districts form partnerships with an online learning firm that tracks open seats in online courses and offers them to school districts at discounted rates.

In the typical arrangement, similar to the one described at SOHS, students who take courses online communicate daily with the teacher, who may be in some other part of the country or even in another nation. Yet students do much of their course work independently on their own schedule. Usually, a school guidance counselor stays in touch to make sure students are keeping pace with the work required from the online course. Naturally, some students are better at independent work than others; for some students, online courses at the precollege level are not the best choice. The value of an online course depends in part on the individual's maturity, work habits, and motivation.

Online courses can enroll students from many localities and even from many countries. Learning to work with such a diverse group enhances precollege students' abilities to be team problem solvers and to appreciate the contributions of people from radically different environments.

▲ Students are learning over a large distance through videoconferencing. Technology makes virtual classrooms possible.

Ariel Skelley/DigitalVision/Getty Images

What does an online environment mean for teaching? When teachers are asked to develop an online course from a course they are used to teaching face-to-face, the challenge is often transformative. Imagine that you have developed lesson plans for a unit of study, and now you are going to use these lessons online with 15 to 20 students who are working at different paces and at different times around the globe. To make this leap, you have to ask some soul-searching questions, like the ones listed in the box titled "Questions for Teaching an Online Course." In fact, research shows that teaching an online course leads many teachers to reexamine some of their beliefs about teaching and learning. The concepts of teacher–student and student–student communication, as well as student accountability and assessment, change in the online environment. Many tips for teaching an online course involve the importance of planning, setting up an adequate working environment, being sure you have mastered the technology, maintaining a consistent online presence by communicating regularly, establishing deadlines, and asking for help and feedback (Phillips, 2016). Perhaps you will be asked to be part of a virtual high school when you are teaching a face-to-face classroom. You may find it challenging to do both—teach face-to-face and teach online. The intellectual "space" of the online class requires a different type of preparation. You will be happy to know, however, that most students who take online courses feel like they are part of a learning community and value the experience. Most teachers who teach online find valuable suggestions and resources on the Internet.

3D Printing

One of the most exciting technologies is **3D printing**, which refers to the construction of physical objects from three-dimensional digital content such as 3D modeling

---

virtual school An institution that exists in cyberspace, teaching all of its classes online.

3D printing The use of technologies that construct physical objects from three-dimensional digital content.

QUESTIONS FOR TEACHING AN ONLINE COURSE

To prepare for teaching an online course, you need to ask yourself questions like these:

- What do I hope the online students will get out of this course?

- Why have I been teaching this course in this particular way?

- What needs to change for the online environment? Which elements of my lesson plans do I keep? Which do I leave out?

- How do I substitute an online activity for something I have done face-to-face?

- How can I foster group work and collaboration among students who are physically far apart?

- How can I improve the way I communicate with students?

APPLICATIONS OF ONLINE LEARNING FOR INCREASING EDUCATIONAL PRODUCTIVITY

1. **Broadening access** in ways that dramatically reduce the cost of providing access to quality educational resources and experiences, particularly for students in remote locations or other situations where challenges such as low student enrollments make the traditional school model impractical;

2. **Engaging students in active learning** with instructional materials and access to a wealth of resources that can facilitate the adoption of research-based principles and best practices from the learning sciences, an application that might improve student outcomes without substantially increasing costs;

3. **Individualizing and differentiating instruction** based on student performance on diagnostic assessments and preferred pace of learning, thereby improving the

efficiency with which students move through a learning progression;

4. **Personalizing learning** by building on student interests, which can result in increased student motivation, time on task, and, ultimately, better learning outcomes;

5. **Making better use of teacher and student time** by automating routine tasks and enabling teacher time to focus on high-value activities;

6. **Reducing school-based facilities costs** by leveraging home and community spaces in addition to traditional school buildings.

Source: Adapted from the U.S. Department of Education, Office of Educational Technology Report, January 2012. http://www.ed.gov/technology.

software. A 3D printer builds a tangible model from an electronic file, one layer at a time, in an extrusion process using melted plastic filaments and building an object from the bottom up, layer by layer. The printers are affordable personal fabrication tools, compact enough to sit on any desktop. The exploration of 3D printing, from design to production, can open up new possibilities, especially in STEM education (Johnson, Adams Becker, Estrada, & Martin, 2013, p. 9). Students from all over the world can participate in lessons addressing how to use this exciting technology.

In one magnet school in Chicago, a "Makers Lab" employs a 3D printing curriculum and teaches the students about the ways this technology can be used to enhance learning. For example, 3D printers can be programmed to make objects with braille labels for blind students, creating a new tactile learning system (Molitch-Hou, 2014). 3D

printers have become a staple in the maker movement discussed in Chapter 6. Teachers can use 3D printing to provide 3D visual aids and model biological systems that are difficult to show—like organs of the human body, for example. With 3D printers and online collaborations, students participate in project-based learning that is experiential in nature and has real-world applications. In addition to 3D printers, 3D scanners can convert objects into virtual models that can then be 3D printed.

For learning, the 3D applications for the maker movement need to be purposeful and within the **makerspace**; students need to be engaged in solving a problem or learning about a real-world concept in greater depth. A makerspace is a place where students can gather to

makerspace A place where students can gather to create, invent, tinker, explore, and discover using a variety of tools and materials.

WRITING & REFLECTION
CHALLENGES OF TEACHING ONLINE

What would be the greatest challenge for you in teaching an online course? Would you design your course so that it would be accessible on tablets and smartphones?

create, invent, tinker, explore, and discover using a variety of tools and materials (Rendina, 2015). Students can work and learn in a variety of makerspaces, collaborating with each other and with groups online. The mind-set of design thinking informs a lot of what students do in the makerspace. New technologies raise the bar for what is possible when you are solving a design problem; however, in makerspaces, engineering design often begins as tinkering and making objects for hobbies, fun, and creative expression.

The Teacher's Role in a Global Classroom

At this point in the chapter, you may be wondering "Why am I going into teaching if students can get so much information elsewhere and connect so readily to the rest of the world?" That is a legitimate question. The answer lies in the importance of your passion, your curiosity, your capacity to listen to and accept students, to gently challenge their ideas and guide them—these are the qualities that will make you a successful teacher.

Your expertise in your content area must be apparent, but it is less important than your ability to help students navigate the floodwaters of information available to them. Your challenge is to become a teacher who helps students become discriminating consumers of information, capable of validating data by doing research and formulating well-supported opinions. In other words, your message to students is "Now that you know what the raw information says, how do you process it?" As a teacher, you will help students make meaning from the data they find; you will help them draw out the big ideas or core concepts in ways that connect to the real world.

Remember that you are your students' guide through group learning, collaboration, conflict resolution, and socially acceptable communication. You can help them become lifelong creative learners by challenging them with problems and projects that require them to collaborate and share in this new, open-source world. That sounds like a tall order, but more and more it is how we live our lives.

Concluding Thoughts

Why do some things take root and grow while others barely break the surface? How long does something have to be around before we can declare that it's here to stay? What has to happen in order to transform an oasis of change into an entire landscape?

—Ronald Thorpe (2003)

The 21st century challenges us to understand more about how people learn, communicate, and do business in a global environment, or what Friedman (2006) calls the "flat world." Who we become as teachers will reflect the times in which we live—our global interconnectivity and our unending access to information and media.

It is difficult to predict the world in which your students will take part as adults. Think about this: In the years many of today's college-aged students were born, there were hardly any cell phones or digital cameras; no iPhones, iPods, or MP3 players; no iPads; very few Internet sites; no GPS devices; no TiVo or DVRs; and no Google or HDTV. Now, try to think 20 years into the future. Can you even begin to imagine what further changes will occur?

Connectivity, communication, and collaboration have become this century's reading, 'riting, and 'rithmetic—three Cs to replace the traditional three Rs of the 20th century. Of course, we need the three Rs to become adept at the three Cs. Yet the world into which you must guide your students is more complex and demanding than ever before.

Clearly, to teach in this environment, teachers must be students of history and of current affairs, and able to keep pace with constant change. Further, the global community challenges teachers to see beyond our own world and into the worlds of others as a way to make the planet a more tolerant, more sustainable, and safer place. As teachers, our personas are revealed in the classroom: how generous of spirit we become and how capable we are of listening to and learning with our students.

With so much information available through such a large variety of media, today's students have to become masters of the art of multitasking. Barbara Kurshan, executive director of Curriki, a global community of educators, learners, and education experts who are working together to create high-quality online materials for teachers and students, refers to a recent experience she had with a group of middle-school students she encountered in a friend's basement. Some students were on the computer, some were sending text messages via their mobile phones, and others were on Facebook. She asked them what they were doing, and they responded, "Studying." They had been given a problem set and were collaborating on how to find the answers, working together, and reaching out to other friends to see who had the knowledge they needed. "That's exactly what goes on in the work world when solving a problem," she says—and too often, "it doesn't go on in the classroom."

Clearly, the experience that students are having in many schools is linear and disconnected, starting from page one and continuing to the end of the book, and then being tested on the material. In these classrooms, students must disconnect from the electronic communities that keep them anchored and keep them connected to their own communities. A gap is growing between the way students have begun to learn and the way schools continue to teach. It is the wired, connected, and tech-savvy teacher who can use the language of the digital information age to help students to take charge of their own learning.

CHAPTER REVIEW

Key Terms

gaming (p. 131)
global competence (p. 129)
globalization (p. 129)
knowledge economy (p. 127)
makerspace (p. 134)

metacognition (p. 129)
online learning (p. 127)
serious learning games/digital
    learning games (p. 131)

3D printing (p. 133)
virtual school (p. 133)

Review the Learning Outcomes

Review each section of the chapter and answer the following:

LO 8-1 How could online learning meet the needs of diverse populations of students?

LO 8-2 How can global education enhance the lives of students?

LO 8-3 How can serious learning games give students control of their own learning?

InTASC Standards

Review the InTASC Standards for the chapter and explain how the chapter addressed each one.

Standard 3: Learning Environments

Standard 6: Assessment

Standard 8: Instructional Strategies

Journal Prompts

What courses would you like to take online instead of face-to-face? How would that enhance your learning experience?

Get the tools you need to sharpen your study skills. SAGE edge offers a robust online environment featuring an impressive array of free tools and resources.

Access practice quizzes, eFlashcards, video, and multimedia at **edge.sagepub.com/koch4e**.

PART IV

Classrooms, Communities, and You

iStock/monkeybusinessimages

The Classroom as Community

I see what happens to young people, first graders through twelfth, when they come to feel that those who represent an institution have their students' best interests at heart.

—Mike Rose (2009, p. 151)

Learning Outcomes

After reading this chapter, you should be able to:

9-1 Explain how classrooms with diverse students can share a common set of beliefs, values, and goals.

9-2 Examine how classroom communities can help prevent the abusive behaviors of bullying and sex-based harassment.

9-3 Examine ways to prevent school violence.

9-4 Describe the roles of communication and collaboration for classroom communities.

InTASC Standards

- Standard 7: Planning for Instruction
- Standard 8: Instructional Strategies
- Standard 10: Leadership and Collaboration

In this chapter, we explore how to create classroom environments—real or virtual—that are welcoming, caring, and ultimately effective for teaching and learning. The personal nature of teaching distinguishes it from many other professions. Teaching keeps you on your toes and requires self-awareness and a special mindfulness of your actions and intentions. You need this level of consciousness to become an effective teacher. Remember, teaching is about building relationships. Whatever the domain in which you teach, the central question is: "How do I create an environment in which students have respect for themselves and for the other members of the classroom community?"

In the current era, in which schools have focused intensely on the academic proficiency of their students as recorded by standards-based tests, it is important to recognize that academic proficiency is only one of the major goals of education. There are social and emotional goals as well. Students should become learners with the capacity to love, work, and be active community members (Cohen, 2006). Along these lines, the philosopher John Dewey (1916/2004) urged educators to have a sympathetic understanding of learners as individuals to have an idea of what is actually going on in their minds. To show that you care about your students, you must *listen* to them. Teaching depends on understanding what the 20 to 30 different minds in your class are thinking. How do they feel about being in school? About themselves? About you? One fourth-grade inner-city teacher gave her students an in-class assignment to respond to this question: "What do you want Ms. Murray to know about you that she does not know now?"

Building Community in the Classroom

Dewey (1938) asserted that the aim of education is to support the development of the skills and knowledge needed for responsible and caring participation in a democracy. In a sense, then, the question this chapter seeks to answer is this: "How do students become engaged, responsible participants in a democracy, and how does that process start with the environment created in your classrooms?"

Classroom Management and Classroom Community

New teachers often seek to understand more about what is typically called **classroom management**. By management, they mean the ways the teacher can get students to do what the teacher wants them to. Classroom management refers to "the actions teachers take to create an environment that is respectful, caring, orderly and productive. It supports both academic learning and socio-emotional learning" (Ryan & Cooper, 2013, p. 183). Other educators believe that "if a teacher's notion is to manage, his or her style becomes domineering. This results in resistance from students and an adversarial relationship" (Tomlinson & Imbeau, 2011).

As a result, the term *classroom management* is sometimes frowned upon because it can imply that teachers use the power differential between themselves and their students to force students to follow a certain set of rules. Educators interested in classroom management, however, have begun to focus instead on the creation, through various strategies, of a **classroom community** in which each

....

classroom management The ways teachers create an effective classroom environment for learning, including all the rules and conditions they establish.

classroom community A sense of common purpose and values shared by the teacher and students in a classroom so that they see themselves as working together in the process of learning; a classroom atmosphere that emphasizes trust, care, and support.

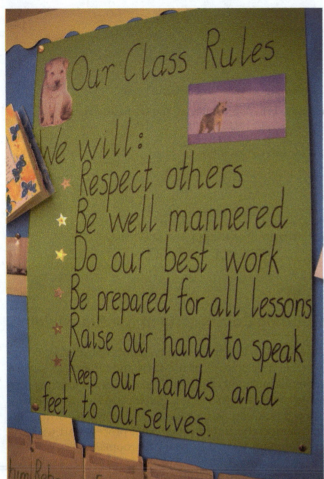

Photofusion/Universal Images Group/Getty Images

participant is invested in the smooth operation of the whole and all participants have an interest in outcomes. In this viewpoint, rules and conditions are not established by the teacher alone but by the group as a whole.

Although structures, routines, and class rules are needed to guide the teaching and learning in classrooms, the way these guidelines are arrived at is crucial. Different teachers have different ways of establishing classroom expectations. When I was chatting with Meredith, who had been in the classroom for 2 years, we explored her experiences as a first-year teacher in an urban school known for its discipline problems. She taught a second-grade class of 30 students, and she felt her first year had been successful and satisfying. I asked her how she felt before the first day of school.

"I was scared. I wanted to meet the children, and I was excited, but before the first day of school, I was told that I had behavior problems in my class. But, after the first five minutes with the class, I was fine. My classroom management skills kicked in, and I was on my way."

When I asked Meredith where she got those skills, she said, "From my mother." I was stunned because I know there are many teaching courses with the title "Classroom Management." Was her mother wiser than professional educators? She elaborated on what she had learned from her mother:

"My mother always expected the best from me, and she was strict and demanding, but I knew she really cared about me and had my best interests at heart. Still, she was a 'no-nonsense mom' who set goals with me and had clear expectations. She checked with me to see how I felt about how I was meeting my goals. I do the same thing with the children in my classroom.

"I ask them what type of classroom will help them learn. I have strict policies, but we discuss each policy and why it makes sense for their learning environment. I hold out the expectation that they will abide by the rules, and I keep my door open. I explain to them that anyone passing our classroom should be able to see a model of students busy with their work and their class discussions. Of course, when they work in pairs or groups, there is some noise, but that is necessary for them to collaborate with their classmates."

When asked if she used any little tricks to keep students focused and productive, Meredith said that she had hand signals to get their attention when they were working in pairs or groups; she introduced those signals on the first day of school. Also, during a group conversation, she would quietly walk over to students who were not paying attention, and her body language helped amend their behavior.

Mostly, Meredith explained, she genuinely cares about her students and expects them to be successful. She wants a classroom that works for both the students and the teacher, and sometimes that means she has to alter her plans. For example, if she notices that the second graders are engaged in a topic and working diligently on task, she extends her lesson, altering her own routine to allow them to go further in an area of study that they find compelling:

"Everything is a collaboration; there is no such thing as teaching separate from learning. It is not always possible to know what curriculum areas will set an entire class on fire—and when one comes up, I hate to let it go just because my plan book says I should."

Good teachers live for those moments when the students are "on fire" (Intrator, 2003)—carried away and enthused by a topic, a project, an experience, or a story. It is at these times, when students are fully communicating with each other, responding to peers and to you, that you think, "Wow, this is why I came to this work!" These experiences engage students' thinking and enthusiasm so completely that they "forget" they are supposed to resist school, and they get carried away by the excitement of the moment.

At these moments, you understand that the classroom is "managed" by the quality of the learning experience, the engagement of the students, and the appreciation of the teacher for the intellectual work that is happening. This is a learning community. It is managed by everyone in it. Let us look at another story about one of my experiences that can tell us more about the foundations of a classroom community:

In an old school building in the East Bronx in New York City, I am trying to bring eighth-grade physical science to life. As part of a unit on the properties of mixtures, we are studying solutions. For this lesson, I want to show the students that, in a solution with water, even though the particles of a solute (the substance that dissolves) seem to disappear, they can be reclaimed. If you boil off the water, the original solute remains at the bottom of the flask. In fact, if you collect the steam and condense it back into water, you can end up with the solute and the water in separate containers—exactly the way they started before the solution was made.

To do this, I set up an apparatus called a Liebig condenser, made popular by the German chemist Justus Baron von Liebig, which makes it possible to collect vapors and turn them back into a liquid. The condenser has an inner tube and an outer tube. The entire apparatus connects to the lab sink in my classroom.

We start with blue crystals of copper sulfate. We stir them into water, making a copper sulfate solution. Then we try to reverse the process. We place the flask containing the solution on a tripod over a Bunsen burner, connecting the open end of the flask to the Liebig condenser with rubber tubing. When the copper sulfate solution boils, the water vapor is collected in the condenser's inner tube, and cold water from the lab sink swirls around the outer tube. Slowly, clear water—the steam turned back into liquid—drips from the condenser into a collecting beaker. The students sit in rapt attention, enthralled.

I ask the class if this process would work if the tube were hooked up to the hot water faucet. All the students shout, "No, it's the cold water that does it!" They seem to understand that the cold turns the steam back into water by removing the heat from the vapor. I do not mind that they are shouting: "Mrs. Koch—look inside the flask—look—the blue crystals are coming back!"

"Yes," I remark, "and how many thought they were gone for good?" Many students raise their hands. They are smiling; they "get it."

They ask if we can try another solution tomorrow. "Sure," I reply, and tomorrow we will try it with salt water. When the students file out at the end of class, some of them call out, "That was so cool, Mrs. K."

I leave the school building elated. I know the students have had a learning experience. They now know more about evaporation, condensation, and the entire process of distillation. As I drive home with a big smile on my face, I am reminded that it is just for days like this that I keep teaching. I say to myself, "It's worth all the preparation!"

Think about what is happening behind the scenes in this eighth-grade classroom. For one thing, the students have learned that I go to a good deal of trouble on their behalf. I have taken the time to set up this complex apparatus and have it ready for their class. They appear to understand that I am deeply invested in their learning and in providing a good science experience. Today will tide us over other days that may not be as exciting, but the students will expect a similarly exciting lab demonstration at some future date.

Over time, as I continued to show my commitment to these students, they never cut science. They were interested. They were well behaved. They managed themselves.

But there are other factors at work here as well. By saying that the students managed themselves, I do not mean that we had no classroom rules; rather, we had rules in which everyone was invested.

Rules, Procedures, and Routines: A Collaborative Effort

To create classroom community, teachers must provide opportunities and structures that can encourage students to help and support one another. To do so, teachers need to offer explicit instruction so that students learn how to support one another (Hittie, 2000).

Rules, procedures, and routines are good examples, and effective teachers use these to manage their classrooms. Too often, however, the decisions about rules, procedures, and routines are solely in the hands of the teacher, and the students have no voice in, and hence no responsibility for, the way their classroom is managed. To build classroom community, a teacher needs to involve the students in establishing the rules and procedures. Remember what Meredith said: "I ask [my students] what type of classroom will help them learn. I have strict policies, but we discuss each policy and why it makes sense for their learning environment."

Now think about my eighth-grade science classroom. The students were all fired up about the distillation experiment, but their behavior stayed well within the limits of appropriate classroom decorum. What rules do you think the class and I developed?

The students and I developed a chart to guide student behavior while watching complex demonstrations. As we made up the chart, the students were creative and inventive, and the result was a true collaborative effort. Rules for observing demonstrations included no crowding around the lab desk; no blocking other students' views; respecting everyone's right to see the demo; and so on. As the story reveals, there was some calling out, and it was a fitting expression of the students' excitement.

Although building a classroom community sounds simple, it requires careful thought and planning. Sometimes, students are reluctant to share their ideas for how the class should function. Encouraging them and then helping the group to reach consensus is what is needed. As you think about beginning your teaching career, consider the steps that you will take to create a classroom community. Some strategies to start thinking about include:

- Take the time to get to know your students and enlist them in their own success.

- Collaborate with your class to create guidelines for appropriate behavior.

- Establish a signal that indicates when students should give you their full attention.

- Give clear directions and create a strategy for the students to seek help.

- Find creative ways to set the mood as the students enter the room. Be consistent.

- Plan a high-quality, exciting, and engaging lesson!

Note: Adapted from "Manage Your Classroom Effectively," by Jennifer Salopek, 2011, *ASCD Update, 53*(11).

Is a Well-Managed Classroom Silent?

Many new *and* veteran teachers confuse a well-run classroom with pervasive silence. As the distillation experiment reveals, appropriate noise related to the activity or experience in which the students are engaged is a healthy aspect of a well-managed classroom. In fact, classrooms in which teachers insist on quiet all the time run the risk of students becoming disengaged and not really present in the social and emotional ways required for learning. As project-based learning experiences proliferate and students work on collaborative teams, the exchange of ideas can be noisy.

In Chapter 4 and throughout this text, teaching and learning are described as active processes requiring thoughtful reflection on challenging ideas and concepts as we make them our own. The best ways to facilitate the process of learning are to first engage students in projects and problems related to the conceptual understanding you are hoping to achieve and then invite students to work in small groups to reach consensus. With all that going on, a classroom can be a noisy place where communication facilitates learning. Today's classrooms have many configurations: Students may be seated at tables, in groups of desks, or, yes, even in rows. But however the classroom is arranged, learning cannot happen in silence. The well-managed classroom usually has groups of students communicating, collaborating with other students, working online, and, yes, making comments that pierce the silence.

▲
At times, the classroom needs to be quiet, with students listening or studying attentively.

iStock/FatCamera

School Community Influences Classroom Community

As you read in Chapter 1, schools have their own climate and culture that often permeate the classroom. In the last 15 years, schools and teachers have been frequently assessed by the scores their students achieve on standardized tests. This test-prep culture has a far reach. In one elementary school in the mid-Atlantic, 10-year-old Sydney recites the suggested dress code for the week before the English Language Arts (ELA) tests. On Monday, the students come to school in pajamas. "Pajama Day," as it is known, stands for "get a good night's sleep before the test." For Tuesday, the students wear their favorite sports teams' jerseys or tee shirts, and this represents the concept of "scoring your best on the test." For Wednesday, the students are asked to wear "readable" shirts, like those that have phrases and sayings on them, representing ELA. By Thursday, the children are all dressed in black representing the need to "fill in the bubbles completely." Finally, it is Friday, the week before the Monday standardized testing commences. The students are asked to wear "fruity colors" to represent eating a healthy breakfast the following school morning. This powerful schoolwide community-building gives students in all classes the message that these tests are important. As a classroom teacher, you will be asked to participate in this test-prep community, being sure to acknowledge that the dress code is optional. However you feel about the tests, you will probably want to be part of the community. As the classroom teacher, the extent to which your classroom community relies on respect, kindness, and mutual appreciation will be the best preparation for your students.

Being Fully Conscious

As a teacher, you are "on" from the moment your school day begins. Everything you say and do may have an effect on your students. For that reason, it is impossible to overstate the importance of being fully aware and in control of your own behavior. As an example, I share the story, as a parent, of an experience my daughter had some years ago. Note the reactions of the student, the teacher, and the parent. What was the effect on classroom community?

At the end of a school day in third grade, my 9-year-old daughter Robin came off the school bus, made eye contact with me, and started to sob. She had held back tears all afternoon and had to struggle to compose herself to tell me about her humiliation by her third-grade teacher.

It appears that left-handed Robin was holding her pencil in an awkward way. Mrs. Owens held her hand up to the class and said, "Class, do you all see the way Robin is holding her pencil? You must never hold your pencil that way." Well, that was it for Robin for the rest of the school day. Humiliated, she retreated quietly into herself and returned home bruised by this criticism in front of her peers.

I visited Mrs. Owens the following day, and before I could recount the episode, she showered me with compliments about Robin. When I shared my concern about the pencil incident with her, she said, "Oh, that was nothing. I didn't mean anything by it. I just want her to hold her pencil correctly."

The teacher reacted impulsively, without regard for how her words and actions could affect her student. Her student's feelings were hurt by the exchange, and she did not even recognize it. As a teacher, you cannot afford to "shoot from the hip." You must be careful to explore ways to change students' habits by engaging in constructive and caring dialogue.

Among the essential qualities teachers need to be successful, one is a clear sense of their own adulthood and a grounded sense of who they are. When you teach, your personality and needs are on display at all times. If you are needy, your students will sense that. You should make certain that your students' needs come before your own needs.

Teachers have different personalities, but what they have in common is that the teacher is the responsible adult in the classroom. As the adult, the teacher is obligated to create a safe, secure, and organized learning environment in which routines and expectations are consistent and respectful.

The Classroom as a Safe Space

In Chapter 6, we discussed the importance of creating a safe school climate. In many ways, a classroom community is a microcosm of the larger school climate. You may not be able to control the climate elsewhere in the school, but you can do a lot in your own classroom.

To foster a sense of community in the classroom, teachers must ensure that the classroom is a safe place—not just a physically safe environment but also an emotionally safe place where students are treated with respect, both by the teacher and by each other. In such a place, everyone is held accountable for what happens. Students come to rely on the teacher's sense of fairness and the consistency with which he or she upholds classroom rules and guidelines.

Some teachers establish a classroom meeting time to help build the sense of community. Teachers may have a "Morning Meeting" every day, or they may have class meetings as needed to discuss a particular event or to handle a problem. Each type of meeting serves a different purpose and contributes to the shared sense of community. The following teaching story illustrates how the meetings work in one fifth-grade classroom:

In a fifth-grade inclusion classroom, Ms. Sanders, who has been teaching for 5 years, has established the practice of daily Morning Meetings. This is a critical part of the day that fosters relationships among the students. The inclusion students, in particular, comment that this is their favorite part of the day.

The four parts of the Morning Meeting are the greeting, the share, announcements, and the news. The meeting takes place at the beginning of each school day on a rug at the rear of the classroom, where students sit on pillows in a circle facing each other, with the teacher positioned in a prominent spot in the circle.

Ms. Sanders views Morning Meeting as a critical event of the day, a time when students are recognized, life stories are heard, and all individuals are valued. She explains, "I make sure I greet each child, even if he or she is going out to a band lesson or early math. I make sure that I talk to them all, and they are greeted by name. I look at Morning Meeting as a place to talk about what is on the kids' minds and what is going on in their lives. Morning Meeting gives the students a place to share with the whole class, not just me. I love it! It really brings us together as a community, and I learn so much about the students as people from this daily exchange."

The students regard Morning Meeting as an important opportunity to share their life outside of school, learn about their classmates, and celebrate their differences. One boy remarks, "We do Morning Meeting, and I especially like the sharing part when you get to bring in something and share it with the class. I always like to see what other people bring in, and when I bring in something, people always come up to me at snack and want to see it. Then when I have a play date they will ask to see the thing I shared, like my arrowhead or rock collection. It makes me feel good inside and kind of special."

Another student says, "I like Morning Meeting the best because you get to hear about current events and what is going on in the world. You also get to hear what is going on in other people's lives during sharing. I really like that."

Ms. Sanders explains: "I think that the personality of the teacher helps the classroom become a warm and caring atmosphere. I think that I am very easygoing and laid back. I am always happy and smiling, and I try really hard to make the class a fun place for all kids. If I come in and I tell the kids a story that happened to me yesterday or a story about my life, then they will share with me. That creates a nice warm environment in which to learn. I try to make the class like a community. I stress that from day one. I promote an environment where they are free to take risks. They can treat each other like friends, and they can count on each other for help."

The students in this class are aware that they are a part of a special classroom community. Their sense of belongingness is not necessarily the norm outside of their classroom. They talk about bullying, ridicule, and aggressive behavior by students from other classes—experiences that occur regularly on the playground, in the lunchroom, and on the bus. Some express outrage at the social injustice experienced by their peers. The students in this class feel a sense of responsibility toward each other, reflecting the care and concern embodied by their teacher, Ms. Sanders.

In this classroom, clearly, the management is handled by everyone. (Reprinted from an unpublished paper by doctoral student Christine Schroder, 2006, Hofstra University, NY).

Ms. Sanders is quite aware of the various ways she encourages a sense of community. She mentions her easy-going personality; her storytelling, which connects her life experiences with those of the students; and her vigilance in promoting a risk-free environment and a safe place for friendships to grow. All of these are critical components in developing a caring classroom.

Morning Meeting in itself is a structure that can build a sense of community and acceptance among the members of a classroom. The daily exchanges among students allow them to

1. feel validated and an important part of the classroom community;

2. make meaning out of new concepts;

3. assist themselves and others in the learning process; and

4. celebrate personal differences.

If you establish a Morning Meeting in your classroom, you may find that students rush to the rug each morning to engage in this community-building ritual.

Research studies have revealed that if students do not feel emotionally and socially safe, the opportunities for them to learn are limited. According to research, a sense of belongingness—of being connected in important ways to others—is one of three basic psychological needs essential to human growth and development, along with autonomy and competence (Osterman, 2000, p. 325). In simple terms, students' learning improves when teachers integrate academic and social learning in the classroom (Bickart, Jablon, & Dodge, 2000; Rimm-Kaufman, 2006). Building classroom community is an intrinsic part of creating academically competent students. In addition to academic performance, researchers have found that

students with a sense of belonging in school feel socially connected, supported, and respected. They trust their teachers and their peers, and they feel like they fit in at school. They are not worried about being treated as a stereotype and are confident that they are seen as a person of value. (Romero, 2015, p.1)

The Responsive Classroom Approach to Community Building

Aligned with the sense of belonging is the **Responsive Classroom**, which introduces teachers to the theory and practice of sound classroom management through democratic principles and practices. The Responsive Classroom approach rests on principles such as:

- The social curriculum and the academic curriculum are equally important.

- How children learn is as important as what they learn.

- Social interaction facilitates cognitive growth.

- Children need to learn cooperation, assertion, responsibility, empathy, and self-control if they are to be successful socially and academically.

- Knowing children individually, culturally, and developmentally is essential to good teaching.

- Knowing children's families is essential to good teaching.

- The working relationships among the adults in a school are critically important to students' learning. (Northeast Foundation for Children, 2007; Rimm-Kaufman, 2006)

Notice that many of these principles rest heavily on the understanding that teaching and learning are about building and fostering relationships—relationships among teachers and students; among students and their peers; and among teachers and other teachers, administrators, and the community at large.

Following these principles, the developers of the Responsive Classroom model recommend a number of specific teaching strategies. They advocate Morning Meeting, for instance. They also recommend *academic choice*, a term that highlights

iStock/Antonio_Diaz

▲
A Morning Meeting is an effective way to create community in the classroom.

Responsive Classroom An approach to teaching and learning, developed by the Northeast Foundation for Children, that seeks to bring together social and academic learning.

WRITING & REFLECTION
THE ORGANIZED TEACHER

How organized are you? Teaching requires attention to so many variables: attendance, lunch money, after-school clubs, individual problems, absentee notes, and on and on.

Reflect upon your own organizational skills. How will being very organized help you to run a smooth functioning classroom? Be specific.

the importance of activities in which students make their own choices, solve problems, and work collaboratively. They even propose strategies for arranging materials, furniture, and displays to encourage independence, promote caring, and maximize learning. You can read more about Responsive Classrooms at http://www.responsiveclassroom.org/.

Tips for Creating a Classroom Community

From what you have read in this chapter, you should already have some good ideas for creating community in your classroom. The most basic suggestion I can offer is to take a genuine interest in your students. Authenticity outs itself. Students can sense when you are honestly interested in them as people as well as learners. Remember, it is often the little things you do that build a sense of trust among your students. For example, elementary school teachers learn quickly that their young students, even in first and second grade, are capable of managing many of the classroom routines—and that doing so gives them a sense of community and responsibility. Giving students classroom jobs facilitates the classroom routines while allowing the students to feel important to the community. These jobs include plant monitor, lunch menu reporter, library helper, whiteboard cleaner, pencil sharpener, and many others. A great deal of psychological research indicates that people, even young children, experience feelings of well-being and happiness when they have a sense of purpose and are of use. Psychologists suggest that this sense of well-being rests on individuals' ability to use their strengths and virtues in the service of something larger than themselves (Seligman, Steen, Park, & Peterson, 2005).

Enlisting your students in service to the classroom community gives them a sense of purpose and allows them to make a contribution to the whole. Even in middle and high school, when your time with the students is of shorter duration, you can make this happen.

Beyond the classroom, your students may have the opportunity to engage in **service learning**—that is, community service done in collaboration with a larger project at the school. This type of learning not only connects students with the larger community but it also forges bonds among

the students as they collaborate to make a difference in their own neighborhoods.

Community-Building in the Secondary Classroom

Think about a middle school in an urban area like Los Angeles. In one classroom, students file in, take their seats, and immediately begin working on a language arts warm-up exercise. While the teacher takes attendance, the eighth graders silently work. When the short exercise has been completed, students raise their hands and wait for the teacher to call on them as they go over the answers together.

Down the corridor, seventh graders stream into another classroom and take over. Some sit on table tops; others wander around the room. As the teacher takes attendance, one boy brushes his hair, three girls suck on lollipops, one girl sings, and a boy in the last row unleashes a barrage of spitballs. The day's warm up is quickly forgotten. Same school, same day, similar students, similar teachers—yet profoundly different behavior (adapted from Mehta, 2009). Educators remind us that the ability to calmly control student behavior so learning can flourish has a huge impact on a teacher's ability to be successful.

Teachers who have good skills in creating an organized classroom community in middle and high school agree on several factors. Most important, an organized teacher who has good communication skills and cares deeply about the students will be able to earn their respect and hence their cooperation. Routines are important, whether in kindergarten or 12th grade. Students feel safe when they know what to expect. The following attributes are helpful, but so is practice! Learn as much about your students as possible, and demonstrate that you are interested in them as people.

Consistency

Teachers should tell students what to expect and then deliver. This applies to all aspects of the secondary classroom, ranging from identifying test days to delivering instruction. Starting every English class, for example, by posing a question for discussion or written response helps establish a routine that students can expect.

service learning Community service done in collaboration with a larger project at the school.

CLASSROOM COMMUNITIES: TIPS FOR TEACHERS

- Teachers can never be overprepared. The first key to a successful teaching experience is to plan, plan, and plan!

- Understand your expectations for students' behavior and share those with them. Show them and tell them what you are hoping for.

- To build a sense of community, develop rules collaboratively with your students, and be clear about these.

- Be consistent. Have clear consequences when rules are broken and follow through!

- Be prepared to admit your mistakes. And use humor when appropriate.

- Make respect central to your classroom culture. Make it clear that you care about your students and that your class will lead to real learning that will benefit them.

- Minimize the power differential in everyday communication. Keep calm in all situations. Whenever possible, connect your classroom discussions and curriculum to students' lives, communities, and culture.

- Learn as much as you can about your students and make connections to their lived experiences.

- Build students' confidence in their own intelligence and creativity.

- Talk about multiple intelligences, if appropriate, and how people can be smart and creative in many ways.

- Have engaging activities prepared for the students when they walk into the classroom. Keep lecturing to a minimum.

- Engage students in group projects, centers, presentations, discussions, or role plays.

- Place the students at the center of the learning experience. Make the classroom about them.

- Remember, the best and most appropriate consequences for students are positive ones—the intrinsic joy that comes from success, accomplishment, social approval, good academic performance, and recognition. Create experiences that enable all students to feel good about themselves.

Source: Adapted from Miller (2010).

Clarity

Teachers must clearly explicate their learning objectives for the course as well their expectations for student behavior. Discuss these topics with students during the first week of class and provide specific examples of what students are expected to accomplish and how they are expected to behave. Practicing classroom rules is not solely reserved for elementary school. By illustrating through role-play with students what is considered appropriate and inappropriate behavior, teachers leave no room for student interpretation on these important points. Ask students to contribute to classroom conduct rules.

Fairness

Show respect for all your students by setting realistic expectations and offering guidance and support to help students achieve those goals.

Foresight

Map out your class in advance with your students. Spend the first few days of class discussing an overview of what you hope to accomplish as far as content, skill development, student behavior, and class format. If students do not abide by class expectations, they know in advance what repercussions they will face.

Preventing Harassment and Bullying

Successful teachers invite their students' lives, languages, and cultures into the classroom. They start building a classroom community on the first day of school. They care about their students, and they create an environment where social justice is both a goal and a reality.

If you say the next person who talks in class will be set on fire and rolled down the hallway, you're in trouble if someone talks and you don't set them on fire and roll them down the hallway.

—Kendra Wallace, Middle School Principal, Los Angeles

In this type of environment, injustices toward individuals or groups of students become readily apparent. Two prominent examples of social injustice in today's schools are sexual harassment and bullying. This section explores these topics and discusses how you can help prevent them from endangering your classroom community.

Sexual and Sex-Based Harassment in School

Under the guidelines established by the federal Office for Civil Rights, sexual harassment is considered a form of sex discrimination and is therefore prohibited by Title IX of the Education Amendments of 1972. Generally speaking, **sexual harassment** is any "unwanted and unwelcome sexual behavior" that interferes with a person's life. Sexual harassment does not include "behaviors that you like or want (such as wanted kissing, touching, or flirting)" (American Association of University Women Educational Foundation [AAUWEF], 2004, p. 11). Sex-based harassment is a broad term including sexual harassment, sexual violence, and gender-based harassment. Sexual harassment and sexual assault begin in elementary schools and occur with alarming frequency in middle and high schools. The victims are girls, boys, and gender nonconforming students.

Sexually harassing behaviors happen in school hallways, stairwells, bathrooms, and classrooms, and they have a negative effect on the emotional and educational lives of students In an AAUWEF national report (Hill & Kearl, 2011), 48% of all students stated that they had experienced sexual harassment in person or online during the previous school year; eight in 10 students experienced some form of sexual harassment during their school lives; 85% of students in Grades 8 through 11 said that students harass other students at their schools; and almost 40% of students reported that teachers and other school employees sexually harass students in their schools. A 2017 report, featuring news from the National Education Association (NEA), emphasized that assaults are often underreported:

> From 2011 to 2015, about 17,000 sexual assaults were committed by U.S. students . . . although the number is likely much higher because assaults are under-reported or mislabeled as bullying, particularly among young victims. About 5% of the victims the AP reported on were 5- and 6-year-olds. (Long, 2017)

In one northern Virginia school district, the family life education curriculum, "which begins in tenth grade and continues through twelfth grade, addresses healthy and unhealthy relationships, definitions of sexual harassment, assault and rape, sex trafficking, and indicators of abuse among students" (Long, 2017). The curriculum also explores the meaning of *consent*:

> Sexual consent, students learn, is when a person clearly agrees to engage in sexual activity with another person. There can be no question about whether they agree, and consent can't be the result of intimidation or pressure. Victims are not at fault if they are engaged in unwanted sexual activity while intoxicated, and it does not matter how a person is dressed or if they did not verbally say no. Silence is not consent. Many

school districts are feeling the pressure of proliferating sexual harassment in their schools and taking this kind of proactive stance. (Long, 2017)

In 1999, the Supreme Court ruled that school districts can be liable for damages under federal law for failing to stop a student from subjecting another student to severe and pervasive sexual harassment (Koch, 2002, p. 262). Title IX also guarantees that hostility and ridicule toward gay, lesbian, and gender nonconforming students that is not immediately acted upon by the school or district may be grounds for a lawsuit against that district. (See Table 9.1 for a simple checklist to determine what has been done to prevent sex-based harassment in the school or district.)

As a teacher, you need to learn about your school or district's policies concerning sex-based harassment and teach them openly to your students. Make sure students know the sanctioned procedures for reporting abuse so they do not needlessly suffer victimization by others. Many schools use role-playing scenarios or videos to prompt student discussion of sex-based harassment issues. Teachers and schools are responsible for creating a harassment-free environment in which all students are safe to learn. The Northern Virginia district described earlier included a concentrated program on sexual violence and the nature of consent.

Establishing a sense of community with your students is a vital means of preventing harassment in school. When students feel responsible for one another and care about their learning community, harassing behaviors are less likely to occur; and when they do, they are less likely to persist. If your classroom community fosters an atmosphere of risk-free communication, your students will be better able to talk about alleged harassment and determine what to do.

Beyond the general principle of making respect central to your classroom culture, you should consider specific guidelines for student behavior that will help prevent sexual

---

TABLE 9.1 ● Sex-Based Harassment Checklist for Schools or School Districts

- Does the school/district have a specific policy against sexual harassment?
- Does the school/district foster an atmosphere of prevention by sensitizing students and staff to issues of sexual harassment?
- Is the school/district prepared to receive and respond to complaints?
- Does the school/district have a grievance procedure for sexual harassment?
- How effective has the school/district been in implementing its antiharassment policy?

Source: Adapted from "Harassment-Free Hallways: How to Stop Sexual Harassment in School," AAUW Educational Foundation, 2004. Washington, DC: American Association of University Women Educational Foundation.

---

sexual harassment Unwelcome sexual advances, requests for sexual favors, or other physical and expressive behavior of a sexual nature that interferes with a person's life.

TYPES OF SEX-BASED HARASSMENT

Title IX requires schools to take steps to prevent and remedy two forms of **sex-based harassment**: sexual harassment (including sexual violence) and **gender-based harassment**. Sexual harassment is unwelcome conduct of a sexual nature. It includes unwelcome sexual advances, requests for sexual favors, and other verbal, nonverbal, or physical conduct of a sexual nature. Sexual violence is a form of sexual harassment. *Sexual violence*, as the Office of Civil Rights uses the term, refers to physical sexual acts perpetrated against a person's will or where a person is incapable of giving consent. A number of different acts fall into the category of sexual violence, including rape, sexual assault, sexual battery, sexual abuse, and sexual coercion.

Title IX also prohibits gender-based harassment, which is unwelcome conduct based on a student's sex—harassing conduct based on a student's failure to conform to sex stereotypes. Sex-based harassment can be carried out by school employees, other students, and third parties. All students can experience sex-based harassment, including male and female students; lesbian, gay, bisexual, transgender, and queer students; students with disabilities; and students of different races, national origins, and ages. Title IX protects all students from sex-based harassment, regardless of the sex of the parties, including when they are members of the same sex. Sex-based harassment creates a hostile environment if the conduct is sufficiently serious that it denies or limits a student's ability to participate in or benefit from the school's program.

Source: U.S. Department of Education, Office for Civil Rights (n.d.). Sex-Based Harassment. https://www2.ed.gov/about/offices/list/ocr/frontpage/pro-students/issues/sex-issue01.html.

harassment. Often, well-meaning teachers ignore certain behaviors, especially in middle and high school, as long as they seem socially acceptable to the students themselves. For instance, teachers may decide that name calling and excessive flirting are "normal" for the students' age, when in fact these behaviors can be disruptive to the victim's well-being. It is important to know how to respond to this type of occurrence. There are many surveys and checklists that help teachers and students recognize sexually harassing behavior. A checklist for teens might suggest, for example, that acceptable flirting makes you feel flattered, whereas harassment makes you feel unattractive or ashamed. The particular guidelines you adopt should take into account your students' age, the cultures represented in your classroom, and your school and district policies.

Bullying

While creating a classroom community that is a safe space for students is a deterrent to negative student behavior, teachers cannot be everywhere. Let us go back to Ms. Sanders's classroom, described earlier in this chapter. Despite the warm and caring environment promoted by her use of Morning Meeting, one of the students reported bullying and teasing on the playground at lunchtime. Because there is a long-standing tradition of the classroom or school bully, this problem is often overlooked. In fact, approximately one in four youth are affected by bullying during the school year, negatively impacting millions of children, parents, and individuals in our schools and communities. Gender nonconforming students are more likely to be victims of bullying (see Figure 9.1).

Bullying implies repeated harmful acts and an imbalance of power. It can involve physical, verbal, or psychological attacks or intimidation directed against a victim who cannot properly defend himself or herself because of size or strength or because of being outnumbered or less psychologically resilient. Bullying includes assault, tripping, intimidation, rumor spreading and isolation, demands for money, destruction of property, theft of valued possessions, destruction of another's work, and name calling (Sampson, 2002). The definition of bullying includes three essential components:

- Bullying is an aggressive behavior involving unwanted, negative actions.
- Bullying involves a pattern of repeated behaviors over time.
- Bullying involves an imbalance of power or strength. (Megan Meier Foundation, 2018)

Many antibullying programs have been put in place, including procedures that students can follow if they feel they are being bullied. Most of the time, however, students do not reveal that they are being bullied, and witnesses tend not to come forward. Although there are more male bullies and male victims, the numbers of female bullies and victims are on the rise (Olweus, 2003). Victimization by bullying has been linked to student depression, eating disorders, and even suicidal tendencies (Sears, 1991).

sex-based harassment A broad term including sexual harassment, sexual violence, and gender-based harassment.

gender-based harassment Harassing conduct based on a student's failure to conform to sex stereotypes.

bullying Repeated cruelty, physical or psychological, by a powerful person toward a less powerful person.

Figure 9.1 ● Percentage of Students Ages 12–18 Who Reported Selected Bullying Problems at School and Cyberbullying Problems Anywhere During the School Year: 2015

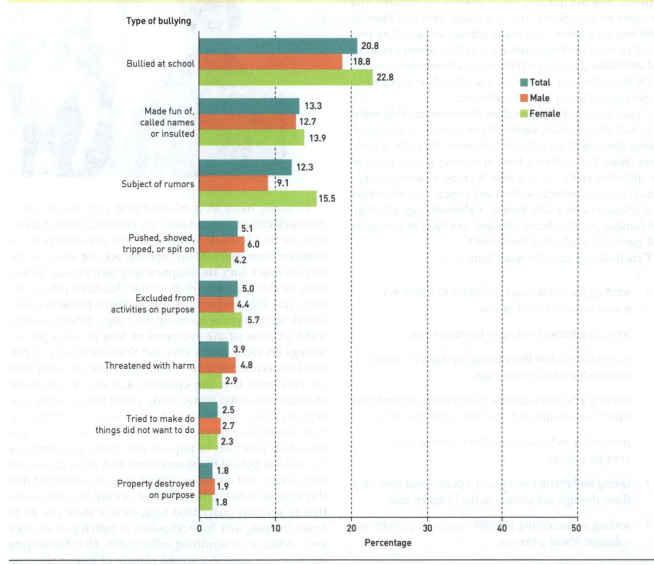

Type of bullying

Bullied at school — Total 20.8, Male 18.8, Female 22.8

Made fun of, called names or insulted — Total 13.3, Male 12.7, Female 13.9

Subject of rumors — Total 12.3, Male 9.1, Female 15.5

Pushed, shoved, tripped, or spit on — Total 5.1, Male 6.0, Female 4.2

Excluded from activities on purpose — Total 5.0, Male 4.4, Female 5.7

Threatened with harm — Total 3.9, Male 4.8, Female 2.9

Tried to make do things did not want to do — Total 2.5, Male 2.7, Female 2.3

Property destroyed on purpose — Total 1.8, Male 1.9, Female 1.8

Percentage (0–50)

Source: U.S. Department of Education, National Center for Education Statistics. (2017e). *Indicators of School Crime and Safety: 2016* (NCES 2017-064), Indicator 11. https://nces.ed.gov/pubs2017/2017064.pdf

Note: "At school" includes in the school building, on school property, on a school bus, and going to and from school. Students who reported experiencing more than one type of bullying at school were counted only once in the total for students bullied at school.

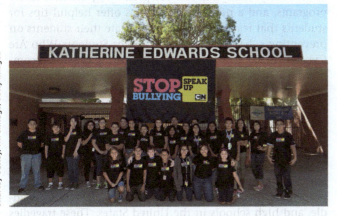

Charley Gallay/WireImage/Getty Images

In classes where a strong sense of community has been created, not only is bullying less likely to occur in the first place, but if it does, the bullying victim is more likely to come forward, as are the witnesses. The emphasis is on the common good and on care and respect for one another.

Cyberbullying

Social networking is a way of life for our nation's youth. They are part of myriad online communities, and with all these opportunities to communicate online, there are hidden dangers. On Facebook, Snapchat, Instagram, Twitter, and other social media, students can send negative and hurtful messages to their peers, creating a sense for the victim of being bullied online. In addition, people can pretend to be someone they are not and entice unknowing children and teenagers to meet them. This is a major source of Internet child and teen abuse, and many schools are adopting programs to warn their students about online sexual predators and establishing ways to report online solicitations. Internet crime is a crime like any other and should be reported to proper local, state, or federal authorities.

Cyberbullying is a prevalent phenomenon that refers to hurtful texts, e-mails, Facebook posts, snaps, or Instagram photos directed at an individual student. It can be a computer crime if it reaches a level of causing serious harm to the intended victim. It is a federal crime to anonymously annoy, harass, threaten, or abuse any person via the Internet or a telecommunications system. Cyberbullying, although not causing physical harm, can lead to effects as damaging and traumatic as physical harassment.

Cyberbullying can take many forms:

- sending mean messages or threats to a person's e-mail account or cell phone;

- spreading rumors online or through texts;

- posting hurtful or threatening messages on social networking sites or web pages;

- stealing a person's account information to break into his or her account and send damaging messages;

- pretending to be someone else online to hurt another person;

- taking unflattering pictures of a person and spreading them through cell phones or the Internet; and

- sexting or circulating sexually suggestive pictures or messages about a person.

Additionally, a person's e-mail account or cell phone can be broken into, allowing the victim to appear to be sending damaging messages to others. Cyberbullying can be very painful for adolescents, leading to states of anxiety and depression and even suicide (adapted from http://www.bullyingstatistics.org/content/cyber-bullying-statistics.html, retrieved March 25, 2018).

Bullying is all about power. The bully has it; the victim does not. Technology accelerates bullying as social media make it easy for bullies to enlist large, usually anonymous groups to carry out relentless attacks with text messages, Facebook posts, e-mails, snaps, and compromising digital photos that may be sexts. Adults are removed from this assault and are not present electronically to intervene. Victims often feel ashamed, powerless, and fearful of retaliation if they report the bully or bullies.

iStock/Highwaystarz-Photography

Facebook has a stop cyberbullying page (https://www.facebook.com/stopcyberbullying); however, most students who are on Facebook continue to post the most personal items on their pages. Many students are not aware of the ways in which they are compromising their privacy. Unless users are extremely careful about their Facebook privacy settings, just about everything that is posted becomes public knowledge to anyone accessing their page. School communities are now raising awareness of how to select privacy settings on social media sites and thus add a layer of personal protection for today's students. There are many who are concerned that the openness and ease of electronic communication has inured many young people to the concept of privacy and personal boundaries. In cyberbullying, these boundaries are consistently violated, and the victim often feels powerless to respond effectively. Cyberbullying is a serious, behind-the-scenes event that often occurs not only during, but also after, school time. It is essential that this type of bullying be addressed openly in schools and that all students understand what each of them can do to report bullying they have witnessed or bullying where they are a victim or an unwitting collaborator. All cyberbullying interventions require a school climate of trust and caring that ensures all communications with school personnel are confidential.

The most important action a student can initiate if he or she is experiencing cyberbullying is to tell someone immediately. Many schools are promoting Internet safety programs, and a number of websites offer helpful tips for students that teachers can use to educate their students on preventing cyberbullying (see "Tips for Students Who Are Cyberbullied"). Creating a safe and trusting classroom community extends to protecting your students from online abuse.

School Safety and Gun Violence Prevention

Since 2000, conservative estimates suggest that there have been more than 130 school shootings at elementary, middle, and high schools in the United States. These tragedies resulted in the deaths of about 60 people at the elementary

---

cyberbullying Bullying or harassment through electronic means such as e-mail, website postings, instant messaging, text messaging, blogs, mobile phones, or chatrooms; also called *online bullying*.

TIPS FOR STUDENTS WHO ARE CYBERBULLIED

- Tell a trusted adult, and keep telling him or her until action is taken.
- Never open, read, or respond to messages from cyberbullies.
- If it is school related, tell your school. All schools have bullying solutions.
- Do not erase the messages. They may be needed to take action.

- If bullied through chat or instant messaging, the bully can often be blocked.
- If you are threatened with harm, call the police.

Source: iSAFE, Inc., "Beware of the Cyberbully," https://www.isafe.org/imgs/pdf/education/CyberBullying.pdf, retrieved March 20, 2018. Reproduced with permission.

level and almost 70 people at the high school level (Bump, 2018). Programs for the prevention of gun violence and the maintenance of safe schools are being developed all over the country. The NEA (n.d.) suggests the following keys to school safety and gun violence prevention:

1. Increase access to mental health services within the school, including school counselors, school social workers, and school psychologists.

2. Provide a safe and secure learning environment by being equipped with an updated structural and technological support foundation to help protect students and educators from danger and providing professional development about bullying, mental and behavioral health, cultural competence, appropriate classroom management, and safety.

3. Take meaningful action on gun violence prevention by ensuring that guns don't end up in the hands of people who shouldn't have them. The NEA believes that everyone who wants to purchase a firearm should go through a background check, regardless of where they are purchasing the weapon.

Source: National Education Association, Three Keys to School Safety and Gun Violence Prevention, at http://www.nea.org/home/54092.htm, retrieved March 28, 2018.

There is little national research being done on gun violence; however, in the wake of school shootings, schools and districts are preparing teachers to enforce lockdown and shelter in place procedures that help mitigate the loss of life in the event of a gun emergency. These professional development initiatives are required as a step toward ensuring the safety of students and all school personnel.

School safety affects all communities and requires vigilance and dedication to cooperate with community leaders and law enforcement officials. The teacher's role in this broad area of concern is to maintain an awareness and understanding of the roles of **school resource officers (SROs)**

....

school resource officers (SROs) Law enforcement officers specially trained to work with and in schools, addressing a safe school climate and preventing crime.

if they are present in your school building. There are many challenges that exist when it comes to law enforcement—a key partner—working in collaboration with schools to help ensure safety. Because law enforcement and school personnel differ in so many ways, they face challenges in the areas of communications, perception, roles, responsibilities, and data sharing.

SROs are specially trained law enforcement officers who are responsible for maintaining school safety and crime prevention. The specially designed training programs in which these law enforcement personnel participate emphasize school–community partnerships and the role of SROs as mentors and resources for youth. Their role is to create a safer environment for both students and staff. SROs can engage in productive, cooperative efforts to prevent, intervene in, and suppress crime-related behaviors in schools. Good school community partnerships foster mutual respect among law enforcement officials like SROs and the teaching and administrative staff (Rosiak, 2009).

Classroom Community and Goodness of Fit

As we mentioned earlier, good classroom management requires that you be fully conscious in the classroom. It requires what Jacob Kounin (1970) called "withitness," a concept sometimes interpreted as having "eyes in the back of your head" to ward off any undesirable behavior. I prefer to think of withitness as a broad awareness that you have about yourself and your students together. Do you have a centered presence in the classroom? Are you aware of the students' dispositions on any given day as they enter your room? At any moment, do you know whether the principles of classroom community that you and the students have developed are working?

These are important matters to take into consideration when deciding on the "goodness of fit" between yourself and the teaching profession. Think about the following concepts:

- Good teachers are usually interested in learning as much as they can about their students.
- Effective teachers are organized and plan ahead.

- New teachers frequently imagine how they will speak and act in front of a class.

- Good teachers care deeply about listening to and valuing their students' ideas.

- Teachers need to be fully conscious or "with it" at all times, and especially in a large group of students.

- Effective teachers are often role models for their younger, less empowered students.

Concluding Thoughts

Clearly, good communication and collaboration with your students are vital for creating a classroom in which everyone feels responsible for managing the environment and working toward the common good. As a teacher, you should identify the most effective rules for your classroom and seek the students' assistance in establishing these as classroom priorities. When you involve your students in setting guidelines for everyone to follow, you help them emotionally invest in an environment where everyone can learn and occurrences like bullying and sexual harassment are stopped in their tracks.

Classroom community relates to the principles of teaching and learning we have discussed throughout this book. When you have your students work in groups, develop their own strategies for solving problems, and apply their concepts to meaningful real-world projects, you not only help them learn individually but you also foster their sense of the classroom as a learning community. When you honor diversity and use culturally relevant pedagogy, you create the same effect. All of these practices are good teaching methods *and* good classroom management strategies.

Finally, your ability to be honest with your students and to show your interest in their lives will go a long way toward earning their trust and turning the classroom into a safe place and a genuine learning community.

CHAPTER REVIEW

Key Terms

bullying (p. 148)

classroom community (p. 139)

classroom management (p. 139)

cyberbullying (p. 150)

gender-based harassment (p. 148)

Responsive Classroom (p. 144)

school resource officers
(SROs) (p. 151)

service learning (p. 145)

sex-based harassment (p. 148)

sexual harassment (p. 147)

Review the Learning Outcomes

Review each section of the chapter and answer the following:

LO 9-1 How do you establish shared goals, values, and routines in your classroom?

LO 9-2 What role does community building have in preventing bullying and harassment?

LO 9-3 How may school violence be prevented?

LO 9-4 What are the most important steps for building community in the classroom?

InTASC Standards

Review the InTASC Standards for the chapter and explain how the chapter addressed each one.

Standard 7: Planning for Instruction

Standard 8: Instructional Strategies

Standard 10: Leadership and Collaboration

Journal Prompt

What personal characteristics must a teacher have in order to create an effective classroom community?

Get the tools you need to sharpen your study skills. SAGE edge offers a robust online environment featuring an impressive array of free tools and resources.

Access practice quizzes, eFlashcards, video, and multimedia at **edge.sagepub.com/koch4e**.

iStock/monkeybusinessimages

Making the Decision to Become a Teacher

Most good teachers leave the classroom in June and ask how they can do it better in September. They spend their summers taking workshops, going to conferences, and seeking professional development on a variety of topics . . .

—Judy Logan (1999)

Learning Outcomes

After reading this chapter, you should be able to:

10-1   Explain how teachers in the 21st century are challenged in ways that their predecessors were not.

10-2   Examine the requirements of your state for earning a teaching certificate.

10-3   Analyze the roles of the American Federation of Teachers and the National Education Association for beginning teachers.

10-4   Discuss how a teaching portfolio can demonstrate your talents for teaching.

10-5   Analyze the self-reflections that lead you to believe that teaching is for you.

InTASC Standards

- Standard 6: Assessment

- Standard 7: Planning for Instruction

- Standard 9: Professional Learning and Ethical Practice

- Standard 10: Leadership and Collaboration

At this point in your journey, you would be correct to conclude that teaching and learning are highly sophisticated activities. A career in education requires careful planning, the capacity for spontaneous decision making, and actions based on careful personal reflection. In this final chapter, we examine some ways of thinking about the teaching profession in the hopes that it will help in your decision-making process. Moments of absolute certainty are rare, but there are signs that can help you make your choice.

Goodness of Fit

You have to love kids and want to connect with them—because if you don't connect with the kids, you will never be able to convey the materials; if you cannot feel the music, you cannot play the music. . . . I can teach anyone about pedagogical strategies, but I cannot teach a person to love kids. And you can feel it in a classroom as soon as you walk in.

—Christopher Day (2004)

As was mentioned in Chapter 1, *goodness of fit* is a term used in descriptive statistics to mean a match between a theory and a set of observations. By using the term to refer to the match between a teacher candidate's attributes and the job of a teacher, this text has invited you to consider your own suitability for the teaching profession.

Think about what you have learned about teaching and what you have recognized about your personal attributes. Remember that there is no one definition of a "good" or a "successful" teacher. The power of a teacher cannot be overestimated. You will be responsible for the education of tomorrow's thinkers and leaders, and you will learn the

joy of making a contribution to other people's growth and development.

Research has found that people are often happier when they are making a contribution to others (Seligman, 2002), and that is certainly true of teaching. But considerable evidence also shows that people are more successful when they are engaged in work that plays to their strengths. If teaching does not play to your own strengths, perhaps it is not the best profession for you. An article written for *The New Yorker* magazine (Gladwell, 2008) discussed how difficult it was for professional sports scouts to determine, based on observing college athletes at play, who would be the best draft pick for particular positions, in this case in football. Titled "Most Likely to Succeed," the article emphasized how difficult it is to predict how someone will do in a position once he or she is hired, no matter how much you learn about the person beforehand. Nowhere is this as serious an issue as when hiring a new teacher. This is mainly because research tells us that really good teachers have profound effects on student learning and can positively influence a child's life. This is a good time to consider how you may be able to tell if you are a good fit for teaching. These are some attributes of good teachers that form only the beginning of a list. You probably have others and can make this list even longer. Many individuals who succeed as teachers have

- a centered presence in the classroom,

- a sensitivity to the classroom setting,

- an ability to respond thoughtfully to each student,

- a personal capacity for juggling many tasks at once,

- an appreciation of how children and young adults grow and change,

- an understanding of the ways our students bring their outside worlds into the classroom,

- a desire to help students feel capable and competent,

- an ability to listen to others, and

- a generosity of spirit.

The Importance of Observing and Participating in the Field

As we mentioned in Chapter 1, visiting a school and spending time in classrooms can provide a sense of the school culture and the school climate. This is important to gain a real-time, current look at the life of teachers and students. Your first formal experience in a classroom will probably be through your **field placement**. The field placement is an opportunity for you to serve as an apprentice and learn from the regular classroom teacher and from your own experience of working with the students.

In some formal field experiences, you begin by making observations. Keep some of the attributes just mentioned in mind as you observe in the classroom setting. In other placements, you may be considered a **participant-observer**. While participating in the life of the classroom, you make careful observations and study the classroom environment to learn about child and adolescent development and teaching methods. Usually, participant-observers are not required to spend the entire school day in the field placement; rather, they must be immersed in the school for a specific number of hours each week.

In other field placements, you are considered a **student teacher**. In this arrangement, you are assigned to a teacher, usually called the *cooperating teacher*, on a daily basis for a specified period of time, such as 10 to 12 weeks. Student teachers at the secondary level often receive two placements, one in a middle school and the other in a high school. At the elementary level, depending on your state's requirements, you may receive one placement in Grades K–2 and another in Grades 3–5.

As a student teacher, you will be expected to teach the class at prearranged times. During some of these teaching experiences, you will be formally observed by a supervisor assigned by your institution. Student teaching is a special time when you develop a clear idea of what the life of a classroom teacher is all about. It is an important part of your professional preparation.

Before you start your field experience, it is important to learn as much as possible about the school and classroom to which you are assigned. Be certain that you understand your role in the classroom and that you are aware of the dress code for teachers in the school. Ask questions. Be gracious, and be sure to thank the teacher in whose classroom you are gaining experience.

The Purposes of Public Education and the Role of the Teacher

Above all things, I hope that the education of the common people will be attended to, convinced that on their good sense we may rely with the most security for the preservation of a due degree of liberty.

—Thomas Jefferson, in a letter to James Madison, 1787

Chapter 3 described the vital role public education has played in American democratic society since the early days of the nation. As the quotation from Thomas Jefferson indicates, U.S. public schools have always been expected to fulfill certain public missions that go beyond the purely academic.

Today, as you have seen throughout this book, **public education** serves the basic function of preparing young people to lead productive lives by increasing their academic achievement and improving their readiness to secure jobs in an increasingly global economy. In addition, however, public education helps equip our youth to become responsible and active citizens in a democratic society. In other words, it prepares them to participate in decisions that contribute to the social good (Kober, 2007).

Although the current era of standards-based assessments emphasizes quantifiable academic achievement, it is useful to envision your career in education as serving a broader purpose. The Center on Education Policy is a national independent source for research and information about public education (https://www.cep-dc.org/). In 2007, it described the mission of public education in terms of six main themes. Those themes resonate today as we examine the purposes of public schooling:

1. To provide universal access to free education
2. To guarantee equal opportunities for all children
3. To unify a diverse population
4. To prepare people for citizenship in a democratic society
5. To prepare people to become economically self-sufficient
6. To improve social conditions

field placement An opportunity for you to serve as an apprentice in a classroom and learn from the regular classroom teacher and from your own experience of working with the students.

participant-observer While participating in the life of the classroom, one who makes careful observations and studies the classroom environment to learn about child and adolescent development and teaching methods.

student teacher One who is assigned to a teacher, usually called the *cooperating teacher*, on a daily basis for a specified period of time, such as 10 to 12 weeks, to start practice teaching a specific number of lessons a week.

public education Education that is publicly financed, tuition-free, accountable to public authorities, and accessible to all students. The term covers various types of public schools, including traditional schools, charter and magnet schools, vocational schools, and public virtual and alternative schools.

In Chapter 9, we explored how classrooms can create a sense of community, a social group mindful of the needs of each of its members. In this sense, creating a classroom community becomes more than a tool for effective teaching and learning; it becomes a model for social justice and social participation in the microcosm of the classroom. Clearly, the important goals of education include helping students develop their abilities to think critically, appreciate diverse cultures, maintain curiosity about the world, and show confidence in expressing their own ideas. Helping your students to feel capable and competent is an important role for the teacher you become.

In Chapters 1 and 2, we explored the experiences of a diverse group of teachers. Now that we have come to the end of this text, I invite you to think about the profession of teaching as requiring an overriding commitment by its members to the well-being of their students. *Teaching is not an ordinary job.* It is a profession that establishes our identities and reveals our values. Remember, we teach who we are!

Most important, the functions and responsibilities of teachers are not confined to the classroom. Central to your work as a teacher is devoting time and energy to professional communities, activities, conferences, and workshops. Teaching is an opportunity for intellectual development, both through professional teacher development courses and through your own intimate contact with new books, ideas, and technologies. Few teachers who are not also intellectually curious are successful.

Further, teaching in the 21st century requires guiding students through the huge quantity of information that enters their lives daily. It is your job to help them understand what is valid and what needs to be discarded. All this has to be accomplished as you prepare your students for frequent standardized testing and find creative ways to help them to be successful. In some locations, teacher performance evaluations are starting to include your students'

test scores. This reality means you want a prepared class but not a class that has suffered from test preparation! These contemporary teaching needs make the teacher's role more complex and ever changing as compared to any previous era. Luckily, you can find support through various professional organizations and on many online sites, in chat rooms, and on blogs.

Recently, seasoned teachers were interviewed about why they remain teachers when there are so many demands from standards and testing (Nieto, 2015). These teachers' responses remind us of the rewards and responsibilities that accompany being a teacher. They include a belief that "all kids deserve an education that honors and validates who they are, that makes room for their questions and concerns, and that challenges them to think deeply and helps them to find meaning in a sometimes hostile and confusing world" (Nieto, 2015, p. 55).

One Size Does Not Fit All

In Chapter 3, when we explored the history of U.S. public education and the many reform movements that have dotted the landscape of teaching and learning, we saw that public education is a large mosaic. Methods are varied, and successes and failures weave their way through each successive period of history. There is no one right way to teach; there are many right ways—and many incorrect ways as well. Teaching is as variable as the types and personalities of teachers. Often, teaching online requires a set of skills that enables you to communicate thoughtfully with your students despite the absence of face-to-face meetings.

The challenge is to imagine you are on a journey of both inward and outward exploration. You will explore your own personality traits, subject areas of expertise, capacity for generosity, and school stories. Try to remember the special moments that made you feel like school was the best place in the world. Also recall those times when being a student was painful or you were victimized by a teacher, knowingly or unknowingly.

One of your most useful tools is your capacity for reflection, along with your humility. It is profoundly moving to affect the lives of young people; it is also an extraordinary responsibility.

Find a way to connect with colleagues or classmates with whom you can have a conversation about teaching. Learning to teach is very much about having conversations and exchanging stories with willing colleagues. These discussions will help you discover the ways teaching will be a personal expression of yourself.

iStock/BanksPhotos

WRITING & REFLECTION
YOUR FIELD EXPERIENCE

What is your most memorable field experience so far? What did you learn from it? In what ways did you feel successful with the students? How, if at all, did you wish you had done things differently?

Creating a Culture of Caring

The key to creating a learning community is to manage your classroom with heart—and, by that, I mean permeate the classroom atmosphere with caring concern. This involves care in interactions with students, lesson planning, seating chart decisions, discipline concerns, grading, and more. Putting care for your students first creates a learning community that inspires them to be their best selves, both in school and out in the world.

—Ridnouer (2006)

Many teachers talk about the importance of caring about students so that they see themselves as valuable and capable of learning. Creating a caring environment has a deep effect on you as well. Building relationships with students changes you in ways that you cannot predict. I remember, as a young middle school science teacher, I would see my students' faces in my dreams long after the school year ended. My first years of teaching were filled with successes and disappointments. I decided to leave the profession and went into business where I was successful but feeling like something was missing. After 2 years in the business world, I returned to the classroom. I felt it was my "calling"; I instinctively knew I belonged there and was determined to find the balance between caring deeply for my students and caring for myself as well. By that, I mean finding the balance between taking care of my students and taking care of myself. This is important as teachers create caring environments. Teaching can be very draining, and learning how to take care of yourself physically and emotionally is very important. My story is a reminder that the early years of teaching confront us with many challenges. Working with young people is often unpredictable and can shake one's confidence. Feelings of frustration are not uncommon; however, they are often counterbalanced by a sense of profound accomplishment when students have that aha moment and demonstrate that they really "get it." Becoming proficient in our chosen profession takes time. Being patient with yourself as you begin is an important attribute.

David Levine (2015) described ways to create a caring culture in your classroom. He suggested asking yourself four questions:

1. What do my students need to succeed?

2. What principles do I need to instill in my classroom in order to meet my students' needs?

iStock/skynesher

▲ Communication, collaboration, and connection are the hallmarks of 21st-century teaching and learning.

3. What behavioral guidelines would I like to see my students follow?

4. What social skills are most important to help my students behave in a principles-based fashion?

In answering these questions, you may want to consider giving all students the opportunity to be heard, helping students to listen to one another, collaborating with students on the rules of behavior, and posting guidelines for helping students create a caring community in the classroom. If you value who the students are, not just how they score on tests, the students know it and feel heard and validated. The authenticity of your feelings "out" themselves.

One teacher described it this way:

I identify as a teacher. It's what I am meant to do, and it is as rewarding to me as art is to the artist, a great play is to the athlete, and the correct diagnosis is to the doctor. When I see students grapple with a concept and come away with new understanding of the material and a new respect for themselves, the long hours I invest hardly matter. (Ridnouer, 2006, p. 1)

The next story offers another perspective on a new teacher and the culture of caring she has created:

Jaime Barron started teaching the fourth grade in an urban area where poverty is commonplace, most children are from minority backgrounds, and more than 90% have lived all or some of their lives in homeless shelters. The students come to school with little social capital. Many are from single-parent families where their responsibilities include the care of younger siblings. All of the students receive free breakfast and lunch daily.

Because Jaime's experience with these fourth-grade students was very positive, she asked if she could "loop" with this class to fifth grade. (*Looping* is the process of sending an entire class together into the next grade level with the same teacher. In some school districts, it requires parental approval.) When I visited her and her class, it was the middle of the fifth grade, and the 29 students were working in seven groups on projects that involved designing model ecosystems for different animals around the world.

Jaime's room is covered with print; student work hangs everywhere. There are posters hanging from clotheslines strung across the room. The posters explain group-work rules that include taking turns, listening to others, and offering ideas. For these students, working independently is a challenge, but they enjoy working on projects and accessing information on the computer, and they tell me they really like Ms. Barron.

The classroom is small and crowded, and there are not enough resources. The students have little knowledge about environments beyond their urban apartments and shelters. Doing group projects that construct environments far beyond their streets is a new experience for them. To aid their imagination, a world map hangs in the classroom. Their city is circled in red.

All the students, who range in age from 10 to 13, appear to have a fundamental understanding that Ms. Barron cares about them. They respond to this. Each morning they bring her enormous plan book to her and ask, "What are we doing today?" They understand that she prepares for them. She is calm and firm; she never yells; she never takes unacceptable behavior personally. Jaime knows that the students with whom she works struggle in their environment. She reminds them of rules and structures they have developed to keep the class running smoothly and to maximize learning. The students tell me they feel safe in her class and are lucky to be with her. "She never yells." Jaime tells me there is little truancy in her class.

I ask Jaime if she will remain in this school next year, when her current students move on to middle school. Yes, she will stay, she explains, because she feels she is making a difference and she is needed here.

It will come as no surprise to you that, to Barron, teaching is much more than a job. It is an authentic commitment to working on behalf of her students. Her clarity about her purpose finds its way into the classroom community that she and her students have created. The students trust her

and know she will not harm them, demean them, scream at them, or use her power over them. Her calm voice and caring manner are accompanied by classroom structures that keep the students productive and safe.

Jaime is extremely well prepared all the time. She consistently has a creative, activity-oriented experience in which to engage the class. She takes the students on field trips, monitors their homework, and works with them one-on-one during lunchtime.

Jaime also actively reflects on her teaching. She has some days that are worse than others, some days that are better, but throughout the ups and downs, she loves her work and cannot imagine doing anything else.

Looking Again at Multiple Ways of Teaching and Learning

In my classroom, my world, the most important people are not the policy makers and textbook companies; they are my students and their families. This is how I navigate the stormy seas as I try to calm the national storm that rages [around education]. . . .

—Mary Jade Haney
(as cited in Nieto, 2014 p. 105)

Throughout this text, we have visited different types of classrooms with varying approaches to teaching. As we have seen, studies in neuroscience show that, for a concept to get hooked into their prior knowledge, individuals need to construct meaning for themselves. We have explored project- and problem-based learning as ways to place the students' own construction of knowledge at the center of their learning experience.

Many educators see student-centered learning as an "anything goes" method. On the contrary, student-centered environments seek to draw out students' ideas to deal with the misconceptions that often accompany the learning of something new. Unless we understand what students are thinking about the material in which we engage them, we cannot know if they "get it."

Do remember, however, that student-centered environments use multiple teaching strategies, ranging from direct explanations to project- and problem-based learning. The successful teacher learns how to adapt the materials to the class in a way that reaches the individual students and asks them to demonstrate their understanding. Hence, student-centered classrooms invite learners to create explanations, demonstrate meaning, and come up with their own ideas and questions related to the content area.

Using Current Technologies

Today, making connections to students' lived experiences means accessing the wired world of cyberspace in ways that enhance students' critical thinking and their abilities to understand a concept. In previous chapters, we emphasized the growing effect of technology on education. *Connect, communicate,* and *collaborate*—these are the three Cs of the newest wave of technology use in the classroom. Teaching can involve creating a class website for which all of the students collaborate to determine the content or using smartphones to tweet about a lesson. Students may publish digital videos related to a topic of study or create blogs that can be reviewed by their peers. The smartphone and computer apps like Facebook, Snapchat, Instagram, and YouTube give users ready access for creating content.

Technology offers two more benefits that are not always appreciated:

1. Learning is more powerful when students are prompted to take information presented to them in one form and "represent" it in an alternative way. The technology now available for teaching and learning helps students do just that. When students create their own representations of information, they provide clues about their thinking and give teachers a view of the accuracy of their conceptions.

2. Media convergence on the Internet can help students integrate information from multiple modalities, ensuring that all students, no matter what their learning style, have the opportunity to grasp key concepts.

Consider your teaching role in a "flat" world, and take an interest in other languages and the global community. Explore possibilities for linking your class with classes in different regions of the country or in foreign countries. The opportunity to engage your students in communication on a global scale is one of the most exciting teaching challenges of teaching and learning.

Learn about your students' uses of technology and their possible lives as gamers, and try out some serious learning games. Be ever vigilant about potentials for online bullying and harassment.

Get a head start and investigate the technological capacities of the schools or districts in which you find yourself observing and practice teaching—and do the same when you get your first teaching job. Remember that your students will be deluged with data and that one of your critical roles will be helping them assess the value of the information to which they are exposed.

Know Your Acronyms

The Common Core State Standards (CCSS) and the Educative Teacher Performance Assessment (edTPA) are two more acronyms to add to a long list of abbreviations for movements and assessments in contemporary education. The Elementary and Secondary Education Act (ESEA), first described in Chapter 3 of this text, was renamed the No Child Left Behind (NCLB) Act in 2002. The Every Student

The technology revolution has made possible collaboration across classroom, state, and country borders.

Succeeds Act (ESSA) is the name of the reauthorization of NCLB, and it is the current education law of the land. It differs from NCLB in several ways, especially by giving states more control over student testing and teacher evaluation, and it is the way in which public schools are funded today. The U.S. Department of Education must approve plans submitted by each state that adheres to the specific guidelines of ESSA.

The **Partnership for Assessment of Readiness for College and Careers (PARCC)** is the commonly used test that assesses Common Core principles in mathematics and English. Many states are pushing back against the administration of these tests, and their presence on the elementary school scene may be waning due to the passage of ESSA. As noted in Chapter 6, the last several years have seen an emphasis on STEM education, addressing science, technology, engineering, and mathematics. Educators in the arts have advocated for STEAM education, ensuring that the arts are integrated in the STEM areas. The Next Generation Science Standards (NGSS) have begun to be implemented in schools and districts across the country, ensuring that students have opportunities for problem solving, design, and construction and an in-depth analysis of disciplinary core ideas.

Being a savvy educator requires that you understand the external forces bearing upon public education today while at the same time drawing upon your inner vision and strength to make classrooms joyful places for children and young adults. In the next section, yet another acronym will be explored, the InTASC Standards, which have been guiding teacher preparation and to which the edTPA standards are aligned. The InTASC Standards describe the areas requiring proficiency for those who want to become teachers.

Partnership for Assessment of Readiness for College and Careers (PARCC) The commonly used test that assesses Common Core principles in mathematics and English.

iStock/Wavebreakmedia

WRITING & REFLECTION
KNOWING YOURSELF

The prevalent theme throughout this text has been the importance of your own metacognition as you embark on a career in education. What are your strengths? Your weaknesses?

How would you match your strengths to the demands of teaching? What personality traits do you want to "work on" as you consider becoming a teacher?

▲ Learning to teach requires observing, participating, and practicing in real classrooms.

Getting Started in the Teaching Profession

If you follow a traditional path toward becoming a teacher, you will receive guidance along the way and help in finding the full list of requirements for your state. As mentioned previously, field experiences play an important role in teacher preparation. Many states require professional certification, and, although the exact process for becoming a teacher varies from state to state, there are some common requirements.

Certification and Standards

Becoming a teacher in the public schools requires **certification** by your state. A state teaching certificate or license shows that you have met the state's requirements for becoming a teacher at specific grade levels and (especially for higher grades) in a certain subject area. For instance, your certificate might be for elementary education (Grades K–6), for middle school social studies, or for middle school and high school biology.

Your state's Department of Education website will describe the range of areas for which you can be licensed. Requirements for teacher certificates or licenses vary from state to state. Some states are relatively compatible with other states in their certification requirements; some states are more individualistic. Of course, your teacher education program will go a long way toward preparing you for state

iStock/FatCamera

certification, but it is important to understand the certification requirements beyond completing your program.

The Praxis Tests

> *Praxis is the doctrine that when actions are based on sound theory and values, they can make a real difference in the world.*
> —Freire (1970)

Most states require that future teachers pass a state exam or series of exams. The Educational Testing Service has developed **The Praxis Series** of professional assessments for beginning teachers. (As used by social scientists, the term *praxis* relates to action based on principles and theories that have a sound basis in research and experience.) A large number of states use this series of tests to assess your knowledge of subject matter and pedagogy.

The Praxis Series consists of three separate kinds of tests:

1. The Praxis I tests measure basic academic skills in reading, mathematics, and writing. Usually, you take these tests before entering your teacher education program or before your student teaching or internship.

2. The Praxis II tests measure knowledge about specific subject areas and about principles of learning and teaching. Generally, you take these tests when you complete your teacher preparation program.

certification The process of obtaining state authorization to teach in the public schools.

The Praxis Series A series of assessments used by many states as part of the teacher certification process.

3. The Praxis III assessment focuses on actual classroom performance. If your state requires Praxis III, the assessment usually takes place in your first year of teaching and leads to a higher level of certification. It includes direct observation of your classroom practice, review of a video or other documentation you send in, and interviews.

Several states offer their own assessments for certification and licensing, but these tests are typically similar to the Praxis tests. These states include Alabama, Arizona, California, Colorado, Florida, Georgia, Illinois, and Massachusetts. To prepare for the Praxis tests, visit their website for advice on how to prepare for taking these tests (www.ets.org/praxis).

The InTASC Standards

Many of the requirements for certification are based on standards and principles called the Interstate New Teacher Assessment and Support Consortium (InTASC). They have been developed by a national organization, the Council of Chief State School Officers (CCSSO). Established in 1987, InTASC represents a combined effort by numerous state education agencies and national educational organizations to reform the preparation, licensing, and professional development of teachers. The CCSSO is a nonpartisan, nationwide nonprofit organization of public officials who head departments of elementary and secondary education in the states, the District of Columbia, the U.S. Department of Defense Education Activity, and five U.S. extra-state jurisdictions. The CCSSO provides leadership, advocacy, and technical assistance on major educational issues. In 2011, the CCSSO issued the InTASC Model Core Teaching Standards that outline what teachers should know and be able to do to ensure every K–12 student reaches the goal of being ready to enter college or the workforce in today's world. These standards address what effective teaching and learning looks like in our contemporary public education system. The recent update of these standards is designed to address the fact that teachers are now being held to new levels of accountability. The purpose of these standards is to describe a new model of teaching that matches today's public school culture. The broad standards topics listed here can be accessed in greater detail on the InTASC website. Recent updates to the standards group them as follows:

The Learner and Learning

Standard #1: Learner Development

Standard #2: Learning Differences

Standard #3: Learning Environments

Content

Standard #4: Content Knowledge

Standard #5: Application of Content

Instructional Practice

Standard #6: Assessment

Standard #7: Planning for Instruction

Standard #8: Instructional Strategies

Professional Responsibility

Standard #9: Professional Learning and Ethical Practice

Standard #10: Leadership and Collaboration

Source: Available at https://www.ccsso.org/sites/default/files/2017-12/2013_INTASC_Learning_Progressions_for_Teachers.pdf

Each of these standards relates to teaching practices and dispositions that have been addressed in this text, including understanding how people learn; differentiation; school climate and culture; knowing and applying content; assessment; and professional development and team work with colleagues, students, and families in your teaching life. For each of these standards, InTASC has performance expectations that match what the CCSSO is hoping excellent teaching performance may look like.

The National Board for Professional Teaching Standards

As mentioned in Chapter 1, the National Board for Professional Teaching Standards (NBPTS, http://www.nbpts.org/) offers a national system for certifying teachers who meet rigorous standards. These standards are relevant to what you have already explored about teaching and learning. It is an advanced teaching credential but does not replace a state's teaching certificate or license. National Board Certified Teachers (NBCTs) embody these "Five Core Propositions":

- **Proposition 1:** Teachers are committed to students and their learning.

- **Proposition 2:** Teachers know the subjects they teach and how to teach those subjects to students.

- **Proposition 3:** Teachers are responsible for managing and monitoring student learning.

- **Proposition 4:** Teachers think systematically about their practice and learn from experience.

- **Proposition 5:** Teachers are members of learning communities. (NBPTS, n.d.)

These themes are familiar to all those who are preparing to become teachers. The National Board has used these general propositions to establish standards for certification in many areas of teaching, from early-childhood education through middle-childhood education to the various academic specialties in secondary education. National Board standards are created by committees of educators who are accomplished professionals in their fields.

The process of becoming an NBCT is arduous and has many steps. To seek this certification, you must

- hold a bachelor's degree;

- have 3 full years of teaching or counseling experience; and

- possess a valid state teaching or counseling license for that period of time, or, if you are teaching where a license is not required, have taught in schools recognized and approved to operate by the state.

Compared with an ordinary teaching certificate, National Board certification is recognized in all states as a higher level of achievement. To obtain this certification, you must meet the requirements of a portfolio assessment that includes videos of your teaching, samples of your students' work, and details of your accomplishments outside of your school experience. In addition, you must take an exam that assesses your content knowledge in your certificate area; test centers are located across the country.

Teaching Positions Here and Abroad

Teachers are in demand throughout the United States and all over the world. In the United States, the teaching areas in shortest supply include, but are not limited to, special education; bilingual education; earth science; chemistry; physics; mathematics and computer science; and foreign languages. Of course, these shortages vary by region and demographics.

As Chapter 8 indicated, though, the world has shrunk tremendously because of technology. You may want to challenge your thinking by going to a foreign country and gaining firsthand experience teaching there. If you decide to do this, it is wise to find others who have traveled this path before you and learn from them what the experience was like. There are groups of teachers who have taught abroad and can serve as resources for you. You can access these groups through teaching-abroad websites, blogs, Facebook pages, and Twitter feeds.

What kinds of positions are available in foreign countries? Although there are teaching opportunities in all disciplines and languages, the majority of positions available are for native English speakers teaching English as a foreign language. To be eligible for these positions, you usually must hold a certificate for Teaching English as a Foreign Language (TEFL). Native English speakers may take an online course to become certified in TEFL. A number of websites list opportunities for teaching abroad and offer information about TEFL courses.

In addition, there are more than 300 American international schools overseas. These are typically private,

nonprofit schools based on a U.S. or British model. Often, the schooling they provide leads to the International Baccalaureate diploma, an international credential that is offered at some schools in this country as well. To explore U.S. international schools, visit the International Schools Services website (http://www.state.gov/m/a/os/c16899.htm). Half of the staff members at these schools are from North America. Before signing up for a position at an international school, be certain to follow the reviews of others who have had this experience. Those reviews and contacts are readily available over the Internet.

Tips for New Teachers

As you begin your fieldwork or your work in your own classroom, remember that as a teacher you are an educational leader. The following list offers some tips as you get started.

- **Learn as much as you can about your school environment.** Learn everything you can about the school in which you will be doing your field placement work or getting your first teaching job. Do your homework. Be prepared.

  o How long has the school been in this community?

  o How many students and teachers are there?

  o How many administrators are there?

  o Who are the students? What types of homes, apartments, or other forms of housing arrangements do they live in?

  o Can you expect a student body that is diverse ethnically? Socially? Economically? How many inclusion classrooms are there?

  o What is the technological capacity of the school? How many SMART Boards are in the school?

  o What does the school website have to say? Is this school or district known for any particular achievements?

  o Do classes have their own websites?

  o How do the students perform on mandated assessments? These scores are a matter of public record.

  o If this is your field placement, from whom do you need permission?

  o Are visitors and invited guests required to sign in? What is the correct protocol?

  o Is there a dress code for students? Teachers?

  o Does the school offer online courses?

Your teaching is as much a product of who you are as of how you implement strategies.

- **Keep a journal.**
  - Record your experiences as you begin. Include your fears and your questions. If you have a smartphone, an iPad, a netbook, or another small electronic device, save these journal entries and look back on them as you continue.
  - Be fully conscious in the classroom. Journaling can help you stay conscious so you do not "shoot from the hip."

- **Join a collegial group and find a friend.** Become part of a new-teacher group, either in your school or college or in your community. If you cannot find one that meets face-to-face, check for responsible groups online. In the most trying of times, it is often your colleagues who offer the most support and help you move forward. This point was made clearly by the teachers who shared their stories in Chapter 2.

If you are lucky, you will find one particular person in your new school with whom you can connect and share your experiences of teaching. This kind of relationship often builds into a lasting friendship.

- **Find a mentor.** Connect with an experienced teacher whom you trust, and communicate your hopes and fears to this person. Being a teacher means you are always a learner: learning about yourself, your content area, and your students. There is much to learn from mentors, so seek out a person who can fill this role for you.

- **Remember that teaching is not telling.** Teaching is not about you; it is about the students. Your focus should be on them. How will you engage them? What will you do on behalf of their learning? *Listen* to them and really hear what they have to say.

- **Plan for creative experiences and activities.** Prepare lessons in which the students' active engagement is at the center, and listen to their ideas. Showing your students that you value what they think is priceless.

- **To create a safe environment, show that you are human.** Do not believe that you have to know everything and do everything right. Model vulnerability for your students; show them that you can laugh at your own mistakes. Students will feel more comfortable when you show that you are learning as well. This does not mean that you are not credible; it simply means that as humans we all make mistakes.

- **Be passionate.** Teachers express their passion for teaching in different ways, but being delighted to be with your students, coming in well prepared, and having a specific plan in mind are all ways to show the students that you care.

- **Differentiate instruction.** Remember that treating all students equally does not ensure equality of outcomes. Equitable and fair-minded teaching considers the ways all of our students, in all their diversity, learn best.

Educational Associations

Dozens of professional organizations provide continuing support of one kind or another for teachers. These range from national associations that offer professional development resources to local union affiliates that may negotiate your next contract with the school district.

Professional organizations have the potential to create learning communities among their members. They offer rich resources for you to use in planning lessons and expanding your professional knowledge. Some of them also help improve your salary and working conditions and protect your professional rights.

Two of the most prominent organizations are the American Federation of Teachers (AFT) and the National Education Association (NEA). There are also many subject- and grade-level-specific groups that provide resources, grants, and guidance for you as you begin your professional career.

The American Federation of Teachers

The AFT is a union affiliated with the American Federation of Labor and Congress of Industrial Organizations (AFL-CIO) and was founded in 1916 to represent the interests of classroom teachers. Its first member, John Dewey, recognized the importance of teachers having their own organization. Today, one visit to the organization's website (http://www.aft.org/) reveals a wealth of resources for the classroom teacher and for other education personnel as well. For example, the site provides information about professional development opportunities and grants.

In addition to being a valuable resource, the AFT directly represents teachers in many school districts around the country. The organization has 43 state affiliates, more than 3,000 local affiliates, and more than 1.5 million members. You may find, particularly if you teach in a large urban school system, that the AFT negotiates contracts for the teachers and other school employees in your district. If so, you will probably become a member of the union, and you may want to take an active role in the local affiliate.

The National Education Association

The NEA, founded in 1857, has more than 3 million members and more than 14,000 local affiliates representing every state. In addition to its Code of Ethics, the NEA provides job searches, teaching tips and tools, important resources for your professional development, and activities and workshops

Peggy Ashbrook

of interest in your state. The organization's website (http://www.nea.org/) is a valuable point of entry to these resources.

Since the 1960s, the NEA has functioned as a union, conducting collective bargaining on behalf of teachers and working to protect teachers' rights as employees of a school district. It also acts as a lobbying organization on educational issues, and it helps set professional standards for the teaching profession.

Most teachers belong to either the AFT or the NEA, and some belong to both. Your decision about membership may be governed in part by local conditions, such as which organization represents the teachers at your school. Remember that an important benefit of membership is that it provides links to other teachers for professional collaboration.

Build Your Teaching Portfolio

Developing a portfolio is an excellent way to organize your thinking about teaching and to display some of your accomplishments on this journey (see Appendix 1). You should continue to update the portfolio each year you teach. It is your professional and personal record, and it demonstrates your knowledge and beliefs as well as your accomplishments. What you choose to include in your portfolio is a statement of what you think is important.

When you begin to look for a job, you will need a version of your portfolio to present to prospective employers, either on a thumb or jump drive, or in the form of a URL for a personal website. The portfolio you show others should be concise, clear, readable, and well organized.

Here are some suggestions for preparing your portfolio:

- Your portfolio should be easily accessible online.

- Include a table of contents so that viewers can skip to parts that particularly concern them.

- Begin with a short essay introducing yourself. In a few paragraphs, describe your interest in teaching and learning and what you have accomplished. See the box for a sample introductory essay.

- Describe your educational philosophy, what you believe a good teacher needs to understand about teaching and learning.

- Discuss your classroom management theory. If your focus is on building community in the classroom, be specific about how you plan to do that.

- Become familiar with the new Common Core State Standards for mathematics and English.

- Become familiar with the Next Generation Science Standards.

- Describe your student teaching experience with specific mention of the grade levels you taught and the lessons and activities you prepared. If you have copies of supervisors' observations that attest to your abilities, include them.

- Include photos or electronic files of a few samples of student work from your field experience.

- If you have approved photos of yourself and a class in action, or even a brief video (no more than 3-minutes long), include them. ("Approved" means that you have received consent forms from the other people shown in the photos or video.)

A SAMPLE INTRODUCTORY ESSAY FOR A PORTFOLIO

I have just graduated from Hofstra University, where I majored in biology and secondary education. I have always loved science and enjoy sharing it with others. I have had experience student teaching in Grades 7–9 and 10–11. My certification area in biology and general science prepares me to teach Grades 7–12 in New York State. I have passed all the exams and requirements for this initial certification.

For my field experience, I have been a participant-observer and student teacher in Grades 8 and 11, and I feel equally comfortable in the middle school and the high school. I have also spent two summers as a counselor at an environmental education camp in Maine, where I enjoyed working with teenagers in a natural setting. I believe my organizational skills, my ability to plan, my understanding of the content area, and my passion for teaching will enable me to be a successful teacher.

- Include your resume, certifications, awards, and letters of reference.

- Do not overdo it. We live in a fast-paced culture, and people do not have a great deal of time to read your portfolio. Be concise and to the point.

Concluding Thoughts

The author Thomas Friedman talks about something he calls the *passion quotient* for teaching. He tells the story of a young child who receives his or her first fire truck or doctor's kit and wants to be a fireman or a doctor. That innocent passion for a certain job, without knowing the salary or the working hours or the preparation required, is what you need to get back in touch with. You need to discover your inner passion, and when you find it, you will know it.

You may already know that your passion is teaching, in which case you will be eager to explore the professional organizations described in this chapter. Or you may still be searching and wondering. If we are going to be successful,

what we select as our life's work must bring us joy, especially if it is teaching. Remember, it is fine to change your mind and say, "I thought this was for me, but now I see I'm better suited to another career."

I want to remind you, though, that teaching is wonderfully satisfying work. The feeling you get when you realize that you have made a contribution on behalf of someone else's development is indescribable. I remember my first year of teaching like it was yesterday. I was nervous, overprepared, and in the end overjoyed. Although I needed the paycheck (which in 1966 was quite meager), I would forget to pick it up at the main office of the junior high where I taught science. The school secretary used to tease me, but one day she gave me a wonderful compliment. She said, "Judging by the smile I always see on your face, I can tell that you get paid for this job in other ways." I was touched by this statement (although my landlord, of course, needed payment in cash).

Becoming a teacher is a commitment to a life of service that has the potential to bring you great joy and personal satisfaction. My best wishes to you on this journey.

CHAPTER REVIEW

Key Terms

certification (p. 161)
field placement (p. 156)
participant-observer (p. 156)

Partnership for Assessment of Readiness for College and Careers (PARCC) (p. 160)

The Praxis Series (p. 161)
public education (p. 156)
student teacher (p. 156)

Review the Learning Outcomes

Review each section of the chapter and answer the following:

LO 10-1 Why is teaching today especially challenging?

LO 10-2 What must you go through to get certified to teach in your home state?

LO 10-3 How does the NEA and the AFT help beginning teachers?

LO 10-4 What would you include in your teaching portfolio?

LO 10-5 What personal attributes lead you to believe that teaching *is* or *is not* for you?

InTASC Standards

Review the InTASC Standards for the chapter and explain how the chapter addressed each one.

Standard 6: Assessment

Standard 7: Planning for Instruction

Standard 9: Professional Learning and Ethical Practice

Standard 10: Leadership and Collaboration

Journal Prompt

What do you see as the biggest challenge facing you on your journey to become a teacher?

$SAGE edge™

Get the tools you need to sharpen your study skills. SAGE edge offers a robust online environment featuring an impressive array of free tools and resources.

Access practice quizzes, eFlashcards, video, and multimedia at **edge.sagepub.com/koch4e**.

• Appendix 1 •
Building Your Teaching Portfolio

Using the "Writing & Reflection" activities and questions found throughout this text, you have been asked to reflect on the topics addressed in each chapter as a way of compiling your teaching portfolio. Developing a portfolio is an excellent way to organize your thinking about teaching and to display some of your accomplishments on this journey. You should continue to update the portfolio each year you teach. It is your professional and personal record, and it demonstrates your knowledge and beliefs as well as your accomplishments. What you choose to include in your portfolio is a statement of what you think is important.

When you begin to look for a job, you will need a version of your portfolio to present to prospective employers. This version should be presented electronically. Many of the previous chapters' portfolio suggestions, as well as the additional prompts that follow, can find a place in this presentation version. The portfolio you show others should be concise, clear, readable, and well organized.

How Do You Document Your Professional Journey?

You may want to document your work in your professional courses and your school field-based experiences. Some teachers collect artifacts, keep a journal, gather their thoughts electronically, or use a formal format to create a portfolio or a personal notebook. Whatever process works best for you, begin to document your journey as a way to reflect on your professional and personal growth as you continue your coursework and fieldwork to become a teacher with your own class or classes. Remember, teaching is something you have to work at: It takes time to prepare, it takes time to practice, and it takes time to process feedback from your students and revise your plan accordingly. It will take time to create your portfolio, too; do not try to compile it all at once, but use it continuously as a place to collect your thoughts and document your journey. You can always go back and edit it later.

Additional Portfolio Prompts

Use these additional prompts as you read through the chapters of the book to add to your portfolio your thoughts on the topics presented.

Reflections on Your Journey. Build on your personal philosophy of teaching by reflecting on the teaching stories in Chapter 2. Address the following questions in a document that you can add to your portfolio.

- Do you think you have a "learning life"?

- How do you anticipate working with and communicating with parents?

- What did you learn from your interview with a classroom teacher that can inform your teaching philosophy?

- How does your religion or culture affect your philosophy of teaching?

Building Your Personal Philosophy. Add to your portfolio by identifying elements of essentialism, perennialism, progressivism, and other philosophies discussed in Chapter 3 that you believe in. Use these to build on the personal philosophy that you have already begun to develop.

It is not enough to interpret what you have read. The well-prepared teacher must explain his or her rationale for designing a learning experience in a particular way. Be sure to express why you believe what you do.

Relating Learning Theories to Your Teaching Philosophy. Reflect on the learning theories presented in Chapter 4 and select a theory that can help you make sense of your personal teaching philosophy. You may use more than one theory to pull together a teaching approach that makes sense to you. Include your reflections in your portfolio. Remember, it is subject to change as you progress on your journey.

Reflecting on Student Diversity. After reading Chapter 5, address the following questions in a document that you can add to your portfolio.

- What is your reaction to the various types of student diversity that were discussed and to the ways students can be the same as and different from each other?

- Reflect on where you see yourself headed as a teacher. Do you have a calling, for instance, to work with at-risk students? Are you motivated to create a gender-fair classroom? What, specifically, speaks to you?

- This chapter has an important message: Different is just different; it is not lesser. Can you teach those who are different from you in ways that do not make their difference "lesser"? Describe how you would do so.

Trends You Find Appealing. **Think** about all of the trends and issues presented in Chapter 6. Add to your portfolio by writing about the current educational trends you find most appealing as a future teacher. Explore the ways you can see yourself involved in this type of change.

Your Thoughts About Using Technology in Teaching. **Describe** the ways you anticipate integrating your life as a technology user into the work you will do with your students. What are the possibilities? Collect your thoughts in your portfolio.

Designing an Activity to Promote 21st-Century Skills. **Chapter** 8 emphasizes the importance of developing your students' 21st-century skills. As an exercise for your portfolio, imagine you are teaching at a grade level of your choice. Think of one activity you could undertake with your class to enhance your students' capacity for thinking critically about a topic. Describe this activity as specifically as possible.

Your Plans for Creating a Classroom Community. There is a great deal of content to digest in Chapter 9. In your portfolio, include your plans for creating classroom community. Think deeply about how you will translate the principles discussed in the chapter into your own practice. Be honest with yourself; if you have concerns, write about them.

Your Choice. Upon completing this book, reflect on your choice to become a teacher. How have your coursework and this book informed or influenced your choice? Do you feel more or less sure now than you did at the beginning of the course? What are your fears or anxieties? Your hopes and dreams? Once you have chosen the path of teacher, a wonderful portfolio addition would be a short essay responding to the simple, yet complex, question:

Why did you choose to become a teacher?

Suggestions for Preparing Your Portfolio

Use a website URL or a software program to store the contents of your portfolio. Print the pages and keep one print copy in a folder. Remember, less is more. Select your favorite artifacts and reviews to show your prospective employer.

- You should prepare a version of your portfolio that is available electronically, either on a personal professional website that you have developed (templates for this are available online or as software applications) or on a USB flash drive that you give to your prospective employers. You can create a PowerPoint file, a Word document with appropriate images, or a PDF.

- Include a table of contents so viewers can skip to parts of the portfolio in which they have a particular interest. Begin with a short essay introducing yourself. In a few paragraphs, describe your interest in teaching and learning and what you have accomplished. See Chapter 10 for a sample introductory essay.

- Describe your educational philosophy—that is, what you believe a good teacher needs to understand about teaching and learning.

- Discuss your classroom management theory. If your focus is on building community in the classroom, be specific about how you plan to do that.

- Describe your student teaching experience with specific mention of the grade levels you taught and the lessons and activities you prepared. If you have copies of supervisors' observations that attest to your abilities, include them.

- Include photos or electronic files of a few samples of student work from your field experience.

- If you have approved photos of yourself and a class in action, or even a brief video (no more than 3-minutes long) that you have burned on a DVD or a USB flash drive, include them. ("Approved" means that you have received consent forms from the other people shown in the photos or video.)

- Include your college transcript, resume, certifications, awards, and letters of reference.

- Do not overdo it. We live in a fast-paced culture, and people do not have a great deal of time to read your portfolio. Be concise and to the point.

Good luck on your journey!

• Appendix 2 •
How to Contact Your State's Teacher Licensure Offices

Here you will find the teacher licensure websites for each of the 50 states plus the District of Columbia, the U.S. Virgin Islands, Puerto Rico, and the U.S. Department of Defense. Keep in mind that you will need to meet an individual state's licensure requirements in order to teach in public schools in that state. If you have a teaching license or certificate in one state, it does not automatically transfer to another state. Some states have reciprocity with other states. This list should help you get started.

Alabama
https://www.alsde.edu/sec/ec/pages/home.aspx

Alaska
https://www.teachercertificationdegrees.com/certification/alaska/

Arizona
http://www.azed.gov/educator-certification/

Arkansas
http://www.arkansased.gov/divisions/educator%20effectiveness/educator-licensure

California
https://www.ctc.ca.gov/

Colorado
https://www.cde.state.co.us/cdeprof

Connecticut
http://portal.ct.gov/SDE/Certification/Bureau-of-Certification

Delaware
https://www.doe.k12.de.us/Page/3476

District of Columbia
https://dcps.dc.gov/page/teacher-certification-and-licensing

Florida
http://www.fldoe.org/teaching/certification/

Georgia
http://www.teaching-certification.com/georgia-teaching-certification.html

Hawaii
http://www.hawaiipublicschools.org/ConnectWithUs/Employment/LicensureAndCertification/Pages/home.aspx

Idaho
http://www.sde.idaho.gov/cert-psc/cert/

Illinois
https://www.isbe.net/licensure

Indiana
https://www.doe.in.gov/licensing

Iowa
http://www.boee.iowa.gov/index.html

Kansas
http://www.ksde.org/Agency/Division-of-Learning-Services/Teacher-Licensure-and-Accreditation

Kentucky
http://www.teaching-certification.com/kentucky-teaching-certification.html

Louisiana
https://www.teachlouisiana.net/

Maine
http://www.maine.gov/doe/cert/

Maryland
http://www.marylandpublicschools.org/about/pages/dee/certification/index.aspx

Massachusetts
http://www.doe.mass.edu/licensure/academic-prek12/teacher/license-types.html

Michigan
https://www.michigan.gov/mde/0,4615,7-140-5683_14795---,00.html

Minnesota
https://education.mn.gov/MDE/Lic/lic/index.htm

Mississippi
https://www.mdek12.org/OTL/OEL

Missouri
https://dese.mo.gov/educator-quality/certification

Montana
https://opi.mt.gov/Educators/Licensure/Become-a-Licensed-Montana-Educator

Nebraska
https://www.education.ne.gov/tcert/

Nevada
http://www.doe.nv.gov/Educator_Licensure/

New Hampshire
https://www.education.nh.gov/certification/

New Jersey
http://www.nj.gov/education/educators/license/

New Mexico
https://webnew.ped.state.nm.us/bureaus/licensure/

New York
http://www.highered.nysed.gov/tcert/certificate/

North Carolina
http://www.dpi.state.nc.us/licensure/

North Dakota
https://www.nd.gov/espb/licensure

Ohio
http://education.ohio.gov/Topics/Teaching/Licensure

Oklahoma
http://sde.ok.gov/sde/teacher-certification

Oregon
http://www.oregon.gov/tspc/Pages/index.aspx

Pennsylvania
http://www.education.pa.gov/teachers%20-%20
administrators/certifications/pages/default.aspx

Puerto Rico
https://www.wgu.edu/wgu/tc_state_info/online_
teaching_degree_puerto_rico

Rhode Island
http://www.ride.ri.gov/TeachersAdministrators/
EducatorCertification.aspx

South Carolina
https://ed.sc.gov/educators/certification/

South Dakota
http://www.doe.sd.gov/certification/

Tennessee
https://www.tn.gov/education/licensing.html

Texas
https://tea.texas.gov/Texas_Educators/Certification/

Utah
https://www.schools.utah.gov/curr/licensing

Vermont
https://alis.edlicensing.vermont.gov/

Virginia
http://www.doe.virginia.gov/teaching/licensure/

Washington
https://www.teachercertificationdegrees.com/
certification/washington/

West Virginia
https://wvde.state.wv.us/certification/

Wisconsin
https://dpi.wi.gov/tepdl/licensing

Wyoming
http://ptsb.state.wy.us/Licensure/BecomingLicensed/
tabid/65/Default.aspx

U.S. Virgin Islands
http://www.vide.vi/general-certification-requirements
.html

U.S. Department of Defense
https://www.dodea.edu/

• Glossary •

A Nation at Risk: The Imperative for Educational Reform A 1983 federal report that found U.S. schools in serious trouble and inaugurated a new wave of school reform focused on academic basics and higher standards for student achievement.

academic language The language of the discipline that students need to learn and use to participate and engage in meaningful ways in the content area.

academy A type of private secondary school that arose in the late colonial period and came to dominate American secondary education until the establishment of public high schools. Academies had a more practical curriculum than Latin grammar schools did, and students typically could choose subjects appropriate to their later careers.

aesthetic education Traditionally, this term referred merely to education in the fine arts, such as painting and music. In the broader view of Maxine Greene and other recent philosophers, however, it means education that enables students to use artistic forms and imagination to approach all fields of learning, including the sciences, and to share their perspectives with others.

American Federation of Teachers (AFT) An international union, affiliated with the American Federation of Labor and Congress of Industrial Organizations, representing teachers and other school personnel as well as many college faculty and staff members, health care workers, and public employees.

assessment Collecting information to determine the progress of students' learning.

assistive technology (AT) A device or service that increases the capabilities of people with disabilities.

augmented reality (AR) AR is a live, direct or indirect, view of a physical, real-world environment whose elements are augmented by computer-generated sensory input such as sound, video, graphics, or GPS data.

authentic assessments Assessments that ask students to perform a task relating what they have learned to some real-world problem or example.

behaviorism The theory that learning takes place in response to reinforcements (for instance, rewards or punishments) from the outside environment.

bilingual education Educating English-language learners by teaching them at least part of the time in their native language.

blog (short for weblog) An online journal using software that makes it easy for the user to create frequent entries; typically, visitors can add their own comments and responses.

Bloom's Taxonomy: a classification system of educational objectives developed by psychologist Benjamin Bloom in the 1950s. The taxonomy has three domains: the cognitive, affective, and psychomotor. The cognitive domain was revised in the 1990s to represent a hierarchy of behaviors that include remembering, understanding, applying, analyzing, evaluating, and creating.

Brown v. Board of Education of Topeka, Kansas A 1954 case in which the U.S. Supreme Court outlawed segregation in public education.

bullying Repeated cruelty, physical or psychological, by a powerful person toward a less powerful person.

certification The process of obtaining state authorization to teach in the public schools.

charter schools Publicly funded elementary or secondary schools that are granted a special charter by the state or local education agency.

classroom community A sense of common purpose and values shared by the teacher and students in a classroom so that they see themselves as working together in the process of learning; a classroom atmosphere that emphasizes trust, care, and support.

classroom management The ways teachers create an effective classroom environment for learning, including all the rules and conditions they establish.

cognitive domain The objectives in the cognitive domain of Bloom's Taxonomy represent a natural progression of mental behaviors that are important in learning.

cognitive learning theories Explanations of the mental processes that occur during learning.

Common Core State Standards A state-led effort coordinated by the National Governors Association Center for Best Practices and the Council of Chief State School Officers (CCSSO) to develop a clear and consistent framework to prepare students for college and the workforce through the collaboration with teachers, school administrators, and experts.

common schools A public, tax-supported elementary school. Begun in Massachusetts in the 1820s, common schools aimed to provide a common curriculum for children. Horace Mann, an advocate for the common school, is often considered the "father of the public school."

constructivism A group of theories about knowledge and learning whose basic tenet is that all knowledge is constructed by synthesizing new ideas with prior knowledge. Constructivism holds that knowledge is not passively received; rather, it is actively built by the learner as he or she experiences the world.

cooperative learning An instructional approach in which students work together in groups to accomplish shared learning goals.

culturally relevant pedagogy Teaching practices that place the culture of the learner at the center of instruction. Cultural referents become aspects of the formal curriculum.

curriculum A plan of studies that includes the ways instructional content is organized and presented at each grade level.

cyberbullying Bullying or harassment through electronic means such as e-mail, website postings, instant messaging, text messaging, blogs, mobile phones, or chatrooms; also called *online bullying*.

dame schools Some colonial women transformed their homes into schools where they taught reading, writing, and computation. These schools became known as dame schools.

differentiated instruction/differentiation The practice of using a variety of instructional strategies to address the different learning needs of students.

digital divide The gap between those with regular, effective access to digital technologies and those without.

digital literacy The ability to use information and communication technologies to find, evaluate, create, and communicate information, requiring both cognitive and technical skills.

digital natives People who have grown up using the digital "language" of computers, video games, and the Internet.

dropout rate The percentage of students who fail to complete high school or earn an equivalency degree.

due process A formal process, such as a legal or administrative proceeding, that follows established rules designed to protect the rights of the people involved.

edTPA A new preservice teacher assessment process.

educational autobiography Your own educational history, told by you.

educational objectives Goals identified with specific teaching and learning activities.

embedded assessments Classroom-based assessments that make use of the actual assignments that students are given as a unit is being taught. These can be used to evaluate developmental stages of student learning.

English as a Second Language (ESL) These are "English-only" classroom programs where instruction is solely in English and there is limited access to native language vocabulary.

equity The act of treating individuals and groups fairly and justly, free from bias or favoritism. Gender equity means the state of being fair and just toward both males and females, to show preference to neither and concern for both.

era of testing The period of time since the passage in 2001 of the federal No Child Left Behind Act that mandated standardized testing in mathematics and language arts in Grades 3 through 8.

essentialism An educational philosophy holding that the purpose of education is to learn specific knowledge provided by core academic disciplines such as mathematics, science, literature, and history. Teachers must impart the key elements of these subjects so that all students have access to this basic or "essential" knowledge.

Every Student Succeeds Act (ESSA) Gives states and local districts more flexibility in how they raise standards and undertake essential reforms to improve student achievement and teacher effectiveness.

exceptional learners Students who require special educational services because of physical, behavioral, or academic needs.

Facebook A social networking service and website that by 2018 had over 2 billion users worldwide. Users must register before using the site, after which they may create personal profiles, add other users as friends, and exchange messages, including automatic notifications when they update their profiles.

Family Educational Rights and Privacy Act (FERPA)/ Buckley Amendment A federal law requiring educational agencies to protect the confidentiality of students' educational records.

field placement An opportunity for you to serve as an apprentice in a classroom and learn from the regular classroom teacher and from your own experience of working with the students.

gaming Used in this context, *gaming* refers to playing computer and video games. Video game culture is a form of new media that has enormous potential for teaching and learning.

gender-based harassment Harassing conduct based on a student's failure to conform to sex stereotypes.

gender-fair education Teaching practices that help both females and males achieve their full potential. Gender-fair teachers address cultural and societal stereotypes and overcome them through classroom interactions.

global competence The attitudes, knowledge, and skills to live and work successfully in our interconnected world (Tichnor-Wagner, 2016). Also involves the development of affective skills such as empathy and respect for others in order to be engaged and effective citizens of the world.

globalization The increase of global connectivity, integration, and interdependence in economic, cultural, social, and technological spheres.

goodness of fit A term generally used in descriptive statistics to describe the match between a theory and a particular set of observations; in this book, it means the match between a teacher candidate's personal attributes, values, and disposition and the demands of teaching.

hidden curriculum What students learn, beyond the academic content, from the experience of attending school.

homeschooling Educating children at home rather than in a school; parents typically serve as teachers.

ill-structured problem A problem that lacks clear procedures for finding the solution.

inclusion The practice of educating students with disabilities in regular classrooms alongside nondisabled students.

individualized education program (IEP) A plan, required for every student covered by the Individuals with Disabilities Education Act, specifying instructional goals, services to be provided, and assessment techniques for evaluating progress.

Individuals with Disabilities Education Act The federal law that guarantees that all children with disabilities receive free, appropriate public education.

informal curriculum Learning experiences that go beyond the formal curriculum, such as activities the teacher introduces to connect academic concepts to the students' daily lives.

inquiry A multifaceted activity that involves making observations, posing questions about the subject matter, and conducting research or investigations to develop answers. Inquiry is common to scientific learning but also relevant to other fields.

Instagram A social media app that allows users to maintain a permanent record of favorite photos or videos. Users have a profile and newsfeed similar to Facebook.

instruction The act or process of teaching; the way your pedagogy becomes enacted in practice.

intelligence profile An individual's unique combination of relative strengths and weaknesses among all the different intelligences.

interactive whiteboard A whiteboard that works together with a computer to display and save information.

Knowledge, Comprehension, Application, Analysis, Synthesis, and Evaluation Bloom's original classes of learning behaviors. They were slightly reorganized and renamed with verbs in the 1990s.

knowledge economy An economic system in which the use and exchange of knowledge plays a dominant role. In this kind of economy, knowledge is both an economic asset and a key product.

Latin grammar school A type of school that flourished in the New England colonies in the 1600s and 1700s. It emphasized Latin and Greek to prepare young men for college.

learning communities A classroom, a cluster of classes, or a school organized so as to promote active engagement in learning, collaboration between teachers and students, and a sense that everyone involved shares the experience of being a learner.

learning disability A disorder in the basic psychological processes involved in learning and using language; it may lead to difficulties in listening, speaking, reading, writing, reasoning, or mathematical abilities.

learning style The dominant way in which we process the information around us. Different people have different learning styles.

learning theory An explanation of how learning typically occurs and about conditions that favor learning.

least restrictive environment A learning environment that, to the maximum extent possible, matches the environment experienced by nondisabled students.

LGBTQ An acronym used to represent lesbian, gay, bisexual, and transgender individuals, and includes Q for Queer,

an umbrella connotation that encompasses different ways of experiencing gender and sexuality.

mainstreaming Having students with disabilities participate in general education classes for part of the school day and spend the remainder of the day in a separate, self-contained classroom for students with disabilities. This leads to full inclusion for many students with disabilities.

maker movement Refers to using a wide variety of hands-on activities (such as building, computer programming, and sewing) to support academic learning and the development of a mind-set that values collaboration and experimentation.

makerspace A place where students can gather to create, invent, tinker, explore, and discover using a variety of tools and materials.

metacognition The understanding of your own thinking and learning processes.

model A representation of a system or an object, such as a small physical structure that imitates a larger structure or a computer program that parallels the workings of a larger system.

multicultural education Education that aims to create equal opportunities for students from diverse racial, ethnic, social class, and cultural groups.

National Association for the Education of Young Children (NAEYC) This professional organization is dedicated to improving the quality of education for all children, birth to age 8.

National Board for Professional Teaching Standards (NBPTS) A nonprofit organization that aims to advance the quality of teaching by developing professional standards for teachers.

National Education Association (NEA) The largest organization of teachers and other education professionals, headquartered in Washington, DC.

No Child Left Behind (NCLB) Act Revised the ESEA and called for states to develop content-area standards and annual testing of math and reading in Grades 3 to 8.

normal schools A type of teacher-education institution begun in the 1830s; forerunner of the teachers' college.

online learning The use of the Internet to provide programs of study or individual courses that offer instructional materials and interactions between teachers and students.

parochial schools A school operated by a religious group. Today, in the United States, the term most often refers to a school governed by the local Catholic parish or diocese.

participant-observer While participating in the life of the classroom, one who makes careful observations and studies the classroom environment to learn about child and adolescent development and teaching methods.

Partnership for Assessment of Readiness for College and Careers (PARCC) The commonly used test that assesses Common Core principles in mathematics and English.

pedagogical content knowledge (PCK) The understanding of how particular topics, problems, or issues can be adapted and presented to match the diverse interests and abilities of learners.

pedagogy The art and science of teaching; all that you know and believe about teaching.

perennialism An educational philosophy that emphasizes enduring ideas conveyed through the study of great works of literature and art. Perennialists believe in a single core curriculum for everyone.

personal teaching philosophy An individual's own pedagogy informed by his or her own beliefs and understanding of how students learn best. A teacher's personal philosophy outs itself through the instructional strategies employed with the students.

philosophy of teaching statement A description of your ideas about teaching and learning, and how those ideas will influence your practice. It should be based on your knowledge of educational research.

picting Using images instead of text to convey ideas.

The Praxis Series A series of assessments used by many states as part of the teacher certification process.

problem-based learning Focused, experiential learning (minds-on, hands-on) organized around the investigation and resolution of messy, real-world problems.

professional development Teachers' lifelong effort to improve their skills and professional knowledge. Although professional development often includes advanced courses and workshops, much of your progress will depend on your own continued reading, reflection, and analysis.

progressivism An educational philosophy that stresses active learning through problem solving, projects, and hands-on experiences.

project-based learning A teaching method that engages students in extended inquiry into complex, realistic questions as they work in teams and create presentations to share what they have learned. These presentations may take various forms: an oral or written report, a computer technology-based presentation, a video, the design of a product, and so on.

public education Education that is publicly financed, tuition-free, accountable to public authorities, and accessible to all students. The term covers various types of public schools, including traditional schools, charter and magnet schools, vocational schools, and public virtual and alternative schools.

QR code A type of two-dimensional barcode that consists of black modules arranged in a square pattern on a white background. When scanned, the QR code links to a website or a video or some printed material that is available digitally.

reflective practitioner A teacher who consistently reflects on classroom events (both successes and problems) and modifies teaching practices accordingly.

Response to Intervention (RTI) A service delivery system in schools aimed at preventing academic and behavioral difficulties as well as identifying the best practices for teaching students with disabilities.

Responsive Classroom An approach to teaching and learning, developed by the Northeast Foundation for Children, that seeks to bring together social and academic learning.

rubric A scoring guide for an authentic assessment or a performance assessment, with descriptions of performance characteristics corresponding to points on a rating scale.

school climate and school culture The values, cultures, practices, and organization of a school.

school resource officers (SROs) Law enforcement officers specially trained to work with and in schools, addressing a safe school climate and preventing crime.

Seeking Educational Equity and Diversity (SEED) Project The national project on inclusive curriculum that promotes multiculturally equitable, gender-fair, and globally aware curriculum and pedagogy through professional development and leadership training for teachers, parents, college faculty, and administrators.

serious learning games/digital learning games These games target the acquisition of knowledge as its own end and foster habits of mind and understanding that are generally useful or used within an academic context.

service learning Community service done in collaboration with a larger project at the school.

sex-based harassment A broad term including sexual harassment, sexual violence, and gender-based harassment.

sexual harassment Unwelcome sexual advances, requests for sexual favors, or other physical and expressive behavior of a sexual nature that interferes with a person's life.

sexual orientation An enduring emotional, romantic, sexual, or affectional attraction that a person feels toward people of one or both sexes.

simulation A computer program or other procedure that imitates a real-world experience.

Snapchat A social media app that allows users to send pictures and videos to their friends, and these images disappear within 24 hours.

social cognitive learning theories Explanations that describe how learning involves interactions between the learner and the social environment.

socioeconomic status (SES) A person's or family's status in society, usually based on a combination of income, occupation, and education. Though similar to social class, SES puts more emphasis on the way income affects status.

special education The branch of education that deals with services for students with disabilities or other special needs that cannot be met through traditional means.

STEAM education An initiative that adds the arts to the STEM framework. The STEAM movement asserts that art and design must be central to education in science, technology, engineering, and mathematics.

STEM education A movement that represents science, technology, engineering, and mathematics education. This approach to learning invites students to understand the interconnectedness of science and technology, and the significance of applying mathematical thinking to solving problems.

student teacher One who is assigned to a teacher, usually called the *cooperating teacher*, on a daily basis for a specified period of time, such as 10 to 12 weeks, to start practice teaching a specific number of lessons a week.

students at risk Students in danger of not completing school or not acquiring the education they need to be successful citizens.

teacher burnout The condition of teachers who have lost their motivation, desire, sense of purpose, and energy for being effective practitioners.

tenure A status granted to a teacher, usually after a probationary period, that protects him or her from dismissal except for reasons of incompetence, gross misconduct, or other conditions stipulated by the state.

theory of multiple intelligences The theory that intelligence is not a single, fixed attribute but rather a collection of several different types of abilities.

3D printing The use of technologies that construct physical objects from three-dimensional digital content.

Title I The section of federal education law that provides funds for compensatory education.

Title IX Part of the federal Education Amendments of 1972, Title IX states that "No person in the United States shall, on the basis of sex, be excluded from participation in, be denied the benefits of, or be subjected to discrimination under any education program or activity receiving Federal financial assistance."

tracking The practice of placing students in different classes or courses based on achievement test scores or on perceived differences in abilities. Tracks can be identified by ability (high, average, or low) or by the kind of preparation they provide (academic, general, or vocational).

Twitter An online social networking service that enables its users to send and read text-based posts of up to 280 characters, known as "tweets."

Understanding by Design (UbD) A plan for instruction that starts with the learning goals and assessments and then develops the learning activities and lessons that will lead to those outcomes.

Universal Design for Learning (UDL) Design of instructional materials and activities that allow learning goals to be achievable by individuals with wide differences in their abilities to learn.

virtual school An institution that exists in cyberspace, teaching all of its classes online.

wiki A website or other online resource that fosters collective authoring by allowing many users to add content or edit the existing content.

• References •

American Association of Colleges for Teacher Education. (2015). About edTPA. Retrieved December 10, 2014, from http://edtpa.aacte.org/about-edtpa

American Association of University Women Educational Foundation. (2001). *Hostile hallways: Bullying, teasing, and sexual harassment in school.* Washington, DC: Author.

American Association of University Women Educational Foundation. (2004). *Harassment-free hallways: How to stop sexual harassment in school.* Washington, DC: Author.

American Library Association. (2018). Digital literacy. Retrieved April 18, 2018, from https://literacy.ala.org/digital-literacy/

Anderson, M., Perrin, A., & Jiang, J. (2018, March 5). 11% of Americans don't use the internet. Who are they? Retrieved March 10, 2018, from http://www.pewresearch.org/fact-tank/2018/03/05/some-americans-dont-use-the-internet-who-are-they/

Annie E. Casey Foundation. (2001). *Where kids count, place matters: Trends in the well-being of Iowa children.* Des Moines, Iowa: Kids Count.

Annie E. Casey Foundation. (2006). 2000 census data: Key facts for United States. Kids Count Census Data Online. Retrieved February 10, 2010, from http://www.aecf.org/

Annie E. Casey Foundation. (2016). *Kids count data book.* Retrieved March 21, 2018, from https://www.aecf.org/m/databook/2016KCDB_FINAL.pdf

Annie E. Casey Foundation. (2017). *Race for results: Building a path of opportunity for all children.* Retrieved March 13, 2018, from https://files.eric.ed.gov/fulltext/ED582131.pdf

Balter, M. (2015). Poverty may affect the growth of children's brains. Retrieved March 25, 2018, from http://www.sciencemag.org/news/2015/03/poverty-may-affect-growth-children-s-brains

Barger-Anderson, R., Isherwood, R. S., & Merhaut, J. (2013). *Strategic co-teaching in your school: Using the co-design model.* Baltimore, MD: Brookes.

Barnwell, P. (2016, April 27). Do smartphones have a place in the classroom? Retrieved March 20, 2018, from https://www.theatlantic.com/education/archive/2016/04/do-smartphones-have-a-place-in-the-classroom/480231/

Bavelier, D., & Green, C. S. (2009). Increasing speed of processing with action video games. *Current Directions in Psychological Science, 18*(6), 321–326.

Bennett-Goleman, T. (2001). *Emotional alchemy: How the mind can heal the heart.* London, England: Harmony Books.

Bickart, T., Jablon, J., & Dodge, D. T. (2000). *Building the primary classroom: A complete guide to teaching and learning.* Washington, DC: Teaching Strategies.

Blad, E. (2017, March 7). How many transgender students are there? *Education Week.* Retrieved March 20, 2018, from https://www.edweek.org/ew/articles/2017/03/08/how-many-transgender-children-are-there.html

Bloom, B. S., Englehart, M. D., Furst, E. J., Hill, W. H., & Krathwohl, D. R. (1956). *Taxonomy of educational objectives: Cognitive domain.* New York, NY: Longmans, Green & Co.

Bloom, H., & Unterman, R. (2012, January). Sustained positive effects on graduation rates produced by New York City's small public high schools of choice. Retrieved April 6, 2018, from https://www.mdrc.org/publication/sustained-positive-effects-graduation-rates-produced-new-york-city-s-small-public-high

Blythe, Tina. (1998). *The teaching for understanding guide.* San Francisco, CA: Jossey-Bass.

Bolt, D. (2000). *The digital divide.* New York, NY: TV Books.

Boston Historical Society and Museum. (2010). Who were the Puritans? Retrieved July 10, 2010, from http://www.bostonhistory.org/?s=librarymuseum&p=researchguide

Bransford, J., Brown, A. L., & Cocking, R. (Eds.). (2000). *How people learn: Brain, mind, experience, and school.* Washington, DC: National Academies Press.

Bransford, J., & Donovan, S. (2004). *How students learn.* Washington, DC: National Academies Press.

Bristol, T. J. (2015). Recruiting and retaining educators of color. White House Initiative on Educational Excellence for African Americans/Stanford Center for Opportunity Policy in Education (SCOPE). https://sites.ed.gov/whieeaa/files/2014/01/Resource-Slides.pdf

Brooks, J. G. (2002). *Schooling for life: Reclaiming the essence of learning.* Reston, VA: Association for Supervision and Curriculum Development.

Brooks, J. G. (2005). One-to-one interview with Janice Koch. Hempstead, NY: Hofstra University.

Brooks-Gunn, J., Duncan, G. J., & Aber, J. L. (Eds.). (2000). *Neighborhood poverty. Volume 1: context and consequences for children.* New York, NY: Russell Sage Foundation.

Brown-Chidsey, R. (2007). No more "waiting to fail." *Educational Leadership, 65*(2), 40–46.

Bruner, J. S. (1960). *The process of education.* Cambridge, MA: Harvard University Press.

Bruner, J. S. (1966). *Toward a theory of instruction.* Cambridge, MA: Harvard University Press.

Bullough, R. V., & Gitlin, A. D. (2001). *Becoming a student: Linking knowledge production and practice of teaching.* New York, NY: RoutledgeFalmer.

Bump, P. (2018, February 14). Eighteen years of gun violence in U.S. schools. Retrieved from https://www.washingtonpost.com/news/politics/wp/2018/02/14/eighteen-years-of-gun-violence-in-u-s-schools-mapped/?utm_term=.95bdba2a781d

Carnegie Forum on Education and the Economy. (1986). *A nation prepared: Teachers for the 21st century.* New York, NY: Carnegie Corporation.

Carr, N. (2010). *The shallows: What the internet is doing to our brain.* New York, NY: Norton.

Carr, E., & Pratt, C. (2007). Positive behavior supports creating meaningful life options for people with ASD. Retrieved April 12, 2015, from http://www.iidc.indiana.edu/?pageId=445

Carter, G. (2006). Supporting the whole child. *ASCD Education Update, 48*(12), 2, 8.

Cawelti, G. (2006). The side effects of NCLB. *Educational Leadership, 64*(3), 64–88.

Center for Education Reform. (2017). Choice and charter schools. Retrieved April 2, 2018, from https://www.edreform.com/issues/choice-charter-schools/

Center for Poverty Research, UC Davis. (2017). What is the current poverty rate in the United States? Retrieved March 31, 2018, from https://poverty.ucdavis.edu/faq/what-current-poverty-rate-united-states

Children's Defense Fund. (2017). Child poverty in America. Retrieved from http://www.childrensdefense.org/library/data/child-poverty-in-america-2016-1.pdf

Cohen, J. (2006). Social, emotional, ethical, and academic education: Creating a climate for learning, participation in democracy, and well-being. *Harvard Educational Review, 76*(2), 201–237.

Coley, R. L., & Morris, J. E. (2002). Comparing father and mother reports of father involvement among low-income minority families. *Journal of Marriage and Family, 64*(4), 982–997.

Common Core State Standards Initiative. (n.d.). About the standards. http://www.corestandards.org/about-the-standards

Common Sense Media. (2015, November 3). Landmark report: U.S. teens use an average of nine hours of media per day, tweens use six hours. Retrieved from https://www.commonsensemedia.org/about-us/news/press-releases/landmark-report-us-teens-use-an-average-of-nine-hours-of-media-per-day

Condliffe Lagemann, E. (2007). Public rhetoric, public responsibility, and the public schools. *Education Week, 26*(37), 30, 40.

Csikszentmihalyi, M. (1997). *Finding flow.* New York, NY: Basic Books.

Darling-Hammond, L., Goldman, S., & Zielezinski, M. (2014). *Using technology to support at-risk students' learning.* Stanford, CA: Stanford Center for Opportunity Policy in Education.

Davis, G. A., & Rimm, S. B. (2004). *Education of the gifted and talented* (5th ed.). Boston, MA: Allyn & Bacon.

Day, C. (2004). *A passion for teaching.* New York, NY: Routledge.

Deal, T., & Peterson, K. (1999). *Shaping school culture.* San Francisco, CA: Jossey-Bass.

Deci, E., & Ryan, R. (1985). *Intrinsic motivation and self-determination in human behavior.* New York, NY: Plenum.

Dewey, J. (1907). *The school and society.* Chicago, IL: University of Chicago Press.

Dewey, J. (1916/2004). *Democracy and education.* New York, NY: Dover.

Dewey, J. (1938). *Experience and education.* New York, NY: Collier Macmillan.

Dori, Y. J., & Belcher, J. (2004). How does technology-enabled active learning affect undergraduate students' understanding of electromagnetism concepts? Retrieved April 17, 2016, from http://web.mit.edu/jbelcher/www/TEALref/Preprint.pdf

Duckworth, E. (1991, February). Twenty-four, forty-two, and I love you: Keeping it complex. *Harvard Educational Review, 61*(1), 1–24.

Durlak, J. A., Weissberg, R. P., Dymnicki, A. B., & Taylor, R. D. (2011). The impact of enhancing students' social and emotional learning: A meta-analysis of school-based universal interventions. *Child Development, 82*(1), 405–432. Retrieved April 4, 2018, from https://onlinelibrary.wiley.com/doi/abs/10.1111/j.1467-8624.2010.01564.x

Dweck, C. (2006). *Mindset: The new psychology of success.* New York, NY: Random House.

Ebner, T. (2018, February 14). With celebration and support, teachers can help retain each other. *Education Week TEACHER.* Retrieved from https://www.edweek.org/tm/articles/2018/02/14/with-celebration-and-support-teachers-can-help.html

Eliot, L. (2009). *Pink brains, blue brains: How small differences grow into troublesome gaps and what we can do about it.* New York, NY: Houghton Mifflin, Harcourt.

Evans, S. (1989). *Born for liberty: A history of women in America.* New York, NY: Free Press.

Farber, B. A. (1991). *Crisis in education: Stress and burnout in the American teacher.* San Francisco, CA: Jossey-Bass.

Fein, R. A., Vossekuil, B., Pollack, W. S., Borum, R., Modzeleski, W., & Reddy, M. (2004). *Threat assessment in schools: A guide to managing threatening situations and to creating safe school climates.* Washington, DC: U.S. Secret Service and U.S. Department of Education.

Felder, R. M. (2002, June). Author's preface. Retrieved June 30, 2010, from http://www4.ncsu.edu/unity/lockers/users/f/felder/public/Papers/LS-1988.pdf

Felder, R. M., & Brent, R. (2005). Understanding student differences. *Journal of Engineering Education, 94*(1), 57–72.

Felder, R. M., & Silverman, L. K. (1988). Learning and teaching styles in engineering education. *Journal of Engineering Education, 78*(7), 674–681.

Fisch, K. (2006, December 15). This is not education as usual [Web log post]. Retrieved from http://thefischbowl.blogspot .com/2006/12/this-is-not-education-as-usual.html

Freed, R. (2015). *Wired child: Reclaiming childhood in a digital age.* North Charleston, SC: CreateSpace.

Freire, P. (1970). *Pedagogy of the oppressed* (M. B. Ramos, Trans.). New York, NY: Continuum.

Friedman, T. (2006). *The world is flat: A brief history of the twenty-first century* (Updated and expanded ed.). New York, NY: Farrar, Straus and Giroux.

Fry, R. (2006). *The changing landscape of American public education: New students, new schools.* Washington, DC: Pew Research Center.

Ganley, B. (2009). Teaching and learning with technology [video file]. Presentation at the University of British Columbia. Retrieved June 12, 2010, from http://vimeo.com/3008955/

Gardner, H. (1993). *Frames of mind: The theory of multiple intelligences.* New York, NY: Basic Books.

Gardner, H. (2003). *Intelligence reframed: Multiple intelligences for the 21st century.* New York, NY: Basic Books.

Gardner, H. (2006). *Multiple intelligences: New horizons* (Rev. ed.). New York, NY: Basic Books.

Gargiulo, R. M., & Bouck, E. C. (2018). *Special education in contemporary society* (6th ed.). Thousand Oaks, CA: Sage.

Gargiulo, R. M., & Metcalf, D. (2017). *Teaching in today's inclusive classrooms: A Universal Design for Learning approach* (3rd ed.). San Francisco, CA: Cengage.

Gay, Lesbian, and Straight Education Network. (2015). National school climate survey. Retrieved February 2, 2010, from http://www.glsen.org/cgi-bin/iowa/all/home/index.html

Gee, J. P. (2008). Being a lion and being a soldier: Learning and games. In J. Coiro, M. Knobel, C. Lankshear, & D. J. Leu (Eds.), *Handbook of research on new literacies* (pp. 1023–1036). New York, NY: Erlbaum.

Gladwell, M. (2008, December 15). Most likely to succeed: How can we hire when we can't tell who is right for the job? Retrieved from http://www.newyorker.com/reporting/2008/12/15/081215fa_fact_gladwell?currentPage=all

Goleman, D. (2006). *Emotional intelligence: Why it can matter more than IQ.* New York, NY: Bantam.

Graham, E. (n.d.). Using smartphones in the classroom. Retrieved March 10, 2018, from http://www.nea.org/tools/56274.htm

Greene, J. P., Forster, G., & Winters, M. (2003, July). *Apples to apples: An evaluation of charter schools serving general student populations* (Education Working Paper No. 1). New York, NY: Manhattan Institute for Policy Research.

Greene, M. (1978). *Landscapes of learning.* New York, NY: Teachers College Press.

Greene, M. (1995). *Releasing the imagination: Essays on education, the arts, and social change.* San Francisco, CA: Jossey-Bass.

Greene, M. (2001). *Variations on a blue guitar.* New York, NY: Teachers College Press.

Hammerness, K. (2006). *Seeing through teachers' eyes: Professional ideals and classroom practices.* New York, NY: Teachers College Press.

Hart, B., & Risley, T. R. (1995). *Meaningful differences in the everyday experience of young American children.* Baltimore, MD: Brookes.

Herold, B. (2017, June 12). Online classes for K–12 schools: What you need to know. Retrieved from https://www.edweek.org/ew/articles/2017/06/14/online-classes-for-k-12-schools-what-you.html

Hill, C., & Kearl, H. (2011). *Crossing the line: Sexual harassment at school.* Washington, DC: American Association of University Women.

Hittie, M. (2000, June). *Building community in the classroom.* Paper presented at the International Education Summit, Detroit, Michigan.

Hoff, E. (2003). The specificity of environmental influence: Socioeconomic status affects early vocabulary development via maternal speech. *Child Development, 74*(5), 1368–1378.

Hoffman, N. (1981). *Woman's true profession: Voices from the history of teaching.* New York, NY: The Feminist Press and McGraw Hill.

Hopkins, D. (2013). *QR codes in education.* UK: Author.

Information Please Database. (2006). State compulsory school attendance laws. Retrieved February 22, 2010, from http://www.infoplease.com/ipa /A0112617.html

Intrator, S. (2003). *Tuned in and fired up: How teaching can inspire real learning in the classroom.* New Haven, CT: Yale University Press.

i-SAFE America, Inc. (n.d.). *Beware of the cyberbully.* Retrieved March 20, 2018, from https://www.isafe.org/imgs/pdf/education/CyberBullying.pdf

Jackson, P. (1968). *Life in classrooms.* New York, NY: Holt, Rinehart & Winston.

Johnson, L., Adams Becker, S., Estrada, V., & Martin, S. (2013). *The technology outlook for STEM+Education 2013–2018: An NMC Horizon Project Sector Analysis.* Austin, TX: New Media Consortium.

Johnson, M. (2018). The advantages of being a new teacher. *Edutopia.* Retrieved February 6, 2018, from https://www.edutopia .org/article/advantages-being-new-teacher

Joubert, J. (2005). *The notebooks of Joseph Joubert* (P. Auster, Trans.). New York, NY: New York Review Books.

Juvonen, J., Le, V., Kaganoff, T., Augustine, C. H., & Constant, L. (2004). *Focus on the wonder years: Challenges facing the American middle school.* Santa Monica, CA: Rand Corporation.

Kashen, S. (1994). Bilingual education and second-language acquisition theory. In C. F. Lebya (Ed.), *Schooling and language minority students* (pp. 61–63). Los Angeles, CA: California State University.

Kelley, T. (2006, December 18). Talk in class turns to God, setting off public debate on rights. *New York Times*. http://www.nytimes.com/2006/12/18/nyregion

Klein, A. (2016, December 30). Tricky balance in shifting from ESSA blueprint to K–12 reality. Retrieved from https://www.edweek.org/ew/articles/2017/01/04/tricky-balance-in-shifting-from-essa-blueprint.html

Klein, S., Ortman, P., & Friedman, B. (2002). What is the field of gender equity in education? In J. Koch & B. Irby (Eds.), *Defining and redefining gender equity in education*. Greenwich, CT: Information Age.

Klopfer, E., Osterweil, S., & Salen, K. (2009). Moving learning games forward [MIT Education Arcade paper]. Available at http://education.mit.edu/papers/Moving-LearningGamesForward_EdArcade.pdf

Kober, N. (2007). *Why we still need public schools: Public education for the common good*. Washington, DC: Center on Education Policy. Retrieved from https://files.eric.ed.gov/fulltext/ED503799.pdf

Koch, J. (2002). Gender issues in the classroom. In W. R. Reynolds & G. E. Miller (Eds.), *The handbook of psychology, Volume 7: Educational psychology*. New York, NY: Wiley.

Koedinger, K. R., Kim, J., Zhuxin Jia, J., McLaughlin, E., & Bier, N. (2015, March 14–18). Learning is not a spectator sport: Doing is better than watching for learning from a MOOC. Presentation at the Learning@Scale Conference, Vancouver, BC, Canada. Retrieved from http://pact.cs.cmu.edu/pubs/koedinger,%20Kim,%20Jia,%20McLaughlin,%20Bier%202015.pdf

Kohn, A. (1999). *Punished by rewards: The trouble with gold stars, incentive plans, A's, praise, and other bribes*. Boston, MA: Houghton Mifflin.

Korat, O., & Haglili, S. (2007). Maternal evaluations of children's emergent literacy level, maternal mediation in book reading, and children's emergent literacy level: A comparison between SES groups. *Journal of Literacy Research, 39*(2), 269–276.

Kosciw, J. G., Greytak, E. A., Giga, N. M., Villenas, C., & Danischewski, D. J. (2016). The 2015 National School Climate Survey: The experiences of lesbian, gay, bisexual, transgender, and queer youth in our nation's schools. New York, NY: Gay, Lesbian, and Straight Education Network.

Kounin, J. S. (1970). *Discipline and group management in classrooms*. New York, NY: Holt, Rinehart & Winston.

Krigman, E. (2014). Gaining STEAM: Teaching science through art. *U.S. News & World Report*. Retrieved April 4, 2018, from https://www.usnews.com/news/stem-solutions/articles/2014/02/13/gaining-steam-teaching-science-though-art

Krug, E. A. (1964). *The shaping of the American high school, 1880–1920*. New York, NY: Harper & Row.

Kyriacou, C. (2001). *Essential teaching skills*. Cheltenham, England: Nelson Thornes Ltd.

Lareau, A. (2003). *Unequal childhoods: Class, race, and family life*. Berkeley, CA: University of California Press.

Levine, D. (2015, June 30). What we need to build a caring classroom culture. Retrieved March 10, 2018, from https://medium.com/changemaker-education/why-we-need-to-build-a-caring-classroom-culture-d1e541a17e56

Lionni, L. (1970). *Fish is fish*. New York, NY: Scholastic Books.

Logan, J. (1999). *Teaching stories*. New York, NY: Kodansha America.

Long, C. (2017, December 4). The secret of sexual assault in schools. Retrieved from http://neatoday.org/2017/12/04/sexual-assault-in-schools/

Lynch, M. (2016, December 25). Using smartphones in the classroom. Retrieved March 10, 2018, from http://www.thetechedvocate.org/smartphones-in-the-classroom/

Lynch, M. (2018, April 11). 10 ways to use student-created videos in the classroom. Retrieved April 15, 2018, from https://www.thetechedvocate.org/10-ways-to-use-student-created-videos-in-the-classroom/

Maker, J., & Nielson, A. (1996). *Curriculum development and teaching strategies for gifted learners* (2nd ed.). Austin, TX: PRO-ED.

Manning, M. L. (2000). A brief history of the middle school. *The Clearing House, 73*(4), 288–301.

McBrien, J. L., & Brandt, R. S. (1997). *The language of learning: A guide to education terms*. Alexandria, VA: Association for Supervision and Curriculum Development.

McGuire, W. (Ed.). (1954). *Collected works of C. J. Jung* (Vol. 17). Princeton, NJ: Princeton University Press.

Mead, S. (2015, March 19). Charters score in cities. *U.S. News & World Report*. Retrieved April 1, 2018, from https://www.usnews.com/opinion/knowledge-bank/2015/03/19/new-study-shows-charter-schools-making-a-difference-in-cities

Megan Meier Foundation. (2018). Be the change: Stop bullying and cyberbullying. Retrieved March 28, 2018, from https://www.meganmeierfoundation.org/resourcecenter.html

Mehta, S. (2009, December 14). Controlling a classroom isn't as easy as ABC. *Los Angeles Times*, p. A1.

Miller, L. (2010). 12 tips for new teachers. In T. Burant, L. Christensen, K. D. Salas, & S. Walters (Eds.), *The new teacher book: Finding purpose, balance, and hope during your first years in the classroom*. Milwaukee, WI: Rethinking Schools, Ltd.

Mitchell, C. (2016, September 3). Black male teachers a dwindling demographic. Retrieved from https://www.edweek.org/ew/articles/2016/02/17/black-male-teachers-a-dwindling-demographic.html

Molitch-Hou, M. (2014, March 21). Chicago magnet school to launch $40,000 3D printing lab. Retrieved May 15, 2015, from https://3dprintingindustry.com/news/chicago-magnet-school-launch-40000-3d-printing-lab-23941/

Molnar, A. (Ed.). (2017). *Virtual schools in the U.S. 2017.* University of Colorado, Boulder: National Education Policy Center.

Moos, R. H. (1979). *Evaluating educational environments: Procedures, measures, findings, and policy implications.* San Francisco, CA: Jossey-Bass.

Moran, S., Kornhaber, M., & Gardner, H. (2006). Orchestrating multiple intelligences. *Educational Leadership, 64*(1), 23–27.

Musu-Gillette, L., Robinson, J., McFarland, J., KewalRamani, A., Zhang, A., and Wilkinson-Flicker, S. (2016). *Status and trends in the education of racial and ethnic groups 2016.* Washington, DC: U.S. Department of Education, National Center for Education Statistics.

National Assessment of Educational Progress. (2005). *America's charter schools: Results from the NAEP 2003 pilot study* (NCES 2005–456). Washington, DC: U.S. Department of Education.

National Association for Gifted Children. (n.d.). Frequently asked questions about gifted education. Retrieved April 5, 2018, from http://www.nagc.org/resources-publications/resources/frequently-asked-questions-about-gifted-education

National Board for Professional Teaching Standards. (n.d.). *Five core propositions of the National Board for Professional Teaching Standards.* Retrieved from https://www.ctuf.org/wp-content/uploads/2016/08/Five-Core-Propositions.pdf

National Board for Professional Teaching Standards. (2002). *What teachers should know and be able to do.* Arlington, VA: Author. Retrieved January 5, 2010, from http://www.nbpts.org/UserFiles/File/what_teachers.pdf

National Commission on Excellence in Education. (1983). *A nation at risk: The imperative for educational reform.* Washington, DC: U.S. Department of Education.

National Education Association. (n.d.). *Three keys to school safety and gun violence prevention.* Retrieved March 28, 2018, from http://www.nea.org/home/54092.htm

National Education Association. (1899). Report of the Committee on College Entrance Requirements. *Journal of the Proceedings and Addresses of the Thirty-Eighth Annual Meeting, Los Angeles,* 632–817.

National Education Association. (1975). *Code of ethics of the education profession.* Retrieved July 14, 2006, from http://www.nea.org/aboutnea/code.html

National Education Association. (2006, May 2). National Teacher Day spotlights key issues facing profession. Retrieved July 14, 2006, from http://www.nea.org/newsreleases/2006/nr060502.html

National Science Foundation. (2008, July 24). *Study: No gender differences in math performance.* Retrieved March 15, 2018, from https://www.nsf.gov/news/news_summ.jsp?cntn_id=111994

Nelson, C., & Wilson, K. (1998). *Seeding the process of multicultural education.* Plymouth: Minnesota Inclusiveness Program.

Next Generation Science Standards. (2013). *Next generation science standards: For states, by states* (Volume 1 and Volume 2). Washington, DC: National Academies Press.

Nieto, S. (Ed.). (2014). *Why we teach now.* New York, NY: Teachers College Press.

Nieto, S. (2015). Still teaching in spite of it all. *Educational Leadership, 72*(6), 54-59.

Norris, C., & Soloway, E. (2017, May 18). Picting, not writing, is the literacy of today's youth. Retrieved March 10, 2018, from https://thejournal.com/articles/2017/05/08/picting-not-writing.aspx

Northeast Foundation for Children. (2007). *What is the responsive classroom approach?* Retrieved May 29, 2007, from http://www.responsive classroom.org/about/aboutrc.html

Ollove, M. (2018, March 12). Little national research is done on gun violence, so some states are stepping in. Retrieved from https://www.washingtonpost.com/national/health-science/little-national-research-is-done-on-gun-violence-so-some-states-are-stepping-in/2018/03/09/faa3097e-1d5a-11e8-9de1-147dd2df3829_story.html?utm_term=.6af4d9ed6dfd

Olweus, D. (2003, March). A profile of bullying at school. *Educational Leadership, 60*(6), 12–17.

Orenstein, P. (2009, October 25). Stop your search engines. Retrieved from https://www.nytimes.com/2009/10/25/magazine/25FOB-WWLN-t.html

Osterman, K. (2000). Students' need for belongingness in the school community. *Review of Educational Research, 70*(3), 323–367.

Palmer, P. (2017). *The courage to teach: Exploring the inner landscape of a teacher's life* (20th anniversary edition). San Francisco, CA: Jossey-Bass.

Payscale.com. (n.d.). Average salary for all K-12 teachers. Retrieved from https://www.payscale.com/research/US/All_K-12_Teachers/Salary

Perkins, D. (1993). Teaching for understanding. *American Educator, 17*(3), 28–35.

Pew Research Center. (2015). America's changing religious landscape. Retrieved March 2, 2018, from http://www.pewforum.org/2015/05/12/americas-changing-religious-landscape/

Pew Research Center. (2017, March 21). Lower-income Americans continue to lag behind in technology adoption. Retrieved from http://www.pewresearch.org/fact-tank/2017/03/22/digital-divide-persists-even-as-lower-income-americans-make-gains-in-tech-adoption/ft_17-03-21_low-incometech_adoption/

Phillips, J. (2016, October 20). 7 tips on how to prepare for teaching online. Retrieved March 20, 2018, from https://elearningindustry.com/7-tips-prepare-for-teaching-online

Planty, M., Hussar, W., Snyder, T., Provasnik, S., Kena, G., Dinkes, R., . . . Kemp, J. (2008). *The condition of education 2008* (NCES 2008-031). Washington, DC: National Center for Education Statistics, Institute of Education Sciences, U.S. Department of Education.

Prensky, M. (2001, October). Digital natives, digital immigrants. *On the Horizon, 9*(5), 1–6.

President's Memorandum on Religious Expression in Schools. (1995). Retrieved from https://www.nytimes.com/1995/07/13/us/president-s-memorandum-on-religious-expression-in-schools.html

Rasmussen, K. (1997, Summer). Using real-life problems to make real-world connections. *Curriculum Update*. Alexandria, VA: Association for Supervision and Curriculum Development.

Ray, B. (2014). *Research facts on homeschooling*. Salem, OR: National Home Education Research Institute.

Rendina, D. (2015, April 2). Defining makerspaces: What the research says. Retrieved March 26, 2018, from http://renovatedlearning.com/2015/04/02/defining-makerspaces-part-1/

Ridnouer, K. (2006). *Managing your classroom with heart*. Alexandria, VA: Association for Supervision and Curriculum Development.

Rimm-Kaufman, S. (2006). *Social and academic learning study on the contribution of the responsive classroom approach*. Turners Falls, MA: Northeast Foundation for Children.

Rivers, C., & Barnett, R. (2011). *The truth about girls and boys: Challenging toxic stereotypes about our children*. New York, NY: Columbia University Press.

Robinson, K. (2006). Do schools kill creativity? [video file]. Retrieved May 24, 2009, from http://www.ted.com/index.php/talks/view/id/66

Rockoff, J. E., & Lockwood, B. B. (2010). Stuck in the middle: Impacts of grade configuration in public schools. *Journal of Public Economics*, *94*(11–12), 1051–1061. Retrieved April 14, 2018, from https://www.sciencedirect.com/science/article/abs/pii/S0047272710000824

Romano-Arrabito, C. (2017, November 8). Snapchat, Instagram, YouTube, oh my! 4 tools for picting in the classroom. Retrieved March 10, 2018, from https://www.edsurge.com/news/2017-11-08-snapchat-instagram-youtube-oh-my-4-tools-for-picting-in-the-classroom

Romero, C. (2015). What we know about belonging from scientific research. Retrieved from http://mindsetscholarsnetwork.org/wp-content/uploads/2015/09/What-We-Know-About-Belonging.pdf

Rose, M. (2009). *Why school? Reclaiming education for all of us*. New York, NY: New Press.

Rosiak, J. (2009). *Developing safe schools partnerships with law enforcement*. Washington, DC: Forum on Public Policy.

Ryan, K., & Cooper, J. M. (2013). *Those who can, teach*. Belmont, CA: Wadsworth, Cengage Learning.

Sadker, D. M., & Zittleman, K. R. (2009). *Still failing at fairness: How gender bias cheats girls and boys and what we can do about it*. New York, NY: Scribner.

Sadker, M., & Sadker, D. (1995). *Failing at fairness: How our schools cheat girls*. New York, NY: Touchstone/Simon & Schuster.

Sampson, R. (2002). *Bullying in schools* [Problem-Oriented Guides for Police Series, Guide No. 12]. Washington, DC: Office of Community Oriented Policing Services, U.S. Department of Justice. Retrieved January 10, 2010, from http://www.popcenter.org/problems/PDFs/Bullying_in_Schools.pdf

Scarborough, J., & Ravaglia, R. (2014). *Bricks and mortar: The making of a real education at the Stanford Online High School*. Stanford, CA: Center for the Study of Language and Information.

Schaffhauser, D. (2010, April 2). Realityworks teaches business ed with online simulation games. Retrieved from http://thejournal.com/articles/2010/04/02/realityworks-teaches-business-ed-with-online-simulation-games.aspx

Schön, D. A. (1983). *The reflective practitioner: How professionals think in action*. New York, NY: Basic Books.

Schwartz, D., & Gorman, A. H. (2003). Community violence exposure and children's academic functioning. *Journal of Educational Psychology*, *95*(1), 163–173.

Schwerdt, G., & West, M. R. (2013). The impact of alternative grade configurations on student outcomes through middle and high school. *Journal of Public Economics*, *97*, 308–326. https://doi.org/10.1016/j.jpubeco.2012.10.002

Scott, A. O. (2000, November 26). Sense and nonsense. *New York Times Magazine*. Retrieved July 28, 2010, from http://partners.nytimes.com/library/magazine/home/20001126mag-seuss.html

Sears, J. (1991). Teaching for diversity: Student sexual identities. *Educational Leadership*, *49*(1), 54–57.

Seligman, M. E. P. (2002). *Authentic happiness*. New York, NY: Free Press.

Seligman, M. E. P., Steen, T. A., Park, N., & Peterson, C. (2005). Positive psychology progress: Empirical validation of interventions. *American Psychologist*, *60*(5), 410–421.

Shulman, L. (1987). Knowledge and teaching: Foundations of the new reform. *Harvard Educational Review*, *57*(1), 1–22.

Smith, T. W., & Lambie, G. W. (2005). Teachers' responsibilities when adolescent abuse and neglect are suspected. *Middle School Journal*, *36*(3), 33–40.

Snyder, T. D. (Ed.). (1993). *120 years of American education: A statistical portrait*. Washington, DC: U.S. Department of Education, National Center for Education Statistics.

Staker, H. (2011). *The rise of K–12 blended learning*. Retrieved from https://www.christenseninstitute.org/wp-content/uploads/2013/04/The-rise-of-K-12-blended-learning.emerging-models.pdf

Statista. (n.d.). Reach of leading social media and networking sites used by teenagers and young adults in the United States as of February 2017. Retrieved from https://www.statista.com/statistics/199242/social-media-and-networking-sites-used-by-us-teenagers/

Stepler, R., & Lopez, M. H. (2016, September 8). U.S. Latino population growth and dispersion has slowed since onset of the great recession. Retrieved from http://www.pewhispanic.org/2016/09/08/latino-population-growth-and-dispersion-has-slowed-since-the-onset-of-the-great-recession/

Stoker, B. (2017, September 25). 6 internet safety tips for teachers [Web blog post]. Retrieved from https://www.studiesweekly.com/6-internet-safety-tips-for-teachers/

Strauss, V. (2013, October 16). Howard Gardner: 'Multiple intelligences' are not 'learning styles.' Retrieved from https://www.washingtonpost.com/news/answer-sheet/wp/2013/10/16/howard-gardner-multiple-intelligences-are-not-learning-styles/?utm_term=.067c1e9c0976

Style, E. (1996). Curriculum as window and mirror. Retrieved from http://www.wcwonline.org/seed/curriculum.html. First published in *Listening for All Voices*, Oak Knoll School Monograph, Summit, NJ, 1988.

Tamer, M. (2012). Do middle schools make sense? *Harvard Ed. Magazine*. Retrieved April 14, 2018, from https://www.gse.harvard.edu/news/ed/12/09/do-middle-schools-make-sense

Thorpe, R. (2003). Getting the center to hold: A funder's perspective. In N. Dickard (Ed.), *The sustainability challenge: Taking edtech to the next level* (pp. 47–54). Washington, DC: Benton Foundation.

Tichnor-Wagner, A. (2016, August 3). A global perspective: Bringing the world into Classrooms. Retrieved March 15, 2018, from https://www.edweek.org/tm/articles/2016/08/03/a-global-perspective-bringing-the-world-into.html?print=1

Toh, K-A., Ho, B-T., Chew, C. M. K., & Riley, J. (2003). Teaching, teacher knowledge, and constructivism. *Educational Research for Policy and Practice, 2*(3), 195–204.

Tomlinson, C. A. (2014). *The differentiated classroom: Responding to the needs of all learners* (2nd ed.). Reston, VA: Association for Supervision and Curriculum Development.

Tomlinson, C. A., & Imbeau, M. B. (2011). *Managing a differentiated classroom: A practical guide*. New York, NY: Scholastic.

Torp, L., & Sage, S. (2002). *Problems as possibilities: Problem-based learning for K–16 education* (2nd ed.). Alexandria, VA: Association of Supervision and Curriculum Development.

Twenge, J. (2017, September). Have smartphones destroyed a generation? Retrieved March 10, 2018, from https://www.theatlantic.com/magazine/archive/2017/09/has-the-smartphone-destroyed-a-generation/534198/

U.S. Census Bureau. (2017). *Poverty thresholds: 2016*. https://www.census.gov/data/tables/2016/demo/supplemental-poverty-measure/poverty-thresholds.html

U.S. Department of Education, Office for Civil Rights. (n.d.). *Sex-based harassment*. Retrieved March 28, 2018, from https://www2.ed.gov/about/offices/list/ocr/frontpage/pro-students/issues/sex-issue01.html

U.S. Department of Education. (1998). Achieving excellence in the teaching profession. In *Promising practices: New ways to improve teacher quality*. Washington, DC: U.S. Government Printing Office. Retrieved January 4, 2010, from http://www.ed.gov/pubs /PromPractice/chapter1.html

U.S. Department of Education, National Center for Education Statistics. (2012). *Homeschooling in the United States: 1999*. Retrieved from https://nces.ed.gov/pubs2001/2001033.pdf

U.S. Department of Education, National Center for Education Statistics. (2016a). *Digest of Education Statistics (Table 105.40)*. Retrieved from https://nces.ed.gov/pubs2016/2016014.pdf

U.S. Department of Education. (2016b). *The state of racial diversity in the educator workforce*. https://www2.ed.gov/rschstat/eval/highered/racial-diversity/state-racial-diversity-workforce.pdf

U.S. Department of Education, National Center for Education Statistics. (2016c). *Annual Report of the Commissioner of Education February 2016, Table 105.30, Enrollment in elementary, secondary, and degree-granting postsecondary institutions, by level and control of institution: Selected years, 1869–70 through fall 2025*. Retrieved from https://nces.ed.gov/programs/digest/d15/tables/dt15_105.30.asp

U.S. Department of Education, National Center for Education Statistics. (2016d). *State nonfiscal public elementary/secondary education survey data, 2004–05 and 2014–15*. Retrieved February 26, 2018, from https://nces.ed.gov/ccd/stnfis.asp

U.S. Department of Education, National Center for Education Statistics. (2016e). *Table 203.50, Enrollment and percentage distribution of enrollment in public elementary and secondary schools, by race/ethnicity and region: Selected years, fall 1995 through fall 2026*. Retrieved from https://nces.ed.gov/programs/digest/d16/tables/dt16_203.50

U.S. Department of Education, National Center for Education Statistics. (2017a). *Digest of Educational Statistics, Table 105.30, Enrollment in elementary, secondary, and degree-granting postsecondary institutions, by level and control of institution: Selected years, 1869–70 through fall 2027*. Retrieved from https://nces.ed.gov/programs/digest/d17/tables/dt17_105.30.asp?current=yes

U.S. Department of Education, National Center for Education Statistics. (2017b). *Digest of Educational Statistics, Table 209.10, Number and percentage distribution of teachers in public and private elementary and secondary schools, by selected teacher characteristics: Selected years, 1987–88 through 2015–16*. Retrieved from https://nces.ed.gov/programs/digest/d17/tables/dt17_209.10.asp?current=yes

U.S. Department of Education, National Center for Education Statistics. (2017c). *English language learners in public schools*. https://nces.ed.gov/programs/coe/indicator_cgf.asp

U.S. Department of Education, National Center for Education Statistics. (2017d). *Fast facts*. Retrieved March 1, 2018, from https://nces.ed.gov/fastfacts/display.asp?id=16

U.S. Department of Education, National Center for Education Statistics. (2017e). *Indicators of school crime and safety: 2016* (NCES 2017-064, Indicator 11). https://nces.ed.gov/pubs2017/2017064.pdf

Vacca, R. S. (2004, May). Student records 2004: Issues and policy considerations. *CEPI Education Law Newsletter*. Richmond, VA: Commonwealth Educational Policy Institute. Available at http://www.cepionline.org/newsletter /2003–2004/2004_May_stud_records.html

Vilorio, D. (2016). Teaching for a living. *Career Outlook*. Retrieved from https://www.bls.gov/careeroutlook/2016/article/education-jobs-teaching-for-a-living.htm

Vygotsky, L. (1962). *Thought and language*. Cambridge, MA: MIT Press.

Wallis, C., & Steptoe, S. (2006, December 18). How to bring our schools out of the 20th century. *Time Magazine*.

Watson, J., Murin, A., Vashaw, L., Gemin, B., & Rapp, C. (2013). *Keeping pace with K–12 online and blended learning: An annual review of policy and practice*. Retrieved from https://static1 .squarespace.com/static/59381b9a17bffc68bf625df4/t/5949b6 0003596eb369b66b06/1498002966450/KeepingPace+2013.pdf

Wiggins, G., & McTighe, J. (1998). *Understanding by design*. Alexandria, VA: Association for Supervision and Curriculum Development.

Winebrenner, S., & Brulles, D. (2012). *Teaching gifted kids in today's classroom: Strategies and techniques every teacher can use* (3rd ed.). Minneapolis, MN: Free Spirit Publishing.

Winerip, M. (2012, February 12). A field trip to a strange new place: Second grade visits the parking garage. Retrieved from https://www.nytimes.com/2012/02/13/nyregion/for-poorer-students-an-attempt-to-let-new-experiences-guide-learning .html

Wisconsin Education Association Council. (2006). Great schools issue paper: The common school movement. Retrieved March 8, 2010, from http://www.weac.org/professional_resources/ great _schools/issues_papers/index.aspx

Wood, T., & McCarthy, C. (2002). *Understanding and preventing teacher burnout*. Washington, DC: ERIC Clearinghouse on Teaching and Teacher Education, ED477726.

Young, M., Slota, S., Cutter, A., Jalette, G., Mullin, G., Lai, B., . . . Yukhymenko, M. (2012, March). Our princess is in another castle: A review of trends in serious gaming for education. *Review of Educational Research*, *82*(1), 61–89.

Zins, J. E., Bloodworth, M. R., Weissberg, R. P., & Walberg, H. J. (2007). The scientific base linking social and emotional learning to school success. *Journal of Educational and Psychological Consultation*, *17*(2–3), 191–210.

• Index •

NOTE: Page references in *italics* refer to photos and illustrations, page references with boxes, figures, tables, or maps are referred to as (box), (fig.), (table), or (map), respectively.